Intercultural Communication
for Business

Elizabeth A. Tuleja, Ph.D.

With James S. O'Rourke, IV, Ph.D., Editor

GlobeComm Publishing

Published by Dog Ear Publishing
4010 W. 86th Street, Ste H
Indianapolis, IN 46268
www.dogearpublishing.net

ISBN: 978-1-4575-3362-4

Library of Congress Control Number: has been applied for

This book is printed on acid-free paper.

Printed in the United States of America

To my parents, Ted and Doris Sery,
who taught me kindness and compassion

And to my mentor, Prof. James O'Rourke IV,
for 'putting me on the map'

Table of Contents

Foreword..vi
Preface viii

Chapter 1: An Overview of Culture
    Introduction...1
    Evolving Demographics in the Global Village.............................5
    A Rationale for Culture Study 9
    Defining Culture 10
    Perception...15
    Stereotypes and Prototypes...20
    Ethnocentrism 25
    Chapter Summary 29
    Applications in the Global Marketplace 29
    A Case Study—Dewey Ballantine, LLP: Cultural
        Stereotypes 30

Chapter 2: Culture and Communication
    Introduction...37
    Communication...38
    Frame of Reference 44
    Language and Culture..46
    Non-Verbal Communication 49
    Structure of Language..52
    Defining Cultural Dimensions 57
    Context and Communication..60
    Expression and Communication 64
    Persuasion in Intercultural Communication 70
    Rhetoric and Language 72
    Chapter Summary 79
    Applications in the Global Marketplace 80
    A Case Study—Language Barriers in a Dangerous Business........81

Chapter 3: Culture and Identity
    Introduction...86
    The Self—Individualism and Collectivism.................................87
    Learning 98

Outlook on the World 104
Environment 104
Ambiguity, Change, and Uncertainty 109
Time 112
Space 120
Chapter Summary 123
Applications in the Global Marketplace 124
A Case Study—Coca-Cola and the European
   Contamination Crisis 132

Chapter 4: Culture and Power

Introduction 143
Power: Ascribed or Earned 146
Masculinity and Femininity 162
Achievement 165
Respect 170
Long-Term/Short-Term Orientation 175
Chapter Summary 178
Applications for Cultural Dimensions in the Global
   Marketplace 179
A Case Study—Big Dog Software, Inc. 181

Chapter 5: Applications for Intercultural Communication

Introduction 186
Challenges and Solutions 187
Developing Intercultural Competence 196
Review: Dimensions of Culture 198
Chapter Summary 199
A Case Study—Canwall Paper, Ltd.: Canadian and
   Chinese Negotiations 201
A Case Study—The Walt Disney Company: Launch of a
   Hong Kong Theme Park 204

APPENDIX 219

ENDNOTES 223

INDEX 236

Foreword

In recent years, for a variety of reasons, communication has grown increasingly complex. The issues that seemed so straightforward, so simple not long ago are now somehow different, more complicated. Has the process changed? Have the elements of communication or the barriers to success been altered? What's different now? Why has this all gotten more difficult?

Several issues are at work here, not the least of which is pacing. Information, images, events, and human activity all move at a much faster pace than they did just a decade ago. Among the more popular, hip new business magazines in recent years is *Fast Company*. Readers are reminded that it's not just a matter of tempo, but a new way of living we're experiencing.

Technology has changed things, as well. We're now able to communicate with almost anyone, almost anywhere, 24/7 with very little effort and very little professional assistance. It's all possible because of cellular telephone technology, digital imaging, the Internet, fiber optics, global positioning satellites, teleconferencing codecs, high-speed data processing, online data storage and...well, the list goes on and on. What's new this morning will be old hat by lunch.

Culture has intervened in our lives in some important ways. Very few parts of the world are inaccessible any more. Other people's beliefs, practices, perspectives, and possessions are as familiar to us as our own. And for many of us, we're only now coming to grips with the idea that our own beliefs aren't shared by everyone and that culture is hardly value-neutral.

The nature of the world in which we live—one that's wired, connected, mobile, fast-paced, visual, and far less driven by logic—has changed in some not-so-subtle ways in recent days. The organizations that employ us and the businesses that depend on our skills now recognize that communication is at the center of what it means to be successful...and at the heart of what it means to be human.

To operate profitably means that business must now conduct itself in responsible ways, keenly attuned to the needs and interests of its stakeholders. And, more than ever, the communication skills and capabilities we bring to the workplace are essential to our success, both at the individual and at the societal level.

So, what does that mean to you as a prospective manager or executive-in-training? For one thing, it means that communication will involve more than simple writing, speaking, and listening skills. It will involve new contexts, new applications, and new technologies. Much of what will affect the balance of your lives has yet to be invented. But when it is, you'll have to learn to live with it and make it work on your behalf.

The book you've just opened applies to managing in a global world. It's direct, simple, and very compact. Professor Elizabeth Tuleja examines *Intercultural Communication for Business*, looking both broadly and specifically at issues and opportunities that will seem increasingly important as the business world shrinks and grows more interdependent. As time zones blur and fewer restrictions are imposed on the global movement of capital, raw materials, finished goods, and human labor, people will cling fiercely to the ways in which they were enculturated as youngsters. Culture will become a defining characteristic, not only of peoples and nations, but of organizations and industries.

James S. O'Rourke, IV
The Eugene D. Fanning Center, Mendoza College of Business
University of Notre Dame, Notre Dame, Indiana

Preface

In this book, we lay a framework for developing cultural competence. Whether you are a student, instructor or business professional, the ultimate goal of reading *Intercultural Communication for Business* is to assess your own personal awareness and combine that with your awareness of other people or groups and their beliefs, values, attitudes, and behaviors. This text examines the basis for culture, reviewing the work of social scientists, cultural anthropologists, and global managers on this emerging topic. Definitions of culture, issues of communication and culture, and our adaptations to cultural dissonance are included, along with practical examples, case studies and illustrations of how cultural issues are managed both domestically and internationally.

Our primary aim is to be instructive about a variety of intercultural communication concepts, allowing you to immediately put into practice what you read. We have taken the best-known and most fundamental concepts in intercultural communication and sorted through the denseness of terminology and theories usually found in social science textbooks to offer you both interesting discussions and useful examples that are current, relevant, and concise. Each chapter contains a basic discussion of relevant cross-cultural issues, grouped thematically followed by numerous examples and illustrations. The final chapter is a summary of our findings and underscores key points from every chapter.

The issues discussed and highlighted in the cases will be referred to as "frameworks" or "dimensions." While there are numerous ways of discussing culture, for the purposes of this book we will group together similar issues into broad, related frameworks. Each framework will include semantic and behavioral dichotomies that place the various cultural dimensions at opposite ends on a continuum. Over the last sixty years, researchers and practitioners alike have found it useful to compare one culture with another by using these dichotomies, which examine a continuous range of preferences, behaviors, and cultural norms. We will talk about this in greater detail throughout this book, but especially in Chapter 1, about cultural generalizations.

Chapter 1, An Overview of Culture, lays the foundation for talking about culture. We define what culture is and look at how perceptions and assumptions affect our attitudes and interactions with people who are different from us, so that we can move away from stereotypes and ethnocentrism toward a better understanding of others' differences that make life so fascinating.

Chapter 2, Culture and Communication, takes a close look at the interconnection between language and culture. We introduce linguistic frames of reference and then examine the verbal, vocal, and visual context in which communication occurs. We also examine ways in which people express themselves across cultures, and explore influence and persuasion from a cultural perspective. It matters how we organize our thoughts and whether we choose to approach reasoning directly or indirectly.

Chapter 3, Culture and Identity, will focus on two important aspects of culture: understanding individual identity and corporate identity. We will first look at the *internal* influences of culture on the individual and then examine how people respond to and identify with the *external* forces of nature and community. Pertinent questions such as "Are they individualistic or collectivistic in their approach?" will play a big part in this discussion. We then move on to explore the external influence of culture on people. Do they avoid or accept ambiguity and change? Do people tend to live in harmony with nature or try to conquer it? How does time, or the individual's perception of it, affect the way a person views the day? How do we use space to convey relationships?

Chapter 4, Culture and Power, focuses on ways people are affected by how their national culture uses power and authority. Key questions will include whether authority is ascribed or earned and whether a culture places emphasis on being or doing (also known as the masculine-feminine dimensions). We will examine the differences in societies that are regarded as competitive or cooperative, and conclude with a discussion on whether respect is given or earned.

Chapter 5, Applications for Intercultural Communication, will tie all of the concepts and discussions together. We will review the various challenges of identifying assumptions, verbal language, and nonverbal differences, and create a game plan for developing your own intercultural success. Throughout, we take the approach that each of us is responsible for learning about other cultures, and we explore a number of ways in which we can increase awareness, respect, and reconciliation among our differences so that intercultural interactions are mutually beneficial rather than stumbling blocks of confusion and misunderstanding. Finally, the case studies will encapsulate many of the cultural dimensions discussed in this book so that you may use them for individual reflection or group discussion.

In sum, *Intercultural Communication for Business* deals with communication and relational interactions among people from various cultures and backgrounds. To achieve a higher level of communicative competence, we must first be able to look inward and develop an awareness of who we are and what our basic values, beliefs, attitudes, and behaviors are. We then must look outward to observe, inquire, and interact with others so that we can develop a deeper understanding of different forms of human behavior. Interpersonal relationships on the job and in the classroom are not neat, tidy, or simple. Add the multiple hidden dimensions of our values, beliefs, attitudes, and behaviors, and it becomes even more problematic and more of a challenge. Our goal is to address the cultural and communication issues that global managers will surely face on a daily basis.

There is so much to say and only so much that we can include in a book this size. We offer no easy solutions for such a complex and multi-faceted topic. Our purpose will be to sift through and condense a massive amount of information to highlight the most salient points from key thinkers on intercultural communication. We will look broadly at various influences that shape an individual's culture and provide you with some specific ideas that will allow you to make your own decisions and formulate your own response to the cultural forces around you.

Elizabeth A. Tuleja
Mendoza College of Business
University of Notre Dame

Acknowledgments

This text was initially part of a seven-book series edited by Professor James S. O'Rourke IV, Director of the Fanning Center for Business Communication, Mendoza College of Business, University of Notre Dame.

INTRODUCTION

Standing before a classroom of more than a hundred international MBA students, I had a lecture to give during the pre-term orientation. In only one hour and twenty minutes, I had the challenge of condensing mounds of information and research so that I could brief this particular group of students on how to deal with the challenges that our U.S. culture, the culture of others as well as their own, would create while they studied in the United States to earn their MBAs. These students were in their late 20s, sophisticated, savvy, smart, and experienced. One criterion for admission was to have worked for at least five years before attending graduate business school. Many of these students had lived abroad, traveled extensively, and spoke several languages. One would think, therefore, that there would be no need for such a lecture. My experience in teaching diverse groups of students, working with a variety of professional clients, as well as living and working abroad, however, reminded me that no matter how culturally savvy we may be, it is always important to be reminded of the subtleties of culture, or what anthropologist Edward T. Hall calls the "hidden dimensions" of culture.

So, there I stood in a high-tech university classroom, surrounded by eager and enthusiastic students as I broached the topic of what to expect while studying in the United States. My challenge as a teacher was to offer practical information that would be immediately relevant to my students. Quite honestly, I wondered what value I might be able to add to this accomplished and worldly group of young professionals. We have all heard the familiar analogies of walking in someone else's shoes, looking through a different-colored lens, or not just focusing on the tip of iceberg. While these examples are all simplistic representations of culture, they nevertheless remind us it is through our own myopic lenses that we tend to view the experiences of others. This is exactly *why* we need to talk about culture (the underlying values, beliefs, attitudes, behaviors, and norms that are so familiar to us) because we can often overlook the fact that what is familiar to us probably will not be familiar to others. It is human nature to make assumptions about other people's actions and behaviors based on what we know or assume to be the "right" way of doing things.

A story may help illustrate this point. Years ago, Stephen R. Covey was interviewed by *Time* magazine. He had been named one of the top 25 most-influential people of that year because of his ideas on the behavioral habits of leaders and successful people. The journalist who interviewed him challenged him saying, "Mr. Covey, you make millions selling common sense." Mr. Covey's apt reply was, "Yes, of course, but we aren't always aware of what we know and don't always put that common sense into practice." The point is that while we may know *how* to communicate, we often aren't aware of *why* we do things the way we do. Pointing out the obvious (or not so obvious, in the case of cultural clashes) helps us focus on doing what we should do in the first place. Regarding intercultural encounters, we are so accustomed to our culture that it's now second nature to us. We don't notice it because it is ingrained in us or programmed into our minds, as Dutch interculturalist Geert Hofstede explains. Because we're comfortable doing things the way they appear most natural to us, we forget that not everyone approaches life the way we do. In essence, we allow *ethnocentrism* to creep into our thoughts and actions and judge others' behaviors according to our assumptions, which of course, are only natural and "right" to us.

Talking about culture and using familiar analogies is essential because all of our competence as communicators comes from self-awareness and other-awareness. As fellow sojourners in this journey called "life," we intuitively know this to be the case, but are often so caught up in the moment that we may neglect to take a step back and examine our assumptions and our attitudes. This text should appeal to a variety of readers. Whether you are student, working with others in learning teams, an instructor facilitating classroom discussion, or a businessperson on the way to do business with a client in another culture, I think we can all benefit from cultivating greater awareness about intercultural communication.

Taking into account such thoughts, how would *you* have proceeded if you were an instructor giving that lecture? Or, if you were a student listening to the lecture, what would *you* have wanted to know and how would you have preferred the information to be organized and communicated? Or, if you are a business professional who has picked up this book to gather some information as you prepare for a business trip, what are the important elements to help you do your work successfully with someone from another culture?

To answer those questions, I chose to do several things during the brief time I had with the students. What ensued in that brief lecture was a highly interactive discussion that offered the best of key thinkers on culture, along with a dynamic exchange that enabled students to add their own insights and experiences to what would be expected of them in the classroom. Rather than talk abstractly about these issues, I first laid the foundation by identifying several key differences in cultural dimensions. Then I invited students to offer their experiences, and we shared personal stories about how they have dealt with their assumptions, stereotypes, attitudes, and behaviors regarding intercultural communication. What I have learned from years in the classroom as well as in communication consulting is that we learn from a mix of theory and practical application. Sharing experiences of both successes and missteps is beneficial because communication is complicated, multifaceted, contextual, and situational. As we share such stories and try to make sense of them through the use of models and concepts, we can sharpen our understanding of the issues from multiple angles and perspectives.

CHAPTER I

An Overview of Culture

*All persons are puzzles until at last we find in some word
or act the key to the man, to the woman; straightway
all their past words and actions lie in light before us.*[1]

—Emerson

What is culture? How do we identify, let alone define, something so complex and abstract? What are perceptions, and how do they shape our understanding of cross-cultural differences? How do stereotypes and ethnocentric thinking interfere with our understanding of culture and how we communicate with others? These are the key questions we will address in Chapter 1.

EVOLVING DEMOGRAPHICS IN THE GLOBAL VILLAGE

In today's global market and increasingly fast-paced society, we often hear people say that the world is shrinking. In the 1960s, media expert and social visionary Marshall McLuhan coined the term "global village," which accurately forecast many of the changes we see today—changes that are the product of advances in technology through telecommunications, travel, and personal computing.[2] (See Figure 1.1) New technologies have made it possible to rapidly move raw materials, capital, finished goods, and people across oceans, borders, and time zones. We can do that both physically and electronically, transporting whatever we may need from the far corners of the world into our offices, our classrooms, and our neighborhoods.[3]

In today's global market, chances are good that most of what you've worn, driven, operated, or eaten was designed, manufactured, and distributed by firms that are transnational in character, organization, and culture. Your pajamas were probably manufactured in China; your suit tailored in Italy; your cereal produced in the Midwestern United States; your toothbrush made in Taiwan; your wristwatch manufactured in Switzerland. Our day-to-day lives are inextricably bound up with products, processes, and services from all over the world—something that, thirty years ago, was thought to be extraordinary. Imported goods were considered a luxury by

Figure 1.1: Entering the Global Village

your parents. That's no longer the case. Now Chinese factory workers wear New York Yankees ball caps; you wear gloves made in their factory.

We buy brand-name products from companies we think are American (Ford Motor Company, for example), only to discover that most of the component parts were manufactured in Brazil, Portugal, Ireland, or Canada. That German automobile in the neighbor's garage (think of a Volkswagen Jetta) was assembled entirely in Mexico. Your Dell computer was manufactured in Round Rock, Texas, but the tech support at the other end of their 1-800 line is in Bangalore, India. That cell phone made in Finland or Japan doubles as a camera, permitting you to e-mail vacation snapshots anywhere in less than a minute.

Those of us old enough to recall the 1970s and 1980s remember living in a world of rotary-dial telephones, electric typewriters, and manual transmissions. Fast forward to the twenty-first century, and we're awash in an explosion of broadband, digital technology that brings the world instantaneously to our desktops, laptops, and hand-held devices. It's changed the meaning of everything from "library research" to "chatting with a friend."

As finished goods, capital, and the supply of labor move quickly around the world, so does the reality of workplace diversity. Through immigration, increased opportunities for education and advancement, and the upsurge of women and minorities in the workplace, the U.S. workforce is no longer a homogenous group of people who look, think, and behave in the same ways. According to the U.S. Census Bureau's *Year 2000 Census*, among the nearly 300 million people inhabiting the United States, about 200 million are classified as White, about 35 million are African American or Black, more than 35 million are Hispanic or Latino, and more than 10 million are Asian. Some 25 million more are of other races or mixed race.[4]

Also according to the Census Bureau, in the year 2003 there were approximately 33.5 million foreign-born residents in the United States.[5] *The Kiplinger Letter* reports that more than 1.5 million foreign-born people settle in the United States each year, a number that will reach 2 million per year by 2010.[6] In addition, a Northeastern University study reveals that immigrants have accounted for over half of the labor force growth between 1990 and 2001.[7] By 2003, many of the foreign-born residents living in the United States were working for one of the 2,800 foreign firms operating here. That figure doesn't include over 7,200 American subsidiaries, affiliates, or branches of firms from over 79 countries.[8] Statistics from the Institute of International Education also show that by 2003 there were approximately 600,000 international students studying in the United States, up by 6.4 percent from the previous year.[9]

McLuhan's global village is not composed of just those who come to North America. The issues inherent in intercultural communication are important for all those who leave the United States and Canada to live and work elsewhere. Kiplinger estimates that more Americans are living abroad than ever before—nearly four million, not including military and diplomats.[10] As of 2003, there were more than 3,000 American corporations operating overseas to support this large number of expatriates, along with 36,300 foreign subsidiaries, affiliates, or branches from over 187 countries.[11] With so many people coming and going, we have become a mobile, global culture of immense proportions. (See Figure 1.2)

At the same time, an image of a world growing smaller and more accessible, with a more-diverse population, working literally side by side in the marketplace, no longer brings to mind those nostalgic recollections of traveling abroad. The twentieth-century image of foreign travel is one of a tourist, intrigued by unusual or quaint customs as she samples interesting cuisine and buys colorful trinkets, all while conversing in an exotic language in some far-off land. Today, that image is as anachronistic as a steamer trunk. The global village is more than the superficial interaction of a tourist on vacation: It is the current-day reality of savvy business professionals, graduate business students, or the folks next door who interact each day with people from all over the world and from a variety of ethnicities and backgrounds.

Demographic Redistribution in American Cities

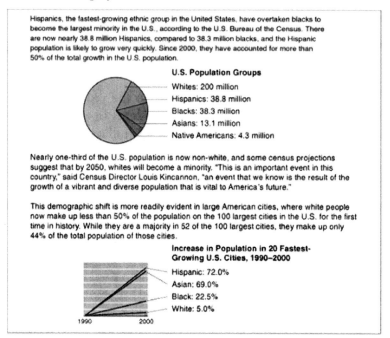

Hispanics, the fastest-growing ethnic group in the United States, have overtaken blacks to become the largest minority in the U.S., according to the U.S. Bureau of the Census. There are now nearly 38.8 million Hispanics, compared to 38.3 million blacks, and the Hispanic population is likely to grow very quickly. Since 2000, they have accounted for more than 50% of the total growth in the U.S. population.

U.S. Population Groups

Whites: 200 million
Hispanics: 38.8 million
Blacks: 38.3 million
Asians: 13.1 million
Native Americans: 4.3 million

Nearly one-third of the U.S. population is now non-white, and some census projections suggest that by 2050, whites will become a minority. "This is an important event in this country," said Census Director Louis Kincannon, "an event that we know is the result of the growth of a vibrant and diverse population that is vital to America's future."

This demographic shift is more readily evident in large American cities, where white people now make up less than 50% of the population on the 100 largest cities in the U.S. for the first time in history. While they are a majority in 52 of the 100 largest cities, they make up only 44% of the total population of those cities.

Increase in Population in 20 Fastest-Growing U.S. Cities, 1990–2000

Hispanic: 72.0%
Asian: 69.0%
Black: 22.5%
White: 5.0%

1990   2000

Sources: S. Schifferes, "Hispanics Overtake Blacks in U.S." *BBC News Online*, June 19, 2003. Retrieved from http://www.bbcnews.com and "Whites a Minority in U.S. Cities," *BBC News Online*, April 30, 2003. Retrieved from http://www.bbcnews.com.

Figure 1.2: Demographic Redistribution in American Cities

As the pace of globalization and contact with other cultures increases, so does the probability that one language will not serve all of your needs. A recent study shows that, across the globe, more people are speaking two or more languages, and the percentage of the global population who learned English as their native language is on the decline.

While many have argued that English is and will continue to be the world language of the twenty-first century, certain researchers studying the future of languages argue that because of population growth in developing countries during the last century, a new "linguistic order" is coming. Studies show that in the mid-twentieth century, about 9 percent of the world's population spoke English as their native language, but that number is expected to decline to about 5 percent by 2050.

Although more than 6,000 languages exist in the world today, more people speak Mandarin Chinese than any other, followed by English, Spanish, Hindi/Urdu, and Arabic. Those four languages will be spoken by roughly equal numbers of people by 2050. (See Figure 1.3) That won't mean English will lose its cachet as a global language, though. English will continue to dominate the content of the Internet, the regulation of international finance markets, international aviation, and air-traffic control. Of course, where there is money, there is influence: English-speaking nations will continue to control a sizable fraction of the world's commerce, capital, and investments.[12]

Languages other than English in U.S.

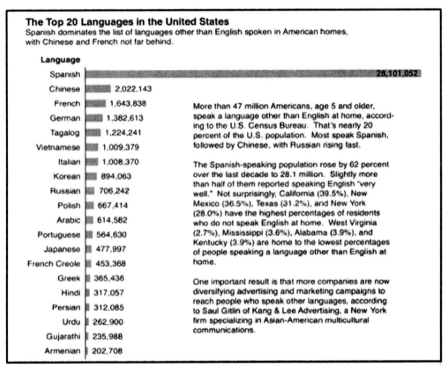

The Top 20 Languages in the United States
Spanish dominates the list of languages other than English spoken in American homes, with Chinese and French not far behind.

Language	
Spanish	28,101,052
Chinese	2,022,143
French	1,643,838
German	1,382,613
Tagalog	1,224,241
Vietnamese	1,009,379
Italian	1,008,370
Korean	894,063
Russian	706,242
Polish	667,414
Arabic	614,582
Portuguese	564,630
Japanese	477,997
French Creole	453,368
Greek	365,436
Hindi	317,057
Persian	312,085
Urdu	262,900
Gujarathi	235,988
Armenian	202,708

More than 47 million Americans, age 5 and older, speak a language other than English at home, according to the U.S. Census Bureau. That's nearly 20 percent of the U.S. population. Most speak Spanish, followed by Chinese, with Russian rising fast.

The Spanish-speaking population rose by 62 percent over the last decade to 28.1 million. Slightly more than half of them reported speaking English "very well." Not surprisingly, California (39.5%), New Mexico (36.5%), Texas (31.2%), and New York (28.0%) have the highest percentages of residents who do not speak English at home. West Virginia (2.7%), Mississippi (3.6%), Alabama (3.9%), and Kentucky (3.9%) are home to the lowest percentages of people speaking a language other than English at home.

One important result is that more companies are now diversifying advertising and marketing campaigns to reach people who speak other languages, according to Saul Gitlin of Kang & Lee Advertising, a New York firm specializing in Asian-American multicultural communications.

Source: Genaro C. Armas, "Census: Big Jump in Non-English Speakers." *The South Bend Tribune*, October 9, 2003, A1, A6.

Figure 1.3: Languages Other Than English Spoken in the United States

A RATIONALE FOR CULTURE STUDY

Before we can understand what makes other people different, and before we can know what makes them tick, we must first understand the basic elements of culture. Those elements are the values, beliefs, and attitudes that serve as the basis for the norms and rules of social interaction, all of which translate into behavior. Knowing something about those will help us to understand another person's world view, and the most basic assumptions he or she holds about others who are different.

Our goal is to have more successful cross-cultural interactions, to become more culturally literate. This book is not a quick fix with instant recipes for success; rather, it is a blueprint. We lay the foundation by first discussing some basic concepts of culture, such as the effects of individual and collective identity; our use of time and personal space; and our use of language, gestures, and more. Once we have some sense of what these things mean and why we use them as we do, we can begin to build our understanding of other cultures. By examining the basic underpinnings of culture (looking at the general), we can translate this into everyday interactions (looking at specific instances). The aim is not just awareness of self and others, but to acquire and use information that will equip us to take action every time we interact with someone who approaches life from a different world view.

Interculturalist Marshall Singer believes that the goal for intercultural communication is not just better communication, since conflict and misunderstanding will always be a part of the human condition. While we can never eliminate misunderstandings because of cultural differences, misperception is less likely if we are aware of the tacit subtleties that create the potential for conflict.[13] By laying out the basic concepts of cultural differences, we hope you will look inward to understand yourself, and then look outward to interact successfully with people who come from different frames of reference.

DEFINING CULTURE

In order to discuss intercultural communication, we must first define the concept of culture. Culture dictates the norms of every group. These norms, or unstated rules, are the accepted and expected ways of behaving and interacting with other people. But culture is something that we don't always see. Culture is something that we learn. From infancy on, we are conditioned to act, react, and learn about how people in our world do things from watching them, conversing with them, and interacting with them. In sum, culture includes our communication patterns; how we solve problems; and how we perceive and pass on our shared values, beliefs, attitudes, and behaviors, including our perceptions of self, group, environment, authority, and power.

Over the last century, key thinkers on culture, including anthropologists, sociologists, psychologists, communication specialists, and business experts, have attempted to define culture from various perspectives, frameworks, and focal points. The notion of culture is so abstract and complex that over 160 more-or less-accepted definitions of the term are in common use.[14]

Anthropologist Edward T. Hall says that culture is about how we communicate, and that it's governed by hidden rules (the silent language and hidden dimension), which are reflected in both language and behavior. Dutch interculturalist Fons Trompenaars says that culture is reflected in how a group approaches problem-solving.[15] Sociologist Geert Hofstede argues by analogy that culture implies a kind of collective "software of the mind," learned over a lifetime of "programming" the way we do things.[16] Kluckhohn and Strodtbeck, well-known anthropologists of the 1960s, construct their definition of culture around six dimensions that delineate cultural differences. Their framework focuses on value orientations (environment, time, people, activity, responsibility, and space), which have become the basis for much of today's research in the area of intercultural communication. [17]

To complicate matters even further as we attempt to define culture, let's look at another perspective from Marshall Singer. He makes an interesting point regarding culture:

> . . . because no person is a part of all, and only, the same groups as anyone else and because each person ranks the attitudes, values, and beliefs of the groups to which he or she belongs differently, each individual must be considered to be culturally unique . . . I am not arguing that every person is a culture unto herself or himself. Culture . . . is a group-related phenomenon . . . each individual in this world is a member of a unique collection of groups. No two humans share only and exactly the same group memberships, or exactly the same ranking of the importance, to themselves, of the group membership they do share. Thus, each person must be culturally unique.[18]

This is an interesting concept: that each of us is culturally unique. While this key thinker on intercultural communication would not go so far as to say that each of us is his or her own culture, the thought of being culturally unique as individuals is provocative. As you can see, culture cannot be neatly packaged into one definition, because it is as broad and complex as the number of people in this world. Culture is dynamic rather than static: it changes with people, geographical and historical events, and technological advances. For example, think about how cell phones and the Internet have changed the way we communicate, which amounts to less face-to-face interaction with other human beings. We now think twice about flying across the continent or to another country if we are able to save time, money, and resources by having a phone or video-conference.

The way we communicate in the twenty-first century is evolving as new technologies come into existence and as we learn to use them in effective and socially responsible ways.

Speaking of Culture

"From an anthropological perspective, every society has a culture and many subcultures. The questions are how to identify their components and how do they work?"

-Melvyn Hammarberg Chair, Department of Anthropology,
University of Pennsylvania

We learn about our culture as we interact with other people while sharing daily life, but we do not necessarily think about the fact that we are living out our particular lives, bound by culture. Most of our day-to-day activities are so natural to us that we have no need to think about why we behave, believe, or think the way we do. For example, we watch television commercials that stress self-actualization and individualism. "Be all you can be; join the army" coaxes young people to attain personal self-actualization. The newer slogan, "An army of one," implies that you can still maintain your individuality even though the purpose of joining the army is to become tightly interwoven in the fabric of the armed forces, with each man and woman depending on one another for their very lives. It is interesting to see how this slogan has evolved in the post-modern world where personal autonomy and self-identification have challenged the former mores of tradition and authority. We consider it natural to listen and accept such slogans without much reflection on or thought to the underlying values that shape these beliefs. We tend to take a more myopic view of culture and focus on what we can see and hear: the language we use, the clothes we wear, the food we eat, and the traditions and customs we uphold. But as we will see in the discussion that follows, there is much more to culture than meets the eye.

AN ANALOGY

An analogy may be appropriate at this point to help us visualize the concept of culture. Imagine that you are standing on the deck of a small tour ship making its way along the spectacular Alaskan coastline. It is close to dusk and you breathe deeply, the cold air filling your lungs as you watch the sun set. In the distance, you see majestic icebergs that ships pass at a respectful distance. Tall, jagged clumps of ice float silently by as the sun reflects its late afternoon glow on a massive expanse of whiteness. You've never seen anything quite like it and the concerns of your day seem to fade along with the setting sun.

As spectacular as it is to see real icebergs up close, we only see—proverbial as it may sound—the very tip. An iceberg is actually an enormous mass of solid ice that has broken off from the polar icecap and, because of its density, floats independently like an ice cube in a glass of water. While what we see above the water level may seem to be massive, in actuality, what's below the water line is even bigger. On average, approximately seven-eighths of an iceberg's mass is submerged.

Culture is, in some ways, like an iceberg. (See Figure 1.4) What we see on the surface is the most familiar and readily identifiable. As we've already seen, the usual associations with culture are a people's language, traditions, customs, food, dress, and more. Such things are noticeable, identifiable, and observable. What we can't see below the surface is what supports those external trappings. What we can see is simply an outward manifestation of all of those underlying factors that inform our behavior and shape and our world view—our attitudes, beliefs, and values.

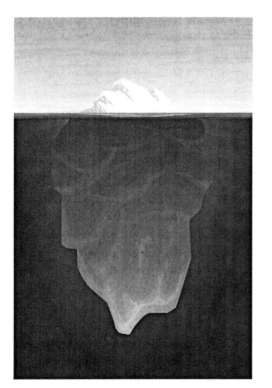

BEHAVIORS

―――――――――――

ATTITUDES

BELIEFS

VALUES

Figure 1.4: The Hidden Dimension of Culture

VALUES

The most basic of those structures are our *values*: those fundamental, unmovable tenets that make us who we are and that shape all other structures in our attitudinal system. They're a psychological assessment, really, of those things, those concepts, those ideas most dear to us. We acquire them at an early age from people we trust, before rational thought begins to play a role in what we know and hold to be true. The world is a particular way for us because that's what our parents, our teachers, our coaches, and our religious figures have told us. We're not in a position to challenge such beliefs—we simply accept them for what they are. Such values can (and do) change, but they do so at glacial speed. Occasionally, as the result of trauma or some cataclysmic event in our lives—a divorce, the death of a child, the loss of a job, a particularly profound betrayal—we'll find that one or more of our basic values has changed. But it's a rare event for most people, and a good thing it doesn't happen more often. Those values serve as the foundation for everything else in our attitudinal system.

BELIEFS

Values provide the basis for our *beliefs*: those truths we hold to be self-evident because they are based on our values. If friendship, for example, is a fundamental value for us, then we believe that genuine friends will behave in certain ways and will expect certain things of us. We, in turn, can expect certain things of them and will be more than willing to go out of our way to help our friends—because we believe in them.

ATTITUDES

Attitudes, in turn, arise from and are consistent with those beliefs. It's a navigational term, really, meaning orientation or position. Thus, an attitude gives some meaning and direction to our beliefs, serving as a guide to general thinking and our views of life over the near term. If a fundamental value of ours tells us that living a healthy lifestyle is important, then a consistent belief might be that smoking cigarettes is not a good idea. The attitude that arises from that belief would tell us, for example, that we not only shouldn't smoke, but that we should encourage others—our children, our employees, and our friends—not to smoke.

BEHAVIOR

Behavior is the direct result of all these structures and is found at the uppermost level of our attitudinal system. It not only gives meaning and life to our more basic attitudes and beliefs, but it is the most visible portion of our system of beliefs. It may be hard to tell what a friend is thinking, but it's fairly easy to see what he or she is doing. We observe behaviors and infer the attitudes and beliefs that animate them. Behavior is often expressed in the form of opinion – for the moment, at least, it's our opinion that we will vote for this person, dine at that restaurant, or purchase a particular brand. It's all subject to change, of course, and is less predictable than the underlying attitudes, beliefs, and values that support it.

Becoming competent in another culture means looking beyond behavior to see if we can understand the attitudes, beliefs, and values that motivate what we observe. By looking only at the visible aspects of culture—customs, clothing, food, and language—we develop a myopic view of intercultural understanding—just the tip of the iceberg, really. If we are to be successful in our business interactions with people who have different values and beliefs about how the world is ordered, then we must go below the surface of what it means to understand culture and attempt to see what Edward Hall calls the "hidden dimensions." Those hidden aspects are the very foundation of culture and are the reason why culture is actually more than meets the eye. We tend not to notice those cultural norms until they violate what we deem to be common sense, good judgment, or the nature of things.

PERCEPTION

The core values that make up our world view also strongly shape our perceptions. Perception is a cognitive process in which we attach meaning to objects, symbols, people, and behavior in order to make sense of them. These mental categories are called schema[19] and help us categorize what we know, for example, about a certain cultural characteristic (such as the meaning behind greetings) in order to better understand it. We each go through a process of receiving, organizing, and translating external stimuli, which influence our behavior and attitudes. For example, in some cultures people shake hands as a means for greeting, while in other cultures people bow and in other cultures they offer a kiss on both cheeks. We go through a cognitive process of receiving information or stimuli (e.g., being kissed on both cheeks) and attach meaning to this action in order to interpret or decode its meaning. During this process, we form mental categories (the schema) in order to help us organize the new information (e.g., the French greet us by kissing and the Japanese by bowing), so when we receive the stimuli, we process that information based on our perceptions and then categorize the information without even realizing it. Thus, it is an unconscious way of making sense out of the unfamiliar.

According to Jean Piaget, a twentieth-century Swiss psychologist who specialized in cognitive development, when we come into contact with something unfamiliar, in order to adapt to that situation, interaction, or environment, we must first assimilate and accommodate those external stimuli. Assimilation means that we process the information and mentally integrate it with our own existing knowledge—technically speaking, into our schema (mental categories). Accommodation means that we go through a process of adjustment or modification of these schemas in order to make sense of this new information.[20]

For example, in the U.S. culture and in other cultures of the developed world, we normally shake hands and look a new business contact in the eye upon meeting and exchanging introductions. When we travel to Japan for the first time and experience our business counterparts bowing rather than, or in addition to, shaking hands, we will try to assimilate or file away that information for future use. The next time we interact with a Japanese businessperson, we are more likely to adjust, or accommodate, our response by anticipating that the business contact will bow. The expectation, then, is that someone from Japan will probably greet others with a bow, so we need to be ready to bow in response.

An awareness of such norms, or unstated expectations of acceptable behavior, is just the beginning of successful intercultural encounters. Many more subtle nuances need to be learned. For example, let's return to the Japanese custom of bowing. While the Japanese are well-versed in U.S. culture and may very well initiate a greeting through a handshake, if they do choose to bow, there are nuances of how to bow appropriately that must be learned. For example, you only bow to the same depth that someone bows to you. Depth of the bow demonstrates the level, or depth, of the relationship and signifies the status of the initiator. If you observe carefully, you will also notice that you must lower your eyes, keeping the palms of your hands alongside your thighs.[21] Our own cultural norms are familiar to us, but often need to be explained to others because the behaviors carry different meaning.

Cultural norms are so pervasive because they are second nature to us, unless someone violates them. What makes understanding core cultural values difficult is that, even when we look below the surface and are aware of those cultural norms that define what people can and cannot do in their culture, our perception of those differences may not be accurate. For example, we may think that a handshake is quite appropriate in any situation and may be insulted if someone won't respond by shaking our hand. Consider the following: A number of years ago when I was a student in the southwestern United States, I remember shaking the hand of a gentleman who was a Native American. My perception of the "normal" way to shake hands was that when you extend your hand both parties should grasp firmly and shake with an up and down motion. However, this man simply offered his hand, which remained limp; he did not shake my hand firmly. I was startled and almost insulted because his cultural norm violated my perception of what a handshake should be: both people participating with a vigorous and firm grasp. At first, I was a little concerned that perhaps I had said or done something wrong. Someone later explained that this is the way someone from his culture shakes hands. My new acquaintance was simply displaying a friendly and appropriate gesture in the way that he shook hands according to the implicit rules of his culture.

Another experience, years later, demonstrated an additional custom regarding how people shake hands—or don't. One of my students at the university had agreed to participate in some research I was conducting and, when I went to greet him and shake his hand, he pulled away from me apologetically, stating that since was a Hasidic Jew he could not shake hands with a woman. I suddenly recalled that I had heard of this tradition before (reaching back into the resources of my memory) so this time, I was not surprised at the response. I had reacted to these two separate instances based upon my own cultural conditioning and the perceptions about "normal" means of behavior. I internalized the data from my experience and was, as a result, able to adjust my expectations and reactions accordingly. The meaning each of these men attached to his style of handshake meant something to him, based on his cultural norms. Each was acting appropriately.

In sum, each of us has core values that affect how we look at the world—in essence, how we perceive ourselves and others. We constantly receive information (stimuli) through a mental (cognitive) process in which we simultaneously attach meaning—that makes sense to us—to that information. We then store away the information as we form mental categories (schema), which we can draw upon for future interactions with others whose actions and words hold different meanings than ours.

Communicative adaptability requires cognitive, affective, and behavioral flexibility. It signals our willingness and commitment to learn from culturally dissimilar others…and support the other's cultural identity and way of communicating.

Stella Ting Toomey, Communicating Across Cultures

Where Big Macs Are Culturally Unacceptable, the Maharaja Mac Is Hot

Check out this article at: http://articles.philly.com/1998-02-08/food/25754686_1_maharaja-mac-ronald-mcdonald-veggie-burgers

Also, take a look at the piece in Foreign Policy regarding different types of McDonald's fare around the world: http://www.foreignpolicy.com/articles/2012/10/08/10_best_mc donalds_meals_you_wont_find_in_the_us

"Two all-beef patties, special sauce, lettuce, cheese, pickles, onions on a sesame seed bun." I remember this slogan being chanted, sung, and stated on T.V., the radio, and in print media when I was a kid. The Big Mac was symbolic of all things American!

However, in order to expand globally, McDonald's has had to adapt its food for the tastes of the local people. For example, in Hong Kong, I remember stopping in a McDonald's to see if they had the famous McApple pie – however, it was not apple but pineapple. And there were cups of corn kernels to suite the vegetable loving palates of the Hong Kong Chinese.

They had Big Macs in Hong Kong – but you won't find that in places like India, where people revere the cow as sacred and don't eat beef. Instead, they have the Maharaja Mac (in this case, it was two all-lamb patties). They also have veggie burgers made from potatoes, peas and carrots ground together with spices (probably *garam masala* which is an important blend of Indian spices that is a staple in every Indian kitchen).

What's interesting about McDonald's outside of the U.S. is that they are more of a meeting and mingling place versus a place to get a quick meal. It's a specialty, a status symbol for the growing middle class, and even a mating site where young people can congregate respectably in public on a date.

' "It's a new craze," said Dilip Odhrani, as his wife [clad in a headscarf], children and friend's children gobbled McChicken burgers, fish filet sandwiches, Vegetable McNuggets, fries, sodas, and more. The first McDonald's franchises in India opened in 1997 in New Delhi and Bombay. Since then, New Delhi has added a dozen more and Bombay nearly that number, all told serving more than 50 million customers.'

How about other tastes for other cultures: Japanese shrimp burgers (Ebi Filet-O), Turkey kabob burger (Kofteburger) made with parsley and mint, Moroccan cumin-infused flatbread beef sandwich (The McArabia), or in France, an open faced ham and cheese sandwich (Croque McDo).

McDonald's has been hailed for its cultural sensitivity regarding the food habits of people around the globe. When asked if McDonald's considers itself to be a multi-national corporation, former Senior Vice President Dick Starmann responded by saying, "Oh, no. We're definitely not multi-national. We're multi-local." All but a few stores, he explained, are owned by local business partners, and everything from the menus to advertising is carefully tuned to local tastes.

Sources: Lini S Kadaba, "Big Mac Nowhere to Be Seen in India, But Maharaja Mac Is One Hot Item," *The Philadelphia Inquirer*, March 9, 1998.

Personal Interview, Richard G. Starmann, former Senior Vice President, Corporate Communications, McDonald's Corporation. Chicago, IL: November 12, 2003.

The idea of perceptions and attaching meaning in order to generalize the behavior of others can lead to a slippery slope if we are not careful how we go about doing this. Before we go much further, we should explain how an understanding of basic cultural dimensions is possible *without* stereotyping. Our goal is to identify basic core values of all cultures—that is, cultural dimensions—to provide a general understanding that we might apply to specific cultures.

As we have discussed, culture is complex, multifaceted, and dynamic. Various areas of culture overlap, such as how we define time, space, equality, achievement, activity, our relationship to people and the environment, and more. There are numerous ways in which to organize the various categories. Since we are drawing on the work of many different experts in the field, you will see a number of similar ideas and concepts in the pages that follow. We will first talk about what is both broad and general in order to highlight some specifics that have particular application to doing business in a global market.

The eight broad categories (also identified as dimensions of culture) we will discuss in subsequent chapters:

-Context in Communication   -Change
-Identity   -Time
-Learning   -Authority
-Environment   -Achievement

We will explore each of these categories in depth but first will examine both the promises and the pitfalls of using our eight categories or dimensions of culture.

STEREOTYPES AND PROTOTYPES

Let's begin by thinking about how people talk about culture, about stereotyping, and culture-bound thinking. First, you should know that not all stereotypes are bad. Stereotypes are actually a way of mentally organizing what is familiar and unfamiliar to us so that we can compare what we do not yet understand with what we already know.

The term *stereotype* was coined by social scientist Walter Lippmann in 1921 when he wrote about why people so readily imagine how other people are, or why they behave as they do, even in the face of ready evidence to the contrary. In his landmark book *Public Opinion* he tells us that to stereotype is to ascribe to all members of a group or class those characteristics or behaviors observed in just one or a few members.[22]

Stereotypes can be grouped into positive, negative, and neutral categories. For example, we might say that the founders of the United States built their nation on the ideas of life, liberty, and the pursuit of happiness; or we might observe that Swedes are blonde; or that Scots wear traditional plaid for special occasions. We recognize that all cultures and subcultures exhibit certain behaviors or possess specific characteristics that are distinguishable from those of other cultures. This helps us sort out and categorize the world with mental processes that are predictable and easy to manage. One helpful way of distinguishing between negative and positive stereotypes is to focus on prototypes, which imply dynamic change, as opposed to stereotypes, which imply limitations. A prototype is an original model upon which we pattern something else. It is a springboard of identification that is the beginning of things yet to come.

For example, the following statement contains information gleaned from objective observations of the Chinese culture: "Building a business relationship may take considerable time with the Chinese." This is a neutral statement that contains information relating to specific cultural norms that have been empirically documented as identifiable patterns within the Chinese culture. After learning more about business practices in Chinese culture, you will come to understand that the Chinese place a very strong emphasis on developing trust over a long period of time and generally do not prefer to rush into business relationships only for the short-term. Further investigation will reveal that the Chinese generally have a long-term view of business; that is why developing relationships over time is so important – generally, the Chinese desire to create long-term relationships and not just focus on the task.

However, the traditional usage of the term "stereotype" sets up limitations for understanding because we can grow inflexible with the ways in which we categorize the behavior of someone from another culture. We run the risk, therefore, of assuming only similarities and may not acknowledge that cultures contain individuals who are capable of acting outside the typical cultural norms. While such generalizations are helpful, they do not take into account the many individual differences that vary from person to person within that culture. Do all U.S. citizens idealize such lofty pursuits? Are all Swedes blonde? Do all Scots adhere to the garb of their ancient clans? The obvious answer is no.

It is what we do with these generalizations that matters. While generalizations of this sort can be helpful in order for us to organize information, we risk becoming rigid in forming categories and assume that what applies to one applies to all. For example, if we use the concept of a family business, you probably think of a small organization employing fewer than a dozen people with annual revenues well below a half-million dollars. You probably also have an image in your mind of a middle-aged (or older) man opening the door in the morning and managing the facility with the assistance of his children or perhaps a few loyal employees. That's just one image of a family business.

In actuality, many family-owned businesses are as large as Campbell's Soup (the Dorrance family), Ford Motor Company (the Ford family), and Hyatt Hotels (the Pritzker family). Many employ professional executives who are unrelated to the owners, and have business interests that extend well beyond the founder's vision. Such businesses are atypical in other ways. Consider Johnson Publishing Company of Chicago, a family business headed by

Linda Johnson Rice, an African American woman who became president and chief operating officer at age 27. She fits hardly *any* of the customary stereotypes of a family business owner.[23]

If we extend this analogy to culture, you will see that, just because a particular culture embraces a certain belief, such as Confucian philosophy, doesn't mean that all people of that culture, such as the Chinese, hold this belief. While it may be helpful to associate Confucianism with Eastern philosophy, we cannot accurately say that all Eastern cultures and their people embrace this philosophy. Therefore, using the term "prototype"[24] may be more helpful (and more accurate), because it focuses more on the dynamic changes and possibilities characteristic of any particular individual, rather than what is both fixed and universal to all in the group. A prototype has the connotation of a framework or a model we can build on. With a prototype view, then, we could say more accurately (and confidently) that while many Eastern cultures, such as the Chinese, may have a belief system founded on Confucian philosophy, others within that culture look to Taoism, Buddhism, or other philosophies—or perhaps nothing at all—because people are both individual and mutable in their beliefs and behaviors.[25]

All cultures have a way of organizing their time, space, social relationships, power, and reactions to uncertainty. Each individual within a culture, however, will behave in his or her own unique ways, which is why we underscore the idea of prototypes. Yet we have a realistic and human need to categorize behaviors and actions that are unfamiliar to us in order to make sense of them. How do we reconcile the two opposing needs of categorization and assumption? The answer isn't simple and this is where it will be important for us to move beyond a superficial awareness of intercultural differences toward action.

We can begin to reconcile these aspects of cultural understanding as long as we don't blindly group all people into one category. Let's say, for example, that you are negotiating a large contract for manufacturing equipment parts from a Chinese vendor. You are aware that, generally as a culture, the Chinese pay specific attention to establishing social relationships as an important part of the negotiation process. Knowing this, you might expect your business client from China to work very hard to establish a relationship through special outings, events, and dinners (as opposed to your own culture's practice of "getting right down to business"). This much is derived from a stereotype of the Chinese. But a prototype approach might also tell you to examine your client's other business relationships, history of business practice in North America, shareholder base, and reputation. Businesspeople behave as individuals and many of them adapt their practices according to the expectations and interests of their customers.

This stereotype-to-prototype model can allow us to use general cultural knowledge as a beginning point in our dealings with others, but to modify our approach as we acquire information specific to the individuals with whom we're hoping to do business. It becomes a way to recognize the many hidden dimensions that implicitly guide our behaviors. This model can also provide us with an opportunity to correct misperceptions, mistaken impressions, and outdated stereotypes that are based on archaic or anachronistic information.

MAKING GENERALIZATIONS

We should also address the problem of approaching intercultural communication from a culture-bound perspective. As we proceed, you'll notice that much of the cross-cultural literature deals with dichotomies, creating polar opposites in order to compare one cultural dimension with another. Various cultures are being held up against one another for the purpose of making comparisons. Since much of the research conducted by the various authors (previously mentioned) is based on a Western thought process and world view, it is important to note that such work is unquestionably culture-bound. It is written primarily by scholars and practitioners from the United States and Western Europe, whose perspectives are informed by Western-style thought and perception. This lens or filter through which these scholars and practitioners view the world is biased because it uses its own culture as the standard or basis for understanding other cultures. With this caveat in mind, we recognize that our basis for understanding others comes largely from a Western perspective. This doesn't mean that Western cultures are dominant; it is simply the perspective through which we will begin to explore differences in intercultural communication. We invite you to explore your own cultural background and experience and bring those perspectives and knowledge to the discussion.

Geert Hofstede, a Dutch social psychologist, has done seminal work in the area of categorizing specific cultural dimensions. Using decades of observational data, his defining research looks at the employees in a multinational company that spans forty countries.[26] While Hofstede's work has been widely cited and is closely associated with intercultural studies, it was never meant to be the final word on identifying certain cultural dimensions and he, himself, has suggested that his work was meant to be a catalyst for other follow-up research. Nevertheless, Hofstede identified five dimensions that describe how the national culture is organized:

- Collectivism/Individualism
- Power Distance
- Masculinity/Femininity
- Uncertainty Avoidance
- Long-Term/Short-Term Orientation

While Hofstede's research is unquestionably culture-bound, he offers both pragmatic and realistic advice for approaching intercultural interactions. He warns us that statements about culture are not necessarily statements about individuals since any of the data he collected specific to each country in the survey is meant to describe the social system. For example, we can be cautious about assumptions regarding values, beliefs, attitudes, and behaviors that say *all* Korean students act a certain way (e.g., they are inscrutable) or that *all* teenagers from the United States who have body piercing are renegades and their behavior will show it.

When Slogans Go Wrong

Communicating with a target market means more than tossing out catchy slogans. A few companies learned this the hard way when they tried to translate their catchy English slogans directly into Spanish.

Braniff beckoned its passengers to "Fly in Leather" and Eastern Airlines proclaimed that "We Earn Our Wings Daily" Both of these now-defunct airlines were terribly mistaken. A Spanish speaker would think Braniff was asking its riders to "Fly Naked" and a Spanish translation of the Eastern slogan evoked a final destination in heaven, following death.

A few classic marketing blunders: General Motors discovered too late that "Nova" literally means "doesn't go" in Spanish. Coors encouraged its English-speaking customers to "Turn It Loose" but the phrased in Spanish meant "Suffer from Diarrhea." Budweiser's "King of Beers" became "Queen of Beers" in Spanish because the Spanish word for beer, "cerveza" has a feminine ending.

These examples show how dangerous it is to assume a good English slogan will be the same in Spanish. But it also shows how important it is for a company to become attuned to the cultural differences within the rapidly growing Hispanic market.

Some companies are now making honest efforts to learn about this growing consumer segment. These efforts create a niche for Hispanic marketing consultants who can design more sophisticated pitches to a Hispanic audience.

Toyota Motor Sales USA, for example, ran a campaign in 1987 asking, "Who Could Ask for Anything More?" The slogan was changed to a more straightforward meaning in Spanish: "Toyota Siempre Le Da Mas" or "Toyota Always Gives You More" McDonald's ran a campaign directly aimed at the Hispanic family, showing three generations of a family that speaks both English and Spanish. McDonald's also used strong community involvement to build up its Hispanic following. McDonald's and Toyota are paying attention to Hispanic cultural nuances. That is the key to reaching this thriving but fragmented market.

Source: David, Helin, "When Slogans Go Wrong" *American Demographics*, February 1992, Vol. 14, Issue 2, pp. 14-17.

Discussion:
1. What were some of the generalization traps made by these companies about doing business in another culture?
2. Identify language or marketing challenges other companies have faced as they go global.

ETHNOCENTRISM

It is human nature to think that all people are just like us. We often assume we are similar rather than different and expect that others will think the same way, perceive the same way, and behave the same way we do. While this is a natural assumption, this way of thinking is actually a form of ethnocentrism. Ethnocentrism is a form of superiority in which you believe your way of doing things is the right and preferable way. It is a way of negatively evaluating other cultures based on your particular cultural standards. (See Figure 1.5) While it may be human nature to do this, becoming an effective intercultural communicator requires that we understand people generally. Hofstede says we may have "different minds but common problems."[27] It is when we project our superiority onto others and judge their "different minds" as inferior that we block the process of understanding intercultural differences. Let's examine one way of looking at ethnocentrism.

HEAVEN & HELL STEREOTYPES

If heaven and hell were seen from a cultural viewpoint, would we bring our preconceptions and stereotypes with us?

Heaven
The cooks are French,
The mechanics are German,
The lovers are Italian,
The police are British,
And it's all organized by the Swiss.

Hell
The cooks are British,
The mechanics are French,
The lovers are Swiss,
The police are German,
And it's all organized by the Italians.

Original source on Internet unknown

Figure 1.5: Heaven and Hell – If heaven and hell were seen from a cultural viewpoint, would we bring our preconceptions and stereotypes with us?

Interculturalist Milton Bennett invites us to think about both the visible and invisible markers of culture as we begin to understand differences. Cross-cultural problems arise from differences in behavior, thinking, assumptions, and values between U.S. people and those from other countries and cultures with whom they associate. These cultural differences often produce misunderstandings and lead to ineffectiveness in face-to-face communication. A deeper understanding of the nature of cultural differences would increase the effectiveness of U.S. people in cross-cultural situations. But to reach this goal, Americans must first become more conscious and knowledgeable about how their own culture has conditioned their ways of thinking and planted within them the values and assumptions that govern their behavior.[28]

Cross-cultural problems arise from differences in behavior, thinking, assumptions, and values between U.S. Americans and those from other countries and cultures with whom they associate. These cultural differences often produce misunderstandings and lead to ineffectiveness in face-to-face communication. A deeper understanding of the nature of cultural differences would increase the effectiveness of U.S. residents in cross-cultural situations. But to reach this goal, Americans must first become more conscious and knowledgeable about how their own culture has conditioned their ways of thinking and planted within them the values and assumptions that govern their behavior.[29]

Bennett's framework[30] can help us to become more conscious and knowledgeable about our ways of thinking interculturally. His developmental model walks us through six stages of the process, each representing one aspect of experiencing difference. (See Figure 1.6) This model is set on a continuum in which moving from left to right through the six stages of *denial, defense, minimization, acceptance, adaptation,* and *integration* will bring us to a more interculturally sensitive position. This model is bent toward linear thinking (which we will discuss in Chapter 3), since Bennett stresses that in order to achieve the ultimate goal of "integration," we must move through each stage, one at a time. While a rigid model such as this has its limitations, it is nevertheless helpful to expand on the discussion of stereotypes and ethnocentric thinking. These phases are based on theoretical ideas taken from Bennett's years of teaching in intercultural training programs and are meant simply as a reference to help us analyze ethnocentricity. By identifying particular areas for self-centered thinking as related to cultural perspectives (hence, ethnocentricity), we can examine each of these stages to see where we may be affected. Bennett emphasizes action preceded by self-awareness to correct ethnocentric views and move us towards communication competence.

The first stage is *denial.* Denial means that we see no difference at all, viewing all things from our own world view or experience. It is easy, for example, to lump people into a single category, such as *Asians* or *Americans.* The former means that *all* Asians, whether Chinese, Japanese, Vietnamese, etc. belong to the same culture. The latter usually means residents of the

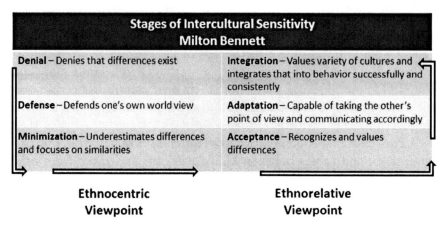

Figure 1.6: Stages of Intercultural Sensitivity by Milton Bennett

United States and neglects the fact that Canadians and South Americans are, in fact, Americans, as well.

The second stage is *defense*. This stage is characterized by excessive hostility against another culture or excessive pride in one's own. This is a stage in which we realize that there are differences but feel threatened by them, so we may insult, antagonize, or diminish others.

The third stage moves to *minimization*. This acknowledges the existence of cultural differences but claims such differences are superficial at best. While we acknowledge differences, we experience a need to maintain our feelings of cultural superiority, so we look for similarities to assuage our fears of difference. For example, if our culture celebrates birthdays in a particular way, we look for similarities in how people from another culture celebrate birthdays. It's clearly superficial, but it makes us feel better.

Moving from the third stage of minimization to the fourth, *acceptance* is the beginning of intercultural understanding. Acceptance recognizes and explores cultural differences by identifying them both by behavior, such as language, styles of verbal communication and nonverbal communication, and by the tacit values of a given culture. These include cultural norms of interdependence and collective work products versus independent and individualistic achievement.

According to Bennett, once we move toward the acceptance stage, we can begin to adapt, the fifth stage. *Adaptation* is the point at which we see and begin to embrace a different frame of reference (we'll talk about this more in Chapter 2). Empathy is a big part of adaptation. We move from simply recognizing and respecting that others are different to sympathizing and then empathizing with them. We try to walk in their shoes and experience (limited as this may be) things from their perspective.

Finally, *integration* is the point at which we all recognize and adapt to the differences, case by case. This final stage is not about simply being sensitive to people from another cultural perspective; it involves building skills and a deeper awareness of what it means to be someone else.

CHAPTER SUMMARY

This first chapter has provided a somewhat broad view of culture to get you thinking about how your own values, beliefs, attitudes, and behaviors may differ from those of the people with whom you interact each day. Using the example of the iceberg, you have seen how behavior is noticeable at the surface, but the reasons for that behavior are submerged deep below. We have examined the nature of perception and how people naturally create mental images that help to sort out interactions, situations, and environments that are unfamiliar to them. We have also discussed the problematic nature of examining culture because each of us approaches life with culture-bound perspectives and sees the world from our naturally biased frame of reference.

The goal for every professional who hopes to be successful in the global market should be to develop a deep understanding of the major cultural dimensions that affect our values, beliefs, attitudes, and behaviors, and which ultimately set cultures and people apart. The explosion of the information age and the interconnectivity that brings people together from the far reaches of the Earth necessitate such an understanding. In the pages ahead, we will examine key cultural dimensions and plumb what lies beneath the waterline in the attempt to understand the tacit, subtle, and often confounding issues that remain hidden from our cultural consciousness.

APPLICATIONS IN THE GLOBAL MARKETPLACE

Culture can affect us in the workplace:

- When stereotypes affect impressions.
- When ethnocentrism interferes with understanding.
- When identifying and communicating differences.
- When trust is not readily established.
- Can you think of a situation in which you encountered difficulties communicating with someone from a different background? What happened and how did you resolve it?

Self-Awareness and Other-Awareness

- What defines you as an individual?
- What are the differences among people in your current work group?
- What makes each person in your work group unique?
- What defines the groups to which you belong?

When Stereotypes Affect Impressions

- Have you ever evaluated someone else according to just one characteristic?
- Can you think of a situation in which you or someone you know has been evaluated according to a stereotype?
- When are we most likely to perceive others selectively? What characteristics are we most likely to focus on in such perceptions?
- Do people you know ever evaluate others based on limited evidence? When are such evaluations most likely to occur? Are they *always* bad?

A CASE STUDY

DEWEY BALLANTINE, LLP: CULTURAL STEREOTYPES AND AN INTEROFFICE E-MAIL

It began, like so many office controversies, with an e-mail message. Responding to a note seeking someone to adopt a puppy, a partner in the London office of the law firm of Dewey Ballantine wrote, "Please don't let these puppies go to a Chinese restaurant!"

Some of the firm's associates found the message offensive and said so; dozens of Asian-American law student associations and bar associations stepped forward to criticize it as well. Senior partners in the firm apologized almost immediately, sending out a firmwide apology. So did the author of the message.[1]

The firm had already put its lawyers through sensitivity training in the wake of a skit performed at a dinner the year before when lawyers infuriated members of the Asian-American community. Their after-dinner parody mocked stereotypical Asian accents to the tune of "Hello, Dolly," singing that they were "so solly" that the firm was closing its Hong Kong office. The firm now no longer even holds that annual dinner. "Somebody made a mistake, and they've apologized," said Morton A. Pierce, a co-chairman at the firm, adding that the partner would be disciplined. "And we keep apologizing," he added.[2]

It is rare but not unheard-of for dog to appear on the menu in a restaurant in rural China, though dog meat is much less likely to be offered by Chinese restaurants in other parts of the world. The message was offensive, associates at the firm say, because it seemed to mock Chinese people. "People say, 'Oh, you're just being over-sensitive,' but I think it's a symptom of something underlying," said Karen Y. Tu, a second-year law student at Columbia who is co-chairwoman of the Asian Pacific American Law Students Association. She later said, "What is going to change this environment? What is going to make it easier? What is going to make Asian Americans comfortable about going back to Dewey?"[3]

DEWEY BALLANTINE, LLP

Founded in 1909, Dewey Ballantine, LLP is an international law firm with offices in key financial centers around the world. For nearly a century, they have provided guidance, experience, and insight to clients on a wide range of complex legal matters. The firm employs 582 attorneys worldwide and specializes in more than 40 separate practice areas, including litigation, taxation, mergers and acquisitions, intellectual property, and banking.[4]

Dewey Ballantine established its London office in 1991. The London office consists of more than 40 attorneys, including 14 partners, qualified in the United Kingdom and the United States, as well as in France, Germany, Ireland, Israel, Italy, Kazakhstan, Russia, and the Ukraine. They provide clients in Europe, the Middle East, and Africa with advice under the laws of those jurisdictions with a focus on capital markets, mergers and acquisitions, private equity, project finance, securitization, structured finance, and international tax. The firm's clients include FTSE 100 and Fortune 100 companies with commercial interests in consumer goods, financial services, infrastructure, oil and gas, power, technology, telecommunication, and transportation.[5]

The company's web site describes the firm as one that "serves a sophisticated and diverse client base."[6] Of 582 lawyers at Dewey Ballantine, 41 are Asian Americans, according to the firm.[7]

THE INFAMOUS DINNER SKIT

The firm issued an apology nearly six weeks after the *New York Law Journal* reported that, at a January 31, 2003 annual dinner, the firm had parodied the closing of its Hong Kong office with a version of "Hello Dolly" re-titled "The Dirge of Long Duck Dong," an apparent reference to the stereotyped Chinese exchange student in the movie *Sixteen Candles*.

The song said the seven-lawyer office, which closed at the end of March 2003, was "Chow Mein" and would get "the gong." "You were the firm's folly," the song intoned, "and now we so solly to be cutting off your source of livelihood." The annual black-tie dinner and its anonymously penned parodies were a longstanding tradition at the firm. Sanford Morhouse and Morton Pierce discontinued the dinner shortly after becoming the firm's co-chairs in October of 2003.[8]

"It was a party culture that had outlived its usefulness," Mr. Morhouse told reporters. But he stressed that neither the dinner nor the e-mail incident in January 2004 should be taken as representative of the firm's character. He said Asian and Asian-American lawyers were "tremendously well-regarded" and "highly valued at the firm."[9]

AN E-MAIL TO REGRET

On the afternoon of Monday, January 26, 2004, Douglas L. Getter, the head of Dewey Ballantine's European mergers and acquisitions practice, returned from lunch to the firm's offices at 1 Undershaft in London's East End. near Lincoln's Inn and the famed Old Bailey courthouse. As he opened his e-mail, Mr. Getter discovered a firm-wide memo in his inbox advertising the availability of some puppies for adoption. He quickly composed a firm-wide reply with the concluding line: "Please don't let these puppies go to a Chinese restaurant!"[10]

By clicking the "reply all" button on the e-mail server, Getter set off a firestorm of criticism, much of which began inside the firm. Within minutes, senior partners began hearing from irate associates and others. Following a brief conversation with Getter, co-chairs Sanford Morhouse and Morton Pierce issued a response. "This afternoon an offensive e-mail was circulated by a partner," they wrote. "Comments of this nature are inconsistent with the values of this firm and will not be tolerated. We extend our immediate apologies to the entire Dewey Ballantine community."[11]

In a press interview the next day, Mr. Morhouse said the firm's executive committee would be meeting shortly to determine what further action to take.

OPPOSITION BEGINS TO EMERGE

Shortly after news of the e-mail message began making its way around the Internet to law firms, law students, public interest groups, and various Internet message boards, a group of Asian American law student organizations sent a letter to Dewey Ballantine asking what proactive steps the firm intended to take to prevent the recurrence of such an incident.

Mr. Pierce responded to critics by saying that it was not clear what the firm should do other than to keep apologizing. "I wish that there were some way we could convince them very easily and quickly that this was truly aberrational with respect to our culture," he said. "But clearly that's not going to happen." Several associates at the firm said they were thinking of leaving to work elsewhere but added that they had already decided to move on before this particular e-mail message was sent. One executive recruiter said that his firm had noted an increase in resumes from Dewey Ballantine associates over the preceding several months, but noted that the trend predated the e-mail message.[12]

News of the incident, however, along with a careful recounting of the dinner skit a year earlier, moved quickly across the Internet and onto a number of weblogs devoted to legal issues and Asian American concerns. One blog poster at *Angry Asian Man* wrote:

It's got to be the world's worst luck for one firm to make national news twice in a twelve-month period for the same kind of incident, and against the same racial group. Various national Asian groups are lining up to excoriate the law firm. I, however, have some mixed feelings. Obviously, Getter's e-mail is more than tasteless and obnoxious; it's culturally insensitive and borderline bigoted. But it's hard to find any criticism of the law firm's response.[13]

Another poster on the same web site disagreed:

As another American of Asian descent who continues to hear the same questions / remarks 'Where are you from . . . . No, I mean your nationality. . . . No, I mean . . . .' And, 'You speak English so well!' . . . The Dewey Ballantine story does not surprise me. Though for the chairman to say this 'may' have been in bad taste? There is NO 'may be' about it. If the parody was made of African-Americans—use your imagination—there is no way the chairman would have simply said this 'may' have been in bad taste.[14]

And yet another shared his personal frustration:

The funny thing is that one of my good friends from law school—also of Asian descent—worked for Dewey as an associate out of law school. (He left long ago). I don't mean to blow this out of proportion, however. Maybe the associates who planned that skit simply lacked decent taste (or sobriety). And to be fair, the firm's chairman did agree that song was 'maybe' in bad taste. Still, this incident reminds me of the many times I've been told, 'Oh, you speak English so well.' I do not have an Americanized given name. But why should it be so surprising?[15]

AN OFFER TO TALK

Senior partners at the law firm met with Asian-American associates on the afternoon of Thursday, February 5, 2004 to talk about the incident. The message, according to Mr. Pierce, was simple: "This isn't Dewey Ballantine; this isn't who we are. This isn't the firm that they joined. It's not emblematic or symptomatic of who we are." The firm said it would hold a special round of sensitivity training in its London office in addition to its twice-yearly firm-wide training.[16]

"There is no defense in these situations," said Roger Cramton, a law professor at Cornell University. He added that law professors have had to rethink the examples they use to illustrate legal issues in classes. "This is such a politically correct world."[17]

Several Asian American lawyers and law students said that the problem was not the e-mail message itself but the fact that the partner who sent it did not stop to think first. "What scares the rest of us," said Andrew Thomas Hahn, a partner at Seyfarth Shaw, LLP in New York, "is [whether] it is pervasive at law firms generally or corporations generally that Asians can be mocked with impunity." Mr. Hahn is president of the Asian American Bar Association of New York. At law firms generally, he thinks, Asians worry that they may be stereotyped as passive and are steered out of certain areas of practice.

Ms. Tu, the law student at Columbia, said that Asian-American law students there were meeting to discuss how to respond. One possible step, she said, would be to boycott Dewey Ballantine during the fall recruiting season—something that might happen informally anyway. "Not as a statement," she said, "but because they don't want to work in that environment." Ms. Tu said that working at big firms can already be difficult for nonwhite lawyers, given their small numbers.

John C. Liu, a member of the New York City Council who has received numerous complaints about the e-mail message, had one suggestion in particular about what Dewey Ballantine could do to assuage concerned Asian-Americans, both within and outside of the firm. "I would like to see them take up a case involving bias against Asian-Americans pro bono. And I have one or two specific cases that I would like to see them take up."

Questions

1. From Dewey Ballantine's point of view, what are the critical issues in this case? Which among them are most important?
2. Who are the principal stakeholders here? What's at stake for each of them?
3. Is this just a temporary matter for the firm, or are complaints and animosity likely to persist? Can Dewey Ballantine take a low profile on this issue and simply wait for the controversy to pass?
4. From a reputation-management point of view, what sort of problems does the firm face?
5. What actions are available to the managing partners? Which actions would you advise they take first?
6. Does Dewey Ballantine need outside communications-management counsel for this matter, or can they reliably handle this with existing staff?
7. Is this, as some observers have said, simply a case of overreaction or political correctness taken to an extreme? Would be it helpful if the firm were to position these events in the context of "good-natured" humor?

CASE SOURCES

1. Jonathan D. Glater, "Asian-Americans Take Offense at a Law Firm Memo," *The New York Times* (February 7, 2004): B1.
2. *Ibid.*
3. *Ibid.*
4. Dewey Ballantine, LLP web page. Retrieved February 11, 2004, from http://www.deweyballantine.com.
5. *Ibid.*
6. *Ibid.*
7. Glater, *supra* n.1, B14.
8. Anthony Lin, "Dewey Partner's E-Mail Causes Upset Over Racial Insensitivity," *New York Law Journal* (January 28, 2004): 1, 2.
9. *Ibid.*, 2.
10. Anthony Lin, "Dewey Partner's E-Mail Causes Upset Over Racial Insensitivity," Law.com. Retrieved February 12, 2004, from http://www.law.com.
11. *Ibid.*

12. Glater, *supra* n.1, B14.
13. *Angry Asian Man* weblog. Retrieved on February 10, 2004, from http://yin.blog-city.com/read/460931.htm.
14. *Ibid.*
15. *Ibid.*
16. Anthony Lin, "Dewey Ballantine Makes Commitment to Sensitivity Training, Working for Diversity," *New York Lawyer* (February 6, 2004). Retrieved February 11, 2004, from http://www.nylawyer.com/news/04/02/020604d.html.
17. Glater, *supra* n.1, B14.

CHAPTER 2

Culture and Communication

Because everyone uses language to talk,
everyone thinks he can talk about language.

—Goethe

Having looked at the fundamentals of culture in the first chapter, it may now be appropriate for us to examine the other half of the equation: communication. Why is it that people consider communication to be so important? How is intercultural communication different from the other communication we engage in? What do people mean when they speak of "sharing the same frame of reference?" Why does context play such a crucial role in the transfer of meaning? How does expression vary from culture to culture, and why do people from various cultures differ in the way they organize and present information? These are just a few of the key issues that lie ahead.

INTRODUCTION

In 1991, the Walt Disney Company encountered difficulty as they tried to communicate the corporation's dress codes to prospective employees in their Disneyland Resort theme park near Paris. At the time, Disney was in the process of hiring about 12,000 staff members at all levels. To maintain the same standards required of employees in the United States, strict rules concerning clothing, hair, facial hair, and jewelry became a major part of applicant screening. Differences in cultural norms regarding appearance quickly turned into a legal dispute, and the company found itself trying to communicate across significantly different frames of reference concerning what is considered appropriate appearance for employees.

The dispute began as French nationals were terminated for not adhering to Disney's strict dress code. A culture clash ensued when the French employees claimed that the U.S.-based company was insensitive to *their* standards of culture, individualism, and privacy. Something as simple as wearing a beard became a legal dispute. Disney executives responded to this protest by claiming that an employee's appearance was related directly to brand image. The controversy accelerated and turned into a labor dispute.[1]

Disney's dress and appearance code was viewed as an affront to European social standards and failed to communicate goodwill toward the company's new employees. Disney held the position that their standards were no different than dozens of other foreign employers, including airlines and professional services firms. While the dispute was eventually resolved, Disney learned a great deal about how to communicate its policies when interacting across cultures with different expectations. The bottom line: when communicating company policies you have to be aware of differing frames of reference.

Speaking of Culture

Communication is at the heart of all organizational operations and international relations. It is the most important tool we have for getting things done. It is the basis for understanding, cooperation, and action. In fact, the very vitality and creativity of an organization or a nation depends upon the content and character of its communications. Yet, communication is both hero and villain—it transfers information, meets people's needs, and gets things done, but far too often it also distorts messages, causes frustration, and renders people and organizations ineffective.

—Philip Harris and Robert T. Moran, *Managing Cultural Differences* [2]

COMMUNICATION

As we think about the act of communicating with someone, it may be helpful to consider the etymology or origin of the word. *Communication* actually stems from the Latin verb *communicare*, "to share or to make common to many."[3] We all know from experience that communicating effectively can be difficult, even with people we know and with whom we share things in common. Add the extra dimension of the cultural norms, which tacitly guide us in the accepted and expected ways of being and doing, and suddenly the process becomes even more complicated. The acts that we associate with communication do not equate to understanding. Two people chatting away, sending and receiving messages in a language they share, aren't necessarily communicating. Thus, communication—truly effective communication between two or more people—is *the transfer of meaning*.[4]

When I understand a subject the way you understand it—with all of the intricacies, complexities, context, and detail—then we have communicated. If I am not only aware of what you *know* about a subject, but how you *feel* about it, then we have communicated. When I comprehend just how important a subject is to you and why you think it's important to take (or avoid) action, then we have communicated.[5] Genuine understanding occurs only when both of us agree not only on the meaning of the verbal symbols (words), but on the nonverbal elements of the transaction (body movement, touch, silence, use of time, and much more) as well. As you will see, language is an important part of this, but there is much more for us to consider.

In our discussion of culture and communication in this chapter, it will be helpful if we view communication as both a process and a product with the main goal of sharing common ideas. The *process* of communication involves simultaneously sending and receiving messages through language and nonverbal messages, which is a form of symbolic cues. The *product* of effective communication is shared meaning among communicators. This shared meaning is the product of a process in which all participants determine the meaning of both verbal and nonverbal messages. Thus, it's fair to say that we do not communicate *to* others, but *with* them.[6] Since language is largely symbolic, we arbitrarily assign symbols to words and expect that everyone involved will share the same interpretation of those words. It is important to observe at this point that communication is a behavior, and behavior communicates. Such behavior frequently produces results—often favorable, but sometimes not.[7]

OUR ROLE IN THE PROCESS

We participate in this process by sending messages through a number of channels, including face-to-face conversation; on the telephone; and through letters, e-mails, text-messaging, and faxes. Each exchange involves a situation or context that will have some effect on participants and the meaning they derive from the process. It may be an inter-organizational teleconference, a convention plenary session in a hotel ballroom, a contentious contract negotiation, a cross-functional group project meeting in a small room, an office-wide social gathering, or a chance encounter in the hallway. The people to whom you send a message must receive the information it contains, perceive and understand the cues that accompany the message, and then interpret all of them according to a personal frame of reference so that they can respond appropriately.

All sorts of distractions, or noise, can interfere with our communication transactions, including *physiological noise* (back pain as you sit through a meeting), or *physical noise* (a siren going off at street level during a business presentation) or *psychological noise* (being anxious or fearful about the presentation itself, or concerns about unrelated issues). The process is often described as transactional because both participants are communicating simultaneously—they transact meaning through the process of clarifying what has been communicated.[9] While one speaks, the other responds through nonverbal—and eventually, verbal—feedback as they exchange meaning and attempt to understand each other within the context and the situation. Thus, the exchange is dynamic rather than static. (See Figure 2.1)

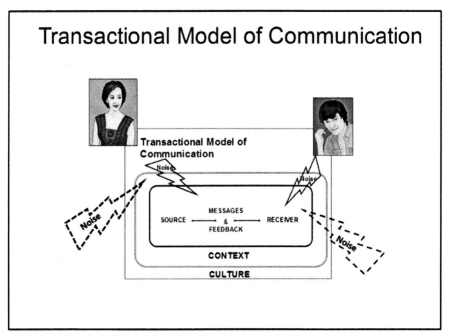

FIGURE 2.1: Transactional Model of Communication[8]

BEHAVIORS ARE CLUSTERED

Communication, as we mentioned a moment ago, is behavioral and involves the interaction of verbal and nonverbal elements. Nonverbal elements can include kinesics or body movement, such as gestures, facial expression, eye contact, posture, and touch. It also includes vocalics, such as tone of voice, inflection, pacing, and pitch. Verbal elements involve the actual words we speak or write. These elements all work together in packages or *clusters* in which the various verbal and nonverbal messages occur more or less simultaneously. Body posture, eye contact, arm and leg movement, facial expression, vocal tone, pacing and phrasing of vocal expression, muscle tone, and numerous other elements all happen at once. It is difficult to isolate one element of the cluster from another without taking all of them into account.[10]

COMMUNICATION BEHAVIORS ARE OFTEN DIFFICULT TO READ

During the 1970s, a number of popular books introduced the general public to communication and its various sub-disciplines. *Body Language*, written by the journalist Julius Fast, described the nonverbal studies of several researchers.[11] That best-seller was followed by others that simplified and popularized research in this area; many of them, however, oversimplified the behavioral science behind the findings in the interest of making a sale, detecting a liar, attracting members of the opposite sex, and so on. According to Professor Mark Knapp, although such books aroused the public's interest in nonverbal communication . . . readers too often were left with the idea that reading nonverbal cues was the key to success in any human encounter; some of these books implied that single cues represent single meanings. Not only is it important to look at *clusters* of communication behavior, but also to recognize that nonverbal behaviors, like verbal, are rarely ever limited to a single denotative meaning.[12]

Speaking of Culture

The unspoken dialogue between two people can never be put right by anything they say.

—Dag Hammarskjöld, United Nations Secretary General, 1953–1961

MANY BEHAVIORS ARE GENUINELY DIFFICULT TO INTERPRET

What may mean one thing in one context, culture, or circumstance may mean something entirely different in another. Professor Knapp goes on to say, "Some of these popularized accounts do not sufficiently remind us that the meaning of a particular behavior is often understood by looking at the context in which the behavior occurs; for example, looking into someone's eyes may reflect attention in one situation and aggression in another." [13] Understanding communication context, just as we would with verbal expression, becomes especially important. In the United States, looking someone directly in the eye may be seen as a sign of respect and honesty. In Japan, it may be seen as an act of hostility and disrespect. Such behaviors are all culturally acquired and context-based. [14]

Different Styles of Negotiating

Nonverbal behavior plays a crucial role in how people from different cultural backgrounds negotiate in business. While it is impossible to understand every nuance of verbal and nonverbal communication, it is still good to gain a general knowledge of what may occur so that you can anticipate the interaction. Obviously, not everyone will behave in the same manner, but awareness can go a long way to a more successful co-creation of communication between people of different cultures. Let's look at three distinctly different ways to negotiate a business contract based on cultural values.

Since the Japanese value emotional sensitivity, they will not express emotion during business deals—self-control and deference are considered essential when responding to clients. For example, when disagreeing about a price it is usual for someone who is Japanese to not argue and to remain silent when he feels he is right.

While still respectful of clients, North Americans have a different way of communicating when negotiating a deal. They typically do not value emotional sensitivity in the same way that the Japanese do and are more straightforward with their demands. Since "saving face" is not a typical value but "cutting to the chase" is, the North American negotiator may come across as being less emotionally sensitive than his or her Japanese counterpart. It has been said that, typically, such a negotiator has no problem being argumentative, but remains detached personally.

In Latin America, like Japan, more attention is paid to emotional sensitivity when negotiating a deal. But rather than hide the emotions, Latin Americans are typically known for displaying emotions and, while they may show such strong emotions, it is usually with the attitude that they will preserve honor and dignity.[15]

Source: Ricky W. Griffin and Michael W. Pustay, *International Business: A Managerial Perspective* (Reading, MA: Addison-Wesley, 1999), 339.

Many Behaviors Are Often Contradictory

Our posture and vocal tone may say one thing, agreeing entirely with the words we speak, but our eyes may say another. We might try to stand up straight and portray a dominant, confident posture, but our hands fidgeting with a pen say may something entirely different. Verbal and nonverbal behaviors come packaged together, and we must carefully examine all of those behaviors before we begin to understand a coherent picture of the person we're speaking with. The obvious problem with such packages or clusters of behavior is that they're not always consistent and not always complimentary. The question is, "Which of them should we believe?"[16]

Some Behaviors Are More Important Than Others

As we examine several behaviors clustered together—vocal tone, pace, and pitch; body posture; pupil dilation; arm and hand movement—it often becomes clear to careful observers that some behaviors are more important than others. For the most part, the relative importance of a behavior is dependent on the habits and usual actions of a speaker. In other words, are the behaviors I'm observing usual or unusual for this person? If they are unusual, do they contradict verbal portions of the message? Some portions of our anatomy are simply easier to control than others: even a nervous person can sit still if she makes a determined effort to do so, but few among us can control the dilation of our pupils or a flush of embarrassment. Many can control facial expressions, but few of us can determine when tears will flow, or when our voices will choke with emotion.[17]

We Often Read into Some Behaviors Much That Is Not There, and Fail to Interpret Some Behaviors That Are Clearly Present

We often look for behaviors that seem most important to us personally: whether a person will look us directly in the eyes as we speak or which direction they've crossed their legs. Such behaviors may be meaningless. We can also misread behavioral cues if we have insufficient information on which to base a judgment. Managers seen nodding off in a conference may be judged as indifferent by their hosts; in reality, it may be jetlag catching up with them.

We're Not as Skilled at This as We Think We Are; Our Confidence Often Exceeds Our Ability

Caution is certainly appropriate as we perceive and process communication behaviors. Even though we've been at this all of our lives, we simply aren't as skilled as we'd like to be. It's easy to misinterpret, misread, or misunderstand someone. It's equally easy to jump to conclusions from just a few bits of evidence. The best advice would be for you to withhold judgment as long as possible, gather as much information—verbal as well as nonverbal—as possible, and then reconfirm what you think you know as frequently as you can. The stakes are high in business and personal transactions—almost as high as the chance for error in decoding communication behavior.[18]

FRAME OF REFERENCE

The product of effective communication is what is actually communicated, whether it's the content of a telephone conversation, an e-mail message, or a formal presentation. When we fail to communicate with one another, it's usually because one of us thinks we've been clear when, in fact, we have not. A frequent source of miscommunication is misreading or missing the *frame of reference*.

The diagram below (Figure 2.2), illustrating Ogden and Richards's "Triangle of Meaning," demonstrates how people share meaning through language. In their schema, a communicator (both sender and receiver) is referred to as an *interpreter*; a *symbol* is anything to which people assign meaning, such as words, diagrams, colors, and so on; and the *referent* is the idea that a symbol will evoke in the mind of an interpreter. So, when we act as interpreters, we hope to select symbols that others will understand in precisely (or approximately) the same way we do. In other words, we're hoping our receivers will assign the same meaning to a word that we have. If we use a symbol that means something different to the person we're addressing than it does to us, then we create faulty "referents" in our minds. In essence, we're not on the same wavelength. Communication, then, occurs only when *meaning* is agreed upon. We can certainly create meaning through nonverbal signals and signs, through graphic images, and other means. But, like it or not, language remains the most powerful tool for humans to share meaning.

There is a great cartoon by Scott Adams where Dilbert is talking to his date over coffee. In the first screen Dilbert asks his date what she thinks of him. In the next screen, she responds, "You remind me of Elvis." The last screen shows each of them and what they are thinking – Dilbert is thinking, "Sexy!" but his date is thinking, "Dead!" In the cartoon our hero Dilbert hears from his date that he reminds her of Elvis. This is an obvious mismatch of frames of reference, the *meaning* (or referent) she assigns to Elvis's name (the symbol) isn't "sexy," but "dead." Things don't look good for the rest of their evening.

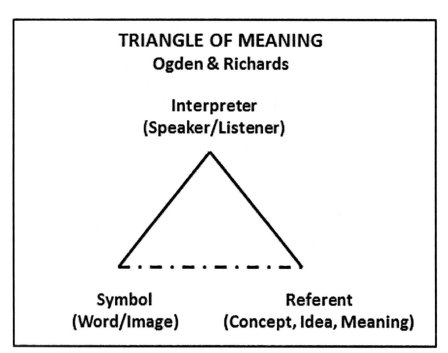

TRIANGLE OF MEANING
Ogden & Richards

Interpreter
(Speaker/Listener)

Symbol
(Word/Image)

Referent
(Concept, Idea, Meaning)

FIGURE 2.2: Ogden and Richards's Triangle of Meaning[19]

The tragedy of Dilbert's love life will have little effect on us, but miscommunication *can* have catastrophic results. Here is an excerpt from the transcript of an air-traffic controller's exchange with the flight deck crew of Avianca 052 in the autumn of 1990, just prior to a crash on New York's Long Island.

Captain to co-pilot:	"Tell them we are in emergency."
Co-pilot to controller:	"We are running out of fuel. . . ."
Controller to co-pilot:	"Avianca zero-five-two, climb and maintain three thousand feet."
Co-pilot to controller:	"Uh . . . we are running out of fuel."
Controller to co-pilot:	"I'm going to bring you about fifteen miles northeast and then turn you back. Is that fine with you and your fuel?"
Co-pilot to controller:	"Uh, I guess so."[20]

The flight crew failed to clearly communicate their emergency to the air-traffic controller. The copilot (from Colombia) used the words, "We are running out of fuel," which obviously made sense to him. The air-traffic controller (from the United States) did not interpret this message as urgent, particularly since he heard, "Uh, I guess so." As a result, the approach controller continued to put the aircraft into a series of turn-and-hold patterns. Eventually, Avianca Flight 052 was cleared to land but missed its first approach, had to circle around for another attempt and crashed. Since the captain spoke very little English, the copilot communicated what he thought constituted an understood emergency, but at no time did he use the words, "in-flight emergency." Rather, he repeated several times, "We need priority." Because the copilot and air-traffic controller had different frames of reference, messages were exchanged, but not an understanding of those messages. Had the air-traffic controller asked a clarification question, such as, "Avianca zero-five-two, are you declaring an in-flight emergency?" then many lives could have been saved.[22] We will return to this example shortly when we talk about context and culture.

Speaking of Culture

In communicating, whatever the medium, the first question has to be, "Is this communication within the recipient's range of perception? Can he receive it?" In communication, people only hear what they want to hear. It is not just what you say but what is understood.

—Peter Drucker, *Management: Tasks, Responsibilities, and Practices* [21]

LANGUAGE AND CULTURE

CODES

Language is really just an arbitrary set of symbols that we use to communicate. To convey ideas or refer to an object, we select from a symbolic code that we hope others will interpret in the same way we do. The grammar, or structure, of a language dictates how we put those words together and in what order. Not all communication takes place through the use of words, so it may be important here for us to distinguish between the *verbal* code, which involves the use of words, and the *nonverbal* code, which amounts to communication without using language. Without getting into the arcane distinctions that make up the study of semantics and linguistics, let's just say that when we use words to communicate, we're communicating verbally. That's true, of course, whether we're speaking or writing. If we're using some other method to communicate that doesn't involve words, we think of that as nonverbal.[23]

A few illustrations may be in order. If I write you a note, I'm communicating verbally but non-vocally. If I speak to you over the telephone, I'm trying to communicate verbally and vocally. But, if I smile and wave as we pass in the hallway, I'm engaging in nonverbal, non-vocal communication. The last possible category might be nonverbal, vocal utterances—clearing your throat to gain attention, or groaning in disapproval. All of this works together.

The nonverbal code includes both *action language* and *object language*. Actions would include all movements that are not used exclusively for communicating. Walking, for example, would serve the functional purpose of moving us from one place to another, but it can also be a powerful communication device if you decide to get up and walk out of a negotiating session. Objects include all sorts of things: materials, artifacts, possessions, and more. This category would include everything from our clothing and jewelry to automobiles, furniture, artwork, offices, and natural surroundings.[24]

The verbal and nonverbal work together in wonderful and sometimes mysterious ways. We judge whether people are happy, angry, or indifferent by their tone of voice. We take our cues from others through eye contact. We judge the status of our co-workers and colleagues by the size and location of their offices, or the style of furniture they have. We often fret about the correctness or propriety of touching someone, even if it's to congratulate or just to reassure. Much of the meaning that we transfer from ourselves to others is contained in those arbitrary symbols we speak or keystroke, but a huge proportion of the meaning others decode comes from the non-symbolic elements of the process. If your boss walks down to your office to pay you a personal visit and ask a favor, that's far more powerful than an e-mail message or a memo on the same subject. Much of our success in the business world (and in our personal lives) will depend on successfully decoding the words, actions, and objects involved in our day-to-day discourse. If we don't get it right, people's jobs, corporate profit, and much more will be at risk. If we're skilled at this, our chances for success are that much greater.

The joy and difficulty of language, then, is that meaning is arbitrarily assigned. There is no logical connection between an object and its name. We simply have to agree on what a word means for us to communicate successfully. Thus, the meaning lies not in our words, but in ourselves.[25] In other words, if I were to ask, "Do words have meaning?" the answer would have to be no. Words by themselves do not have meaning. People do. Rather than asking "What does this sentence mean?" it would be more appropriate to ask, "What do you suppose she meant when she wrote this?" For example, in the Far Side cartoon by Gary Larson, there is a spaceship that has just landed. One of the space aliens is reading a 'human' dictionary and misinterprets, 'Take me to your leader' with the wrong noun – and instead inserts 'stove'. The other alien yells at him for getting the wrong word.

As we expand our discussion about frames of reference, we can easily see that words take on multiple meanings or connotations based on our perceptions of them. As we communicate with people, we can easily misunderstand them by attaching our own set of meanings. For example, if your supervisor were to walk by your desk, hand you a folder and say, "I'm going to need this *soon*," what would your reaction be? If you work in any number of industries, you might think, "by the close of business today," or "within a couple of days." If you're a commodities trader, you would drop what you're doing and attend to the folder immediately. It all depends on the frame of reference for your organization and the industry in which you work.

The development of slang is another example of quick mutation in the verbal code. Words change over time based upon the dynamic changes of culture and the demands of people and institutions. The word *bandit* usually means a "bad guy," especially one who hides in outlying areas of a region. This word originally came from the Latin "bandire," which means "to proclaim." Centuries ago it developed into "bandito" (one who is banned) by the Italians who banished such bad men from their villages, and it was the English who eventually borrowed this term and used it in theatrical plays. As such, this is how a word that initially meant to proclaim something now means a thug or robber.[26] The verbal code is the language that we use to describe people, things, concepts, and ideas. It is both symbolic and mutable because we attach meaning to symbols based on our perceptions and experiences over time.

Speaking of Culture

There are different emphases according to culture about how to begin a business letter. In the U.S., directness and a concise statement of purpose dictate that the point is put in the opening paragraph. While traditionally someone from an Arab background would begin with a lengthy personal greeting that includes background information. In Japan, business letters often begin with an apology and then mention their appreciation for an ongoing business relationship.

—G. L. Grice and J. F. Skinner, *Mastering Public Speaking* [27]

Cultural Challenges:
German Cheerleaders Needed To Smile

Back in 2003, the New York Times ran an interesting article on a new American Football team in Berlin, Germany and focused specifically on the abilities of the cheerleaders. American Football was barely a decade old in Europe and was a bit of an oddity in a sports culture that was enthusiastically devoted to 'soccer'. In European Football, there were no cheerleaders, save for the cheering fans in the bleachers. In general, the young ladies who auditioned for the cheerleading spots did not smile enough. Since the notion of an NFL-type sport was not customary, there was a steep learning curve both through spoken and nonverbal language. The German cheerleaders learned the English chants and had to apply nonverbal communication – such as smiling and nonlinguistic cheers (e.g., shrieks, grunts, etc.).

Source: Y. E. Hong, "Teaching Germany to Grin and Bear Cheerleading," *The New York Times* (November 30, 2003): 8.

NON-VERBAL COMMUNICATION

VOCALICS

An important dimension in nonverbal communication is the *vocal* code, which refers to the manner in which we say things. *Vocalics* or the use of vocal tone, force, pitch, rate, and volume are all nonverbal in nature, but we use them every day to emphasize certain words or to convey certain meanings, including anger, irony, cynicism, or concern. If I say, "Elisa, what were you thinking?" it may be interpreted in any number of ways, depending on which word I use my voice to emphasize. I may emphasize her name or the word *you*, as I turn and speak to her, hoping to include her in the discussion. Or, I may have a scolding tone in mind as I ask, "What *were* you thinking?"

Some languages, such as Chinese, are tonal, in which the meaning of a word depends on the tone with which it is spoken. The word for mother, "ma," is said with a consistent high-level tone. If you use a low rising tone it will mean "horse," but by using a high-to-low tone it will mean "to curse" somebody.[28] Both words *and* tone are used to carry meaning. Eastern cultures, such as China, Japan, and Korea, as you will read in Chapter 3, place great emphasis on establishing relationships before business transactions occur. To facilitate that, language is often indirect and always used with an emphasis on politeness. The Japanese especially like to be precise with their use of language but rely heavily on tone, gesture, and maintaining at least a surface level of harmony. People from the United States tend to focus on the verbal by asking questions in order to look at an issue from all angles, but pay less attention to the vocal cues. People from Japan tend to focus closely on tone of voice, gestures, and often what is *not* said. The following exchange between a North American supervisor and a Japanese subordinate may help to illustrate these differences:

Connor: "How long will you need to finish the project report you're working on?"
(*Connor thinks*: "I need to get this information for planning purposes.")
(*Murakami thinks*: "Why is he asking me this?")

Murakami: "I do not know. When do you want it?"
(*Connor thinks*: "Why doesn't he know? He's certainly in the best position to know.")
(*Murakami thinks*: "He's the boss. He should tell me when he wants it.")

Connor: "I need it as soon as possible. Can you get it to me in ten days?"
(*Connor thinks*: "I'd better press him on this project or else it will never get done.")
(*Murakami thinks*: "I am working as hard as I can. I'm not sure when it will be done. It will depend on what other projects and demands come my way.")

Murakami: "Yes, of course. I will finish it in ten days."
(*Connor thinks*: "That's great! He'll finish it in ten days. I don't have to worry about this anymore.")
(*Murakami thinks*: "He wanted a date, so I agreed. I don't want him to get upset. I will do my best to meet his request.")

In fact, the project report objectively required more than two weeks of work to complete. Mr. Murakami worked overtime to get the job done, but by the end of the second week he was still two days short of completing the report.

Connor: "Do you have that project report? You agreed it would be ready today."
(*Connor thinks*: "I must make sure he complies with his commitment. I can't ever trust Murakami to do what he says he will.")
(*Murakami thinks*: "What's the matter with him? Can't he see I've nearly killed myself trying to meet his timeline, which was unrealistic in the first place? This is an impossible man to work for!")[29]

SYMBOLS, SIGNALS AND SIGNS

A subtle but important distinction exists between the meanings and functions of symbols, signals, and signs. A *symbol* is a semantic device created for the purpose of carrying meaning. It stands for something else. Symbols are usually of two types: verbal and nonverbal. Verbal symbols, or words, may mean whatever we want them to. "Striking" may mean a labor dispute in which workers walk off the job, or it may indicate the price at which an equity option may be traded. Much of the meaning we assign to a verbal symbol, then, depends on context, including our experience, the source of the message, the surrounding words and paragraphs, our social expectations, and much more. *Signals* are much like symbols in that they are created for the purpose of conveying meaning, but they have a much narrower function. A signal is restricted to just one meaning. A traffic signal that flashes red means "stop." It doesn't mean slow down, look both ways, think about it, or go if no one else is coming. It means stop. *Signs* are different from both symbols and signals in a number of important ways. First, not all of them are created by humans, and second, they don't necessarily carry just one meaning. Signs are an indicator, something that suggests the presence or existence of something else, and may be interpreted differently by those who perceive them. Low, fast-moving clouds may be seen as a sign of an impending storm, while silence may be taken by some as a sign of guilt.

The images depicted in Figure 2.3 are simple graphic sketches. They have no meaning in and of themselves, but may be taken to mean something if the people who use them agree on what that meaning might be. The first of the images is a circle with a diagonal line through it. There is no inherent meaning to this symbol except that which we attach to it. This symbol has become known as a deterrent for something that we should not do: No smoking; do not walk on the grass; no littering.

We also assign meaning to shape and color. We have assigned yellow to inverted triangles that mean "yield," and red to octagons that mean "stop." There is no reason why the color green should mean "go." We've simply agreed as a society that it does and we instruct others, including immigrants and teenage drivers, about the meaning of that color. By the way, marketers now say that green is almost universally accepted in the developed world as a package design element indicating low-fat, healthy, or all-natural contents. Meanings can change quickly if you aren't paying attention.

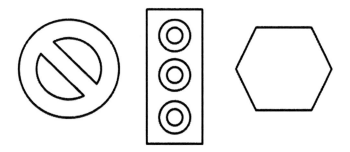

FIGURE 2.3: Symbols, Signals, and Signs

While it is important to interact successfully in the verbal code, whether in a common shared language or in your client's language, we exchange much more than just the words we speak. Vocal and visual codes are informed by cultural values, beliefs, and attitudes that will affect your communication interaction and outcome.

STRUCTURE OF LANGUAGE

Every culture has its own language, or linguistic code, that serves both a function of reporting human experiences as well as defining what that experience is for its speakers.[32] There are approximately 3,000 languages in existence and each of them is a perceptual tool by which its speakers communicate thoughts, desires, beliefs, values, and attitudes. While the words (or verbal symbols) are arbitrary, the structure of the language is not. All language is rule-governed, which means that it has its own structure (also known as syntax) and semantics (the meanings attached to words).[33] The underlying structure of a language's grammar supports both denotative (definition) and connotative (acquired through context and experience) meanings of words. This carries significant meaning to the people who speak that particular language.

Speaking of Culture

The overriding assumption is that if you know something about the way other people communicate, how they use language, you can improve the quality of your communication with them and your understanding of their behavior.

—Lawrence A. Samovar and Richard E. Porter, *Intercultural Communication* [34]

For example, in the English language, our structure or grammar dictates that all sentences follow a simple subject-verb-object pattern. "I go to the office" makes perfect sense to our thought processes. But to a speaker of another language, such as Japanese, the sentence would read more like, "To the office I go," using object-noun-verb. In English, adjectives come before nouns, but in Spanish, adjectives come after. So the English sentence, "I want to drink cold water" differs from the grammatical structure and word usage of the Spanish translation, "Quiero tomar agua frío." To an English speaker, saying "I want to drink water cold," is confusing, but even more so when translated literally into Spanish, "I want to take water cold." English speakers "drink" rather than "take" a beverage. Written Chinese carries no verb tense, which means that the listener must infer time through the context of what is being said. So, "Wo mai shu," could mean anything from, "I bought / buy / will buy a book."[35] And in Arabic, people read from right to left, the opposite of English. English-speaking businesspeople traveling to Arabic countries, such as Egypt, should make sure that their sales documents have an impressive back cover, because their information should start at what they would consider the end of the document.[36] And in some languages, such as French, there are certain personal pronouns that distinguish familiarity and relationship. For example, you should use the more formal, vous (you), when addressing a superior until you are told that you may use the more personal, tu, form of address. In English there is no differentiation for addressing someone in the second person. Such differences in language structure and word usage frequently cause confusion in a non-native speaker's mind.

Language as a Reflection of World View

In Bill Bryson's book, The Mother Tongue – English and How It Got There – he explains that native language speakers are able to instinctively distinguish between shades of difference (in their language) than non-native speakers. He uses the examples of French and Spanish. In French, people do not distinguish between 'house' and 'home' whereas in English you would – a house is a building and a home is where the family is together. Other words without distinction in French are mind and brain; man and gentleman. Grammatically, there is no distinction between "I wrote" and "I have written." In Spanish, the word for 'president' and 'chairman' are the same.

Other examples of instinctive distinction include the notion of 'wishful thinking' for which there is no word in Italian. In Russian, there isn't a word for 'efficiency', 'challenge', 'engagement ring', 'have fun', or, as would be said in English, 'take care.'

This doesn't mean that there are no ways of expressing these notions, ideas or thoughts – there are – they are just different.

In English there are things that cannot be described in one word. For example, in Italian, there is a special word for a water mark from the condensation of a glass on a table, 'culacino'. In Spanish, we borrow the word for 'macho'. And in Gaelic, there is even a word that describes a very specific itch that only that happens on the upper lip as you sip whiskey, 'sgirob'!

Bill Bryson, *The Mother Tongue: English and How it Got that Way*, William Morrow Paperbacks, 2001, p. 6. 37

Language and thought are linked together and, therefore, play an important role in how we perceive things. To this end, one notion of the relationship of language and culture is that the language that we speak (because of its syntax and semantics) shapes how we view the world. This is known as *linguistic determinism:* language determines our perception. A more accepted view, linguistic relativity, takes this concept a little further, saying that, if language shapes our perceptions, then speakers of different languages will view the world differently: *language influences our perception*.[37] A favorite example of this (which is debated by linguists as an urban myth) is Eskimo languages are thought to have as many as 100 separate words for snow, which help them distinguish one type from another. In actuality, the language groups of the Inuit and Yupik attach suffixes to words that could be expressed similarly with compound words or phrases so that similar concepts are expressed but using different combinations of words. Because they live in an arctic environment, there is justification for the various distinctions that they use to describe types of heavy snow, wind-driven snow, icy snow, or powdery snow. English speakers also have many words for snow: blizzard, packed, slushy, flurries, etc., and if, for example, you are a skier in Telluride, then you have the need to distinguish these types of snow. If, however, you live in a tropical climate, like Miami, you probably wouldn't have much need for those words; rather you might find it more useful to focus on words that relate to variance of temperatures in the tropics. Regardless of where one lives and what language is spoken, language and culture have a profound impact on how we interact with others.[38]

Speaking of Culture

In cross-cultural communication we judge the speech of someone else based upon our own standards. With no other frame of reference at their disposal . . . speakers have little choice but to interpret what they hear according to the rules of speaking of their own native speech communities. And since the rules are very likely to be quite different, misunderstandings are almost inevitable.

—N. Wolfsen, *Communicating Across Cultures in South Africa* [39]

This discussion about language and frames of reference, codes, and the structure and meaning of language is crucial if we are to understand the tacit workings of intercultural communication. It is not enough to know the rules for correct grammar and vocabulary of a language. This is just a starting point. To know the rules for language use—*how* to use it—is only part of what makes communicators competent. Remember, simply communicating via language does not guarantee that participants will understand each other. We must each consider our goals for communicating, the key players involved, and what our relationship to them might be. We should consider how the context, backdrop, and circumstance of the interaction may affect what we say, and how we control our tone of voice and body movements as we speak. We must take note of the social norms that affect what we can say or are expected to say. Finally, we must think about channel choice: should we speak in person, on the phone, via e-mail, or in a letter to be delivered by the postal service? Knowing *why* you want to say something, *what* to say, *how* to say it, *when* to speak, and to *whom* to say it constitutes what sociolinguist Dell Hymes calls communicative competence.[40] This concept can help with our understanding of knowing when to speak or not to speak in various business situations. (See Figure 2.4)

For example, if you need to request additional funding from your budget director for your product launch, and if you know that she is preoccupied with other issues in the department, you may hold off until you sense that she is in a better frame of mind to hear what you have to say. Or, if your VP for Sales and Marketing sends you to negotiate a contract with someone from a culture who sees status as important (and, therefore, would expect to close any major deal only with the senior official), you will have to choose very carefully what to say and how to say it to open the door for possible serious conversation.

COMMUNICATIVE COMPETENCE
Dell Hymes, Sociolinguist

It is not enough to know how to speak a language (e.g., the rules of grammar) but we need to know the rules for use as well. Essentially, this means that communication competence is the what, how, when, where, why and to whom of communication. It includes all of the intangible hunches you get while watching and listening during an interaction—the subtext of what is *really* being communicated (not necessarily what is said but what is not said).

Setting	•Time and place (where your communication happens)
Participants	•Relationships (who is involved and what is their status)
Ends	•Goals and outcomes (what do you expect to happen and what *actually* happens)
Act sequence	•Grammar and content (*what* is actually said)
Keys	•Tone or manner (*how* something is said)
Instrumentalities	•Channel (the way the message is sent—e-mail, letter, face-to-face conversation, etc.)
Norms	•Social rules (what is expected of you and your communication partner)
Genre	•Understanding the medium (having knowledge of type of medium—such as the etiquette involved in sending e-mails)

Source: Foundations of Sociolinguistics: An Ethnographic Approach. *Philadelphia: U of Pennsylvania Press, 1974.*

FIGURE 2.4: Communicative Competence – The word *speaking* becomes a mnemonic device to assist in understanding the elements of competence.

Here is an example of how a corporate officer used his communicative competence to know what (or in this case, what not) to say to whom, when, and in what manner. In 2003, when Sam Falcona, Senior Vice President for Corporate Communications at Phillips Petroleum Company, learned that his firm would merge with another petroleum giant, Conoco (formerly Continental Oil Company), he was faced with a serious dilemma. His principal task would be to convince key stakeholders from employees to investors that the merger was a great idea, but until it was a "done deal," he couldn't tell a soul, not even his family. Along the way, he and his small staff would have to prepare for merger by arranging for a new corporate logo, new stationery, business cards, billboards, and signs. Everything from the entrance to the corporate headquarters to the canopies of their gas stations nationwide would have to reflect the new ownership at precisely the same moment. The corporate headquarters and hundreds of administrative and executive staff would have to relocate on short notice from Bartlesville, Oklahoma, to Houston, Texas. Standing in their way were the Federal Trade Commission, the U.S. Securities and Exchange Commission, a circuit court, numerous regulatory officials, and more than a few state and local authorities.

Once Falcona and his team were given the green light, they would have to move the message and its associated products to millions of people across dozens of channels in a very short period of time. "Understanding what we wanted to say, why we had to say it, and to whom we had to say it," Falcona said, "would be crucial. We knew that not all audiences would react the same way. Wall Street thought it would be fabulous. Oklahoma thought it was the end of the world." Communication competence, he added, was greatly helped by the fact that his team was "highly professional and well prepared for this. It wasn't easy," he added, "but we got it done on time and under budget."[41] Sam Falcona assessed his audience well and used his competence as an astute communicator to navigate his way, and his company's way, through a delicate transition.

Having discussed the nature of culture in Chapter 1 and some details about language use in the beginning of this chapter, we'll turn our focus in the remainder of this book to how we put the two together to understand the what, how, when, where, why, and who of communication.

DEFINING CULTURAL DIMENSIONS

Before going any further, let's think for a moment about how we will describe the main cultural dimensions (or categories) that we mentioned in Chapter 1: context, identity, learning, environment, change, time, authority, and achievement. The image in Figure 2.5 is a composite sketch of the *main* cultural dimensions we will discuss throughout the remaining pages of this text. Within each of these categories (or dimensions) you will find additional dimensions, but for the sake of clarity, we will refer to the eight categories listed here as the main dimensions. From time to time, we will refer back to Figure 2.5. We'll use the diagram, labeled "Eight Cultural Dimensions," as a model based on a continuum of polar opposites to make distinctions about specific cultural differences. We'll underscore two things before we continue: first, our definition of a model, and second, how we use language to describe points of cultural difference on that model.

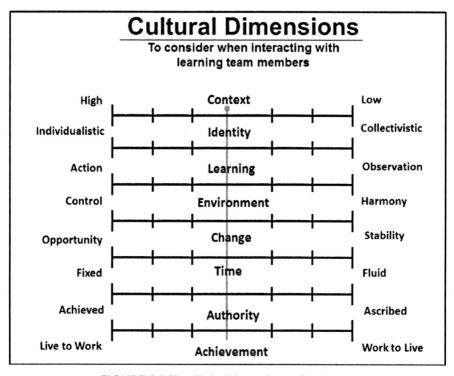

FIGURE 2.5: The Eight Dimensions of Culture[42]

Some may argue that using a particular model to explain any phenomenon is rigid, restrictive, and creates a positivistic outlook about what a concept means. Others may contend that it only serves to reinforce simplistic generalization. On the contrary, we find that, if used appropriately, models can serve as accurate representations to help make abstract concepts more concrete.[43] For example, we may remember being young schoolchildren who eagerly anticipated that special day of show-and-tell.

Rather than sit in a circle and simply tell our classmates and teachers about a favorite possession or hobby in the abstract, we were invited to bring in that object to display; the stuffed animal, worn baseball, or special trinket became a tangible reality for all to see. Holding that favorite treasure in your hand while you told the story behind it made the experience all the more vivid and the tales all the more real. An example from the business world will serve as another illustration. In the automotive industry, design engineers not only create numerous pages of design specifications to accompany drafts of their designs, they also assemble prototypes. Everyone from operations and manufacturing to marketing and sales can see a prototype and form an impression in their minds so that the idea is no longer vague or abstract. Models can represent abstract concepts that help us visualize certain points, key features, ideas, or notions.

We must define our language use as well. North American English uses the language of problem-solving, which translates into cause-and-effect thinking that is very linear: "The decline in stock price followed the announcement of a delay in the rollout of their new product. The delay clearly caused the decline." Or, consider the following: "Our approach is either ethical or it's not." "It's either right or wrong." "The answer is yes or no." In Western culture, we like well-defined ideas and logical connections. In this sense, one way of making comparisons is to do so along a continuum that uses polar opposites. This may also create generalization traps but, as you saw earlier, to reduce confusion (or dissonance) as we try to make sense of conflicting behaviors of people who differ from us culturally, we form mental categories to help us process unfamiliar information. It will be helpful to think of these categories as continua that can vary in degree, depending upon the communicators, context, and setting.[44] We view this model as a continuum of choices[45] and will take into consideration that every culture has certain overarching preferences that define its values, beliefs, attitudes, and behaviors. Within each culture, though, there are many possibilities for behavior among its individuals. While we locate certain cultures at specific places along this continuum to help us make comparisons, we must recognize that each individual from that culture will make her or his own choices within that continuum.

Speaking of Culture

There are two sides to every question.

—Protagorus

CONTEXT AND COMMUNICATION

HIGH VERSUS LOW CONTEXT

We have talked a little about the verbal and nonverbal codes and should now examine how these important dimensions of intercultural communication affect whether a culture tends to favor explicit or implicit communication. When communicating across cultures, communicators must be aware how their culture affects the context of communication.

Anthropologist Edward T. Hall created the notion of high- and low-context cultures. Hall is credited with founding the scholarly field of intercultural communication based on his work with the Hopi and Navajo Indians of the Southwestern United States, as well as his work with the Japanese as a Foreign Service Specialist. From both his research and his foreign-service work, he developed a continuum along which he charted the communication patterns of different cultures.

In *high-context cultures*, meaning is derived from the subtle, tacit actions and reactions of the communicators and not necessarily the words they use. Communication will also be less direct. Relationships are especially important, so the manner in which something is said, and the attention paid to the audience for those remarks are carefully observed. For example, silence can mean that a person is thinking, is showing deference, or is simply taking the time to respond while observing the reactions of the receiver. A speaker from a high-context culture will understand the importance of that silence and will infer that implicit meanings often speak louder than words. A *low-context culture* relies more on the explicit or actual words that are spoken. Emphasis is placed on being direct, and receivers are meant to respond to the verbal code in more literal ways. The task is more important than the relationship, so low-context speakers will use clear language, and a lot of it, to get the point across. Low-context speakers are uncomfortable with silence and quickly will try to fill it with more words. Such speakers may interpret silence as a lack of understanding and will, therefore, feel as if they have to explain in more detail. Figure 2.6 depicts the names of a number of nations plotted along a diagonal continuum. You will notice that the Eastern (Asian) cultures are positioned toward the high-context pole. Arab and Mediterranean cultures are positioned in the middle, while Western cultures (U.S., Canada and Western European) fall closer to the low-context pole.[46]

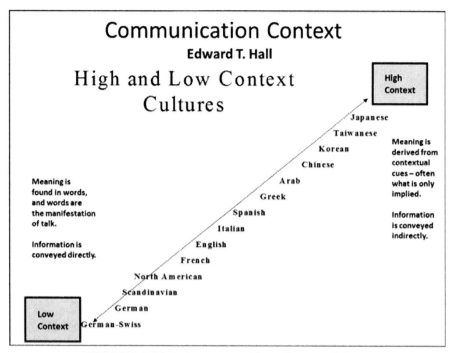

FIGURE 2.6: High-Context and Low-Context Cultures

HIGH-CONTEXT CULTURES

When communicating with someone from a high-context culture (such as Japan, Korea or Taiwan), where context is understood without using words, you must closely observe the nonverbal codes, looking for visual and vocal cues, rather than merely relying on the verbal code, or what is explicitly stated in words. For example, the Chinese take a solidly high context approach as is indicated in their Chinese symbol for listening. (See Figure 2.7) These characters of the eyes, ears, and heart form the symbol for listening: It is impossible to listen, they say, without using the eyes because you need to look for nonverbal communication. You certainly must listen with the ears, since Chinese is a tonal language, and intonation dictates meaning. Finally, you listen with your heart because one must be intuitive and sense the emotional undertones expressed by the speaker. This symbol represents the entire person when communicating. Other high-context cultures, such as Korean, have words that exemplify their communication priorities. In Korean, there is a word, *nunchi*, that when translated into its literal meaning means that you communicate through your eyes. Koreans believe that the environment supplies most of the information that we seek, so there is little need to speak.[47] We will visit this concept again when we talk about Eastern culture and its emphasis on harmony with the environment.

FIGURE 2.7: The Chinese Symbol for Listening [48]

Low-Context Cultures

In the United States, value is placed on verbal and written messages that are clear, concise, and to the point. Any how-to book for the business profession offering speaking or writing tips will say to state your point and support it succinctly. For example, when traveling abroad, a U.S. citizen will not hesitate to go to the front desk and tell the hotel clerk that his or her room is inadequate. A guest who has to wait may become impatient with the clerk by saying, "Excuse me but my room doesn't have the view I was promised." The guest will consider this action both pragmatic and appropriate in order to get what is wanted: a room with a better view. After all, U.S. customer service is built on the motto that "the customer is always right." On the other hand, a Japanese guest staying at the same hotel would not be direct by complaining right away. He or she would assume that the hotel staff would anticipate any problems or needs that would arise so that they might "save face" and not have to complain.[49]

Another aspect of low-context cultures is the amount of time spent (or not spent) in listening. Listening studies estimate that business professionals in the U.S. spend about 45 percent of their time listening, 30 percent speaking, 16 percent reading, and just 9 percent writing. The average person speaks about 12,000 sentences every day and 150 words per minute, but the human brain is capable of attending to approximately 400 words per minute.[50] We are capable of taking in more words than we can actually produce. Those of us from a low-context culture should take this to heart and use the "spare time" or differential between speech speed and thought speed to pay attention to what is *not* being said. While we may *hear* what the speaker is saying, we don't necessarily apply active listening skills. Listening is different than hearing since we need to attend to what is being said and gather information simultaneously. People from low-context cultures would benefit from those in high-context cultures by listening with the heart and eyes and not just the ears.

In sum, the people of high-context cultures place their emphasis on and trust in nonverbal communication, so they are less verbal, more comfortable with silence and "reading between the lines." In low-context cultures, people talk more and depend on verbal more than nonverbal codes, and are decidedly uncomfortable with silence. On the low-context end of Edward T. Hall's continuum are European nations, North America (the United States, Canada, and Mexico), Australia, and New Zealand. High-context countries include Asian, African, and other non-Western cultures.

What does this mean for the business world? Several major themes related to business communication focus on high- and low-context cultures. Low-context cultures, for example, feature less formality in addressing superiors. In the United States, it is common for people to address a superior, one or two ranks up, by first name. Informality is accepted—commonplace, really—because it decreases the distance between the boss and his or her employees. However, executives in the United States expect to have a private office. An office with a door is seen as a status symbol and is respected. Other cultures, such as Japanese, have the opposite approach to formality and office space. Senior management usually has shared office space so that the superior is on the floor with the subordinates. A large percentage of Japanese are of the "old school" that adheres to a strict code of formality called *keigo*, a certain type of honorific language that elevates someone while humbling oneself. To address someone of a higher status or age, you must add the suffix *-san* to the name (e.g., Sakamotosan) to show respect. But Japan's business culture is in a state of flux as more young people enter the workforce and management strives to create a flatter structure, in which employees are making more decisions and sharing ideas even if they are not senior management.[51]

Whether you come from a high-context or low-context culture, it is important to recognize there are clear distinctions among those who feel more comfortable focusing on tasks and being informal in both language and gesture, and those who place greater emphasis on silence, relationships, and formality. Neither is necessarily better. They are simply different ways of expressing cultural values and behaviors.

EXPRESSION AND COMMUNICATION

SAVING FACE

Linked to the issue of whether a culture is high or low in context is how people save face. In higher-context cultures, including Asian societies, saving face and avoiding shame are of high importance. While the concept of "face" is tied directly to respect, we will discuss authority and position power in Chapter 4. Words carry such strong meaning that they must be chosen carefully. It is ultimately better to save face in an Asian culture so that a superior doesn't become embarrassed. For example, the Chinese and Japanese place a high value on harmony, both at home and in the workplace. Since respect for those in higher positions is essential, Chinese and Japanese people will not want to disrupt harmony during a business negotiation by saying no. Often they will respond to questions or comments with a yes—not to mean they agree or accept the deal, but to acknowledge they are listening and hear you. Saving face means that one must be indirect and hint at meanings.

In the structure of the Japanese language, the content of the message is revealed at the end of the sentence rather than the beginning. Since harmony and benevolence are crucial to maintaining strong relationships, the Japanese want to avoid insulting a person from the start. There is no syntactical rule for not placing the word *iie* or "no" in the beginning of a sentence—it is primarily social and consistent with the Japanese style of indirectness. To be straightforward in the beginning is to lack social courtesies of maintaining a harmonious relationship.[52]

U.S. humorist Dave Barry once described the Japanese style of refusal as follows: "To the best of my knowledge, in all the time we traveled around Japan, nobody ever told us we couldn't do anything, although it turned out that there were numerous things we couldn't do. Life became easier for us once we learned to interpret certain key phrases, which I'll summarize in this convenient table. . . .

English Statement Made by Japanese	*Actual Meaning in "American"*
I see.	No.
Ah.	No.
Ah-hah.	No.
Yes.	No.
That is difficult.	That is completely impossible.
That is very interesting.	That is the stupidest thing I ever heard.
We will study your proposal.	We will feed your proposal to a goat."[53]

While we're not completely sure about feeding business proposals to a goat, you get the idea: Japanese businesspeople will go to great lengths to avoid saying no to anyone.

Another time-honored form of saving face is the Japanese practice of what is called *honne* and *tatemae*. *Honne* literally means "truth" and *tatemae*, "façade." This practice of communication begins at the surface level, such as exchanging pleasantries and complements, until a strong and familiar relationship is established so that the true intentions may be revealed to the "friends" or business partners (when you say what you really mean). Since Japanese culture strives to maintain harmony, or *wa*, public confrontations, open displays of emotion, or voicing negative opinions are not the norm.

Business negotiations take on a distinctive manner when we compare cultures like Japan and China to the United States. People from the United States generally do not think twice about open confrontation and often welcome heated debates regarding topics of controversy. In North America, it is not uncommon for businesspeople to state their opinions and press to get their way. The task (getting the contract negotiated at a good price and within time constraints) will take precedence over the relationship. That is not to say that relationships are unimportant—they are— but so is driving a hard bargain. Asian cultures, on the other hand, are embarrassed by open disagreement. Japanese companies will often use an intermediary to deal with problems that may result in conflict. The Chinese have a similar way of dealing with negotiations: They avoid open confrontation and hold to the Confucian mandate of kindness to people. They typically ease into a business proposition by slowly developing a relationship so that both parties can reach mutual understanding. Heavy-handed tactics in international negotiations, such as countering a proposal that is already on the table, will likely cause the Chinese to lose face and be insulted. While contracts may be written and signed, from the Chinese perspective they are not set in stone. Good business relationships mean that contracts and agreements can be changed because of the trust that was painstakingly developed; an oral promise holds more importance than a contract.[54] Saving face and creating harmony are highly respected values in Asian cultures.

EXPRESSION OF EMOTION

As we communicate across cultures, we can misunderstand visual codes in the same way we can misinterpret verbal codes. Because virtually all nonverbal mannerisms are culturally acquired, expressiveness differs from culture to culture regarding emotions. For example, Latin American,

European, and Mediterranean cultures are among the most expressive; North American (the U.S. and Canadian parts of North America), Eastern European, and African cultures vary their levels of expression; and German and Asian cultures are among the most reserved. In Middle Eastern cultures, it is considered natural for people to show warmth and expression by speaking in animated tones, moving close to another person and looking him or her in the eye, or by touching—an arm around the shoulder, a kiss on either side of the cheeks. However, people who come from more-reserved cultures such as Thailand may interpret loudness and animated gestures as a sign of anger or disapproval. In some high-context cultures in which preserving face and following hierarchical rules for respect are important, people may be more comfortable with neutral expressions over expressions of affection.

The anecdote below shows how one person's idea of affirmation and positive response can mean another person's shame and embarrassment. Think about how you would have reacted if you had been in Jane's position and were relieved that someone said something to break the awkward silence.

Baffled in Bangkok

Jane Reynolds, a U.S. America with an upbeat and outgoing personality was just put in charge of making a deal happen with a trade association in Singapore. She was up to this task because she had live there for ten years and had many contacts and established relationships – people trusted her.

Her first task was to chair a conference in Thailand, which meant that she would be the leader of panel discussions. Jane did her due diligence and asked some friends what to expect and their response was that Thai women would probably not speak up in public – there would be hesitancy to provide feedback or opinions in a large group setting.

The very first meeting that morning, several Thai women offered their suggestions, speaking in a subdued fashion and gently provided comments. Jane, being enthusiastic, jumped up from her seat, gestured excitedly and in a loud voice, thanked the women for their insights. She was delighted that she was not meeting resistance, as her colleagues had indicated might happen.

The panel continued with women sharing in small groups around tables. However, Jane noticed that there were no more comments voiced to the large group. She also noted that, when she asked specific questions to the large group, people were quite silent.

Later, two of the women who had initially spoken up quietly approached her, appearing shy and uncomfortable. They asked why she had been angry with them earlier in the morning. Jane was astounded and responded, with a smile, that of course she hadn't been angry with them but that she was excited at their participation.

Trouble, by this encounter and upset that she might have offended the women, she returned to her hotel room, baffled by why these kind-hearted Thai women would have thought she was angry with them! It had all started out so well – what happened?

1. What were Jane's assumptions about the conference attendees?

2. Why do you think the women responded the way they did?

3. What could she have done differently in that situation?

4. Do you think Jane learned from this experience?

5. What would you have done?

Adapted from: Gesteland, Richard R. (2005). Cross-cultural business behavior: Negotiating, selling, sourcing and managing across cultures. Copenhagen, Denmark: Copenhagen Business School Press.

Eye contact and handshakes are two distinguishing features of culture. The eyes are thought to be the most expressive part of the body—some describe them as a window into the soul. Some cultures use more direct and sustained eye contact than others; that can vary based upon gender, age, and status. This is changing, however, as more women throughout the world enter the job market and rise to higher levels. Generally, the Arab world and Mediterranean cultures tend to use intense eye contact, as do Italians and Latin Americans. Northern European and North American cultures are said to have firm eye contact, while Koreans, North Africans, and Thai use moderate contact. Most Asian cultures use indirect eye contact.[56] The handshake and the bow are two of the most common ways for business people to greet each other. People from Western cultures will usually shake hands, while people from Eastern cultures customarily bow. Handshakes can range from the firm and brisk to the gentle and light. While most young people get a 30-second lesson from Mom or Dad on how to shake hands properly, learning how to bow is not so simple. Japanese businesses, particularly those whose employees have regular contact with the public—such as the Mitsukoshi Department Store in Tokyo—regularly conduct seminars on bowing: who must bow first, who must bow deeper, and who must hold or sustain a bow longer. Even the placement of hands (extended at the side for men, extended on the thighs for women) is a matter for concern and repeated practice in such seminars.

Speaking of Culture

Germans are relatively reserved, not given to enthusiastic public displays of emotion, although some southern Germans are a bit more expressive. As opposed to Latin Europeans and Latin Americans, Germans use few gestures or animated facial expressions, and avoid interrupting another speaker.

—Richard R. Gesteland, *Cross-Cultural Business Behavior* [57]

Turn-taking is another aspect of expression. Expressive people may interpret interruptions as a normal part of conversation or negotiation, such as people from Italy or Spain, but Northern European and U.S. and Canadian negotiators may become frustrated at constant interruptions. The Japanese are even more reserved as they are careful not to interrupt their business contacts out of respect and also because they are completely comfortable with silence.[58] Doing business with someone who may potentially counter your particular affective or neutral style means that you will have to make adjustments. International businessman Richard Gesteland gives this advice based on his 35 years of experience in marketing and management: "It is said that 'When in Rome, do as the Romans do.' In a sales meeting it is the seller's responsibility to adapt to the conversational behavior of the customer. But for joint ventures or strategic alliances, it is appropriate to meet each other halfway. The important aspect of negotiating across cultures is to be aware of potential communication conflicts."[59]

Speaking of Culture

In relationships between people, reason and emotion both play a role. Which of these dominates will depend upon whether we are affective, that is we show our emotions, in which case we probably get an emotional response in return, or whether we are emotionally neutral in our approach.

—Fons Trompenaars and Charles Hampden-Turner, *Riding the Waves of Culture* [60]

SILENCE

We are all familiar with the saying "Silence is golden." There is a lesser-known Japanese proverb that says, "He who speaks has no knowledge and he who has knowledge does not speak." People who listen rather than speak demonstrate credibility, from an Asian perspective, because they are seen as reflective human beings. Eastern philosophy does not follow the Western orientation of rationality (objective truth that can be found). Rather than search for truth, they say the truth will find you and reveal itself. Patience in listening and practicing quiet reflection are central values in Eastern cultures.[61] Ambiguity, inference, and the use of metaphor are accepted and embraced in such cultures.

Silence, like speaking, is another type of symbolic resource. Like the mathematical number zero, silence has a distinct function.[62] Min-Sun Kim, a professor of communication at the University of Hawaii at Manoa, gives us a non-Western perspective on the importance of silence in communication:

One of the basic building blocks of communicative competence, both linguistic and cultural, is knowing when *not* to speak in a particular culture. Therefore, to know when, where, and how to be silent, and to understand the meanings attached to silence, is to gain a keen insight into the fundamental structure of communication in that society. . . . Silence is not just the absence of behavior.[63]

Saving face, being affective or neutral with expressiveness, and dealing with silence are all important aspects of intercultural communication. We just mentioned the aphorism "When in Rome, do as the Romans do." Its general meaning is: Don't set your own rules when you are someone's guest. That proverb is often attributed to Saint Ambrose (circa 340–397

C.E.), as liturgical advice to Saint Augustine who was traveling and had asked if he should fast on Sunday as he did in Milan – or on Saturday as was customary in Rome. St. Ambrose responded, "Si fueris Romae, Romano vivito more; si fueris alibi, vivito sicut ibi." Translation: "When you are in Rome, live in the Roman style [fast in the Roman way]; when you are elsewhere, live as they live elsewhere."[64] You'll find many sayings like this in other languages – in Chinese, the translation is "Enter village, follow customs'. In Moroccan, "Do like your neighbor or move your house door." In Polish, "When you fly among crows, you should caw like them." That's good advice. We must each do our best to adapt to the customs, practices, and expectations of others, particularly when we are on their home turf.

Numerous studies have shown that it is difficult (though not impossible) for anyone to adopt a second culture. We are who we were when we grew up. The customs we practice, the manners we exhibit, and the comfort we feel in being around others who do the same are all the product of our enculturation as children. The bad news is that no culture is truly universal. The culture we embrace is the product of our parents, our teachers, and our surroundings as we grew and matured. As we travel and interact with others, we're likely to find that, while we share some things in common, cultural differences will persist. The good news is that, almost without exception, people of other cultures will readily forgive small gaffes and behavioral *faux pas*, as long as you make a sincere effort to pay attention to those issues that matter most to your hosts. You needn't embrace their culture; you must simply respect it.

PERSUASION IN INTERCULTURAL COMMUNICATION

PATTERNS OF ORGANIZATION

We have already discussed the ways in which culture is connected to language and thought processes. We should now focus on how culture and language influence the ways people organize their thinking. Research has shown that people in various cultures have distinct problem-solving approaches and patterns of thought. One of the most noticeable distinctions in the organization of thought processes is linear thinking versus circular thinking. A cognitive psychologist, R. Kaplan, suggests that we can better understand a culture's thought processes by analyzing a paragraph written in that language in order to determine its language-cognition patterns.[65] There is a strong tendency for low-context cultures (cultures that use words more than silence) to employ linear, sequential thinking and to express those thoughts aloud and in writing. Higher-context cultures (those that use silence more than words) show a preference for circular thought processes whose patterns are non-sequential.

Speaking of Culture

Each language and each culture has a paragraph order unique to itself, and that part of the learning of a particular language is mastering its logical system.

—R. Kaplan, *Intercultural Communication* [66]

In a low-context culture such as in the United States, you can pick up any business communication book and find an emphasis on directness, clarity, organization, and support. The saying "Time is money" pervades our business culture and compels us to have our facts in order, present them succinctly, and not take up any more time than we need. The U.S. culture is achievement-oriented, sees time as a precious commodity, and values action over inaction. Famous sayings such as, "Action is character" and "If I rest, I rust" were given to us by the English, but have joined this nation's collection of mottos. This need for conciseness and action is demonstrated in how these texts spur us on to use the active versus passive voice. The active voice (e.g., "John closed the business deal.") demonstrates power, control, decisiveness, and results. The passive implies lack of control, doubt, hesitancy, and incompetence (e.g., "The business deal was closed [by Jack]."). As we saw in Chapter 1, all textbooks are written from a culture-bound perspective, which favors that particular culture's attitudes and values about how things should be. Since language and thought are interconnected and influenced by culture, the grammar of a language influences how speakers communicate information.

While indirectness may not suit most North Americans (U.S. Americans and Canadians), higher-context cultures tend to prefer this method of communication. Harmony with nature and in relationships is nonnegotiable. As you will see in Chapter 3, such cultures are in sync with the external environment and blend with it rather than try to control it. Eastern belief systems such as Confucianism and Buddhism say this brings inner peace and oneness to those who accept such views. It is more appropriate for someone from a high-context culture to spend time in the beginning of a presentation or meeting by thanking the gods, invoking the spirits, or asking Allah's blessing before entering into formal discourse. Speaking patterns in higher-context cultures (such as Arab, African, and Asian) allow speakers to take their time getting to the point, use more eloquent language, and expect ambiguous language or inferences such as metaphors because they save face, are less direct, and require that the listener "read between the lines," using the context of a message to uncover its meaning. This is uncomfortable for low-context communicators because they want the speaker to get to the point. Since the speech or thought patterns are more circular, and a person from a high-context culture takes his or her time to make an important point, there seems to be no logical presentation of ideas, facts, or purposes. This is undoubtedly why high-context cultures can give the appearance of "going in circles" when speaking. The difference is whether the listener uses an inductive or deductive approach to logic, as we will explain in the section that follows.

Speaking of Culture

Literacy entails more than learning how to read and write; it influences thinking patterns, perceptions, cultural values, communication styles, and social organizations as well.

—R. Kaplan, Intercultural Communication [67]

RHETORIC AND LANGUAGE

ETHOS, PATHOS, AND LOGOS

Fourth-century B.C.E. philosopher and teacher Aristotle created a framework for persuasion that has been used throughout the centuries. He identified three elements based on Western philosophy and on forms of reasoning established by both Greek and Roman philosophers that form the basis for argumentation: ethos, pathos, and logos. *Ethos* is the credibility assigned to a speaker by his or her listeners. What are his or her status, background, character, age, and experience? What does he or she know of this subject? *Pathos* is the emotional appeal that a speaker might use in order to evoke various emotions and attitudes related to the audience's needs. *Logos*, finally, is the logic or structure of an argument. Logic, more than any of the other forms of artistic proof, is limited in its utility because of a bewildering series of rules regarding major premises, hypothetical assertions, conditional conclusions, and more. If an argument conforms to the rules of logic, though, speakers have a powerful weapon in their arsenal of persuasion. Valid logic, ethically employed, is difficult to refute.

While Western cultures tend to rely on strong arguments and evidence that is presented directly and succinctly, there are no agreed-upon standards across cultures regarding what constitutes evidence. What is convincing to one may be seen as rubbish to another. But there are preferences for what sort of proof certain cultures favor. Latin American, African, and Arab cultures appreciate narrative stories and parables, especially those with implicit morals. U.S. American, Canadian, German, and Nordic cultures tend to rely on specific, concrete data. *Credibility* is determined in some cultures, especially those which value hierarchy, such as Latin American, East Asian, Indian, and Russian, by position power, status, age, or religion. *Emotional* appeals are common in cultures that are expressive with gestures and feelings, such as Middle Eastern, Latin American, and African, while logical appeals that offer objective data to support claims and assertions are more respected than feelings or opinions.[68]

DEDUCTIVE AND INDUCTIVE REASONING

A couple of definitions may be in order here. *Deductive reasoning* begins with a statement that applies to all members of a group or class and concludes with the notion that "what applies to all must apply to one." It is a form of reasoning that moves from the general to the particular. The principal mechanism for deductive argument is the *syllogism*. A syllogism is really just a series of statements or premises that lead to a valid conclusion. They come in two forms: *categorical* and *hypothetical*.

A categorical syllogism offers claims about categories (of people, things, all sorts of categories), then by including a particular instance in the category, reaches an inescapable conclusion. Here is an example:

Major Premise:	All men are mortal.
Minor Premise:	Socrates is a man.
Conclusion:	Socrates is mortal.

What is true of all in the category must certainly be true of individuals within the category. To refute a categorical syllogism, you would either have to prove that not all men are mortal or that Socrates is not a man. A hypothetical syllogism, on the other hand, begins with a hypothesis, or an "If . . . then" statement. If I can prove that something is true under certain conditions, then all I must to do win the argument is prove that the conditions are present. Here is an example:

Major Premise:	If I eat in the office cafeteria, then I shall become ill.
Minor Premise:	I have eaten in the office cafeteria.
Conclusion:	I shall become ill.

To be valid, the minor premise of a hypothetical syllogism must either *affirm the condition* or *deny the consequent* of the major premise. If I say I've eaten in the cafeteria, then I'm affirming the condition, and if I say I will not become ill, then I'm denying the consequent. Either will work. It won't do, however, for me to deny the condition ("I haven't eaten in the cafeteria; therefore, I shall not become ill"). Many other things could make you ill. Similarly, if I affirm the consequent ("I shall become ill"), it doesn't necessarily mean I've been eating in the cafeteria. Because syllogisms are subject to so many different rules (most of which we won't mention here) to produce valid conclusions, deduction is a tricky and sometimes difficult form of reasoning to use. Deduction is at the heart of logic, though, and it's certainly worth knowing about.[69]

Inductive reasoning, on the other hand, begins with specific examples and tries to draw a general conclusion from them. It's a form of reasoning that moves from the particular to the general. Induction does not follow a specialized form, such as the syllogism, to reach its conclusions; rather, it seeks to convince the listener by the preponderance and proximity of evidence. An example: "My uncle once owned a Yugo automobile and it proved unreliable. My cousin also owned a Yugo and had a similar experience. And, just last week, I read in the newspaper about an accident involving a Yugo. I would conclude, therefore, that the Yugo brand is simply unreliable."[70] Inductive reasoning is how some people use samples of experience to form general conclusions, but it is fraught with problems. First, your cousin and your uncle might have gotten bad samples from an otherwise fine product line. Even the best of motorcars will occasionally experience difficulty, so it may be unfair to draw conclusions based on limited samples or narrow experience. Statistical reasoning, based on induction, actually states the probability that a conclusion might be wrong, based on sample size and error rate. The real difficulty is not that you may be wrong about a particular example, but that you may be wrong about the entire class of objects, people, or phenomena. Inductive reasoning is the basis for stereotypes, and flawed induction may lead to prejudicial thinking. "Pitfalls," said Cicero, "await he who speaks in generalities."

In sum, deduction is more about rules, while induction is more about examples. Having introduced you to these two basic (and ancient) forms of reasoning, we should note that some cultures have a clear preference for one rather than the other. As noted previously, many Western and G7 nations have developed a cultural preference for deductive, analytic logic, while many Eastern, Latin, and African cultures have developed a preference for inductive, example- and story-based reasoning. Let's look at some practical applications for business.

Thinking "Outside The Box" When It Comes To Persuasion

Let's say that you're a marketing director for a large pharmaceutical company and are preparing a presentation of forecasts for a new product that will be introduced into the East Asian market. You put together your information and determine that you will support your message with facts, figures, and the research results of the latest clinical trials. Your information is current, statistical, and objective. You meet with your prospective Chinese counterparts and begin the presentation stating your forecasts for the market are accurate projections and that, since this drug will do well on the foreign market, you need business partners overseas. You want your Chinese clients to provide resources to help pave the way and eventually produce mutual profitability.

This method of organization and support is typical of low-context cultures, which tend to be direct and verbalize objective facts. This is a form of linear, analytic reasoning in which you offer a major and minor premise and then draw a valid (and, let us hope, irrefutable) conclusion. In other words, you put the general issue up front and then move to a specific conclusion. ("This drug, with proper promotion and distribution, is predicted to do well in the Asian market. Your firm can partner with us to provide the proper level of promotion and distribution. Therefore, together we can succeed with this drug.") This method of reasoning, which relies on linear analytics and objectively verifiable facts, is a Western-style organization pattern.

Your presentation to the Chinese may not go over well for several reasons. First, Asian culture is high-context and generally prefers a more inductive approach, which is the opposite of what you have chosen to offer. An inductive approach would provide a number of examples and then draw a conclusion. Because this type of presentation works contrary to linear thinking, you will often hear people (in Western audiences) say, "That's fine, but get to your point!" So, the Chinese approach might be: "Asian business is interested in collaboration with U.S. markets (examples provided); Asian people want to benefit from U.S. products without having to pay costly international prices (more specific examples here); our company has both the interest and the resources that could meet the demands (specific illustrations, once again); *therefore* our company wants to help you market your drug." Asian cultures also favor establishing relationships first, so it might take as many as half-dozen visits to China before you will find a senior decision maker willing to agree to a joint venture.

PRESENTATIONS

Not all societies prefer the same approach to reasoning, whether deductive or inductive. In Asian cultures, it is customary to begin by recognizing and paying respect to the audience, according to rank, followed by an acknowledgment of the developing relationship among those in the room. In the United States and Canada, however, it is more natural for a speaker to begin with the problem and move directly to a presentation of solutions. In French culture, it is customary to give background information about one's organization and the people involved in it.

The French also take the time to gracefully enter a formal presentation. Since they value their language as a national symbol as well as source of beauty, they focus on the style of their language and how creative they can be in presenting their argument. Creativity and cleverness in a business presentation are often regarded as important for their own sake—after all, how could one be practical without enjoying the beauty of the language? A fitting example occurred between a group of management students at the Wharton School in the United States who were preparing to debate (via satellite videoconference) another group of students at the École des Hautes Études Commerciales, an elite graduate school of management in Paris. When the connection was made across time zones, the U.S. students were ready to jump in and begin a debate on the benefits (or faults) of the European Union; however, the French participants had a different idea in mind. Their professor began with a long introduction that explained the history of the university, numbers and types of students who attended, and what types of programs and divisions there were within the university. Both students and professor from the United States were taken aback (although the French counterparts could not see their quizzical looks because of where the camera was placed) because they were concerned about precious time evaporating with every second that passed. The professor from the United States also wondered if she should have prepared some elaborate information that reflected the school's pride and heritage, and how their international counterparts might have perceived a lack of such an introduction.

There are numerous reasons why people from low-context cultures are more direct with their message structure. Getting to the point up front serves as a form of respect. People who are busy do not appreciate having their time taken up with unnecessary explanations and indirect "beating around the bush." The logic of their approach might look like this:

Major Premise:	Time is a valuable commodity to a businessperson.
Minor Premise:	Those listening to me are businesspeople.
Conclusion:	Time is valuable to these people and I should not waste it on trivialities.

The United States is also a visual culture. People are accustomed to the eight-second sound bites captured by aggressive reporters, and the constant change of images in thirty-second commercials. What naturally follows is that making business presentations requires the use of charts, graphs, and visual support. Most businesspeople in the United States are also accustomed to flashy PowerPoint presentations that demonstrate the presenter's expertise and level of preparation for a presentation. To present important data without having at least some visuals to back up and support your key points would mean failure in this culture. However, other cultures can view audiovisual aids as an impediment, a distraction from the personal relationships that prospective business partners must develop before any deal can be made.

The presentation style of U.S. Americans and Canadians often follows the business case framework of problem statement, analysis, and recommendation. Canadians, for example, prefer that a speaker gives the recommendation at the beginning of a report and then provide the rationale and necessary background, emphasizing the practical use of information. This is the typical form of linear thinking in which a speaker pushes for the hard sell: "Here are my data; here is why my data are accurate; and here is why *you* should buy my product." While this process of moving from problem to solution seems perfectly appropriate for this low-context culture, others can easily take offense. Audience members from a high-context culture may perceive this as too forward and would be insulted that you had to state the obvious for them, which should have been carefully implied throughout your presentation. Reactions of this sort are directly related to cultural aspects of perception and frame of reference. What you might consider perfectly acceptable in your culture could be perceived as insulting and ultimately jeopardizing to a business deal in another culture that is less direct and looks for relationships first and the hard sell last (if at all). Table 2.1 shows some differences in how people across various cultures might approach a business presentation, based on generally accepted cultural norms.

Communication In Low Vs. High Context Cultures	
In Low-Context Cultures	**In High-Context Cultures**
+Completing tasks is more important than maintaining relationships.	+ Relationships are worth maintaining and tasks will be completed.
+ Data should be completely objective.	+ Data can include subjective elements.
+ Employees expect detailed information.	+ Employees expect the boss to handle details.
+ People are addressed informally.	+ People are addressed more formally.
+ Executives are awarded private office space.	+ Executives share open office space.
+ An employee's competence is what gives him or her importance (as well as position).	+ An employee's position or status gives him or her a certain amount of power.
+ Meetings stick closely to an agenda.	+ Business meetings can be interrupted at any point while participants multitask.

TABLE 2.1: Low Versus High Contexts

Finally, some high-context cultures find arguments more convincing because of the value they place on stories and analogies, rather than facts and figures. (See Table 2.2) African cultures often place emphasis on storytelling as a ritual process of myth-building and persuasion. In Madagascar, for example, it is common for a merchant to use a four-point organizational pattern in which he first humbly apologizes for taking the listener's time. He then thanks everyone present, from the highest-ranked people in attendance down to the lowest. In the third phase of the speech, he may use everything from illustrations to proverbs, fables, and apocryphal anecdotes in the substance of his proposal. Syllogisms and the formality of logic are far less important to the trader and his audience than the fabric of human experience and its connectedness to nature. Finally, he will thank and bless his listeners.[72]

Some Differences in Presentation Styles Across Cultures		
	U.S. American	**Japanese**	**Arab**
Language	Succinct and to the point	Indirect and circuitous	Elaborate explanations
Persuasion	Factual, concerned and with short-term gains	Look for harmony and long-term gain	Look to national religious overtones to make point
Delivery	Make eye contact and engage the audience	Make use of pause for reflection and use less eye contact out of respect	Display status through gestures

TABLE 2.2: Some Differences in Presentation Styles Across Cultures [71]

CHAPTER SUMMARY

This chapter has examined how culture affects each of us through our thought processes as we use language. Some cultures display a tendency to be direct and focus on purely verbal interactions, while other cultures value indirect and more ambiguous communication through nonverbal gestures, inferences, and metaphor. Content is king in one culture, while others value context. As the process of globalization leads us into more business activities across cultures, we should remember to assess another culture through the perspective of those who know it best. Knowing that certain expectations and preferences are important to the people of another culture will help you to avoid the assumption that your ways of seeing, thinking, and communicating are the right ways (or the only ways). We should pay close attention to the visual, vocal, and verbal cues that people display as they interact with us. We also need to understand something about how the people of another culture save face so as not to embarrass someone. We should know, for example, whether they may be accustomed to publicly displaying emotion and whether or not they are comfortable with silence.

Our goal in communicating across cultures should never be to assume that a business partner will use a more direct style of communication because she comes from the United States, or that a client will prefer an indirect style because he comes from Japan.[73] Focus on *why* these speakers from different cultures behave the way they do by understanding the many hidden dimensions of culture. Moving beyond awareness of communication contexts and into appropriate action means you are becoming a competent communicator because you can engage a variety of audiences in various contexts, knowing *what* to say, *how* to say it, to *whom* you should say it, *when* to say it, and *why*.[74] Just because we can speak the same language doesn't mean we know how to communicate. Our goal in communicating across cultures is to be able to share our ideas and make them common to many by understanding the multiple cultural dimensions that lie below the surface.

APPLICATIONS IN THE GLOBAL MARKETPLACE

The following section is a summary of the dimensions (or categories) of culture that we have discussed throughout this chapter. As you read through each, picture that iceberg we talked about at the beginning of the book. It's easy enough to identify the behaviors above the waterline, but as the cliché makes clear, what you see is only the tip of the iceberg. Once you identify either your behaviors or those of others regarding these questions, take some time to consider what supports them from below: What are the values, beliefs, and attitudes that give meaning to the behaviors we can readily see? For this section you may also consider discussing your responses with people in your learning team or work team.

CONTEXT: HIGH OR LOW

High and low context in intercultural communication refer to whether members of that group prefer to derive meaning from talk (low context) or from observation (high context). Speakers from a high-context culture will be indirect with their messages and expect you to figure out what they mean through contextual cues, nonverbal behavior, silence, or even the use of metaphors. Speakers from a low-context culture, on the other hand, will be much more explicit, offering listeners very little opportunity to "read between the lines."

Helpful Tips

When you know you will be working with people from a certain culture, or traveling to another culture, learn something about that culture's preference for directness so that you will know when to be direct or when to be indirect. You might also want to think about how you would respond to someone from another culture who is even more direct than you are.

Check for clarification. It is reasonable to ask someone if you don't understand a particular custom or what is said. Perhaps you are giving a presentation and have said or done something and sense an uncomfortable feeling that overcomes your audience. As soon as you are able, take someone aside whom you can trust and ask for feedback.

Make sure that you listen carefully to what is being said and pay attention to "turn-taking" while monitoring the flow of the conversation. Display empathy to assess the needs of those with whom you are communicating.

Questions to Ask Yourself Regarding Context And Behavior

Observe yourself as you interact with others. Do you tend to talk more or listen? Do you require complete explanations or can you derive meaning from the context. Keep in mind that this aspect of communication is affected not only by culture but by personality preference as well.

Observe the nonverbal communication behaviors (gestures, silence, rate, posture, eye contact, and more) that you use. Look at the behavior of others. What does this say about you? How do you interpret the nonverbal behaviors of others? How do you react to theirs?

Final Thought

When interacting with people from other cultures, be aware of whether they are direct or indirect with communication. And of course, you should remember that the statements made here about a culture in general are not necessarily statements about individuals.

A CASE STUDY

LANGUAGE BARRIERS IN A DANGEROUS BUSINESS

As they fought a raging wildfire last year in southern Oregon, a fire crew got word that the blaze was approaching rapidly and all workers needed to evacuate. They yelled the directions to a Hispanic crew digging a fire line, but none of them understood English. They stood, confused.

Members of the English-speaking crew ran toward the workers, waving their arms in an attempt to communicate. Eventually, someone who could translate was found and no one was hurt. "That's a dangerous situation," said Ed Daniels, training manager for the Oregon Department of Forestry, who investigated the account. "Knock on wood that no one has died" yet because of language barriers.

The case illustrates a growing language barrier on the front lines of the nation's wildfires as more Hispanic migrant workers rush to firefighting jobs around the West. In Oregon and Washington, contractors who employ the majority of crews fighting forest fires in the Northwest estimate that Hispanics make up more than 60 percent of their crews. Many of those workers cannot speak or understand English.

The prevalence of Spanish spoken on the fire lines has prompted a safety debate among contractors. Despite the influx of Hispanics, the Pacific Northwest Wildfire Coordination Group, which oversees national contract crews, has strengthened language requirements to ensure more firefighters speak English. On any 20-person crew, the boss and the three principal assistants must speak English fluently. All fire communication on the radio must be in English. And firefighting officials are making greater efforts to make sure those hired on crews meet the minimum English requirements.

But many contractors say they prefer to hire Hispanics—regardless of language barriers—because they are very hard workers. "They know how to work," said Jack Neuman, executive director of an association of contracting groups that work out of Washington, Oregon, and Idaho. "They know how to use tools. Most of them are looking for a halfway good-paying job and firefighting does pay a decent wage." Most can earn $5,000 for two months' work, with food and lodging provided. That compares with roughly $1,200 a month working in farming. Neuman added that 98 percent of the firefighters in his association are Hispanic.

Budget considerations and shifting demographics are pushing more non-English-speaking Hispanics onto the fire lines. And huge fires in the West in recent years have boosted demand for fire crews. The pay attracted Vicente Ramirez, a first-year firefighter from Mexico. After years of picking grapes in California and apples in Washington, Ramirez, who doesn't speak English, said he wanted to make more money. "There isn't another job that pays like this," he said.[1]

DISCUSSION QUESTIONS

1. Why is it important for firefighting crews to all speak the same language? For crews in the American West, is English the best choice?
2. What cultural factors may be at work in this case (e.g., frame of reference, contexts for communication)? Why would Spanish-speaking crews be attracted to this line of work, and why would they be particularly good at it?
3. Would the presence of a translator on each crew solve the problem?
4. What nonverbal approaches might the Department of Forestry and Wildfire Suppression Associations consider? How can they work around the language barrier to assure the crews' safety and still provide employment opportunity?
5. What other occupations might experience the same sort of language and culture problems on the job?

CASE SOURCE

1. "Language Barriers in Firefighting: Rising Number of Hispanics Fight Western Wildfires," *The South Bend Tribune*, August 21, 2003, A6.

CHAPTER 3

Culture and Identity

We must learn to speak a foreign culture in the same way that we must learn to speak a foreign language. [1]

—Edward T. Hall

W hat does it mean to express one's identity individually or collectively? How are learning, cognitive orientation, and problem solving influenced by culture? Why is it important to consider how we view our environment? Do we accept it or do we control it? And how do we relate to ambiguity, time, and space? These are the key issues we will examine in the pages ahead as we compare the inward-oriented concept of the Self and the outward-oriented forces of the Universe.

Consider the following scenario, set in West Africa, in which a U.S. American is asked to communicate across cultures about issues related to environment, identity, and ethics. As you read, think about how you might react if you were in Mr. Jackson's position. What would you have recommended? What would you have done?

A Sales Decision in West Africa

Darren Jackson is a VP of international sales with a U.S. based multinational company, ChemicoSpecs that makes specialty chemicals. Recently, the Ministry of Agriculture in one developing nation in West Africa is interested in obtaining large quantities of an insecticide, which they want to extend over several years. The Minister of Agriculture has heard that this particular insecticide will help decrease crop damage. However, Jackson knows that there is another product that would be just as effective but has never been used in the U.S. (it is used in Asian markets).

It is an extremely toxic product but considered safe if used according to the specific instructions. The USDA's testing has concluded that this particular product has the potential to be ingested through residue on vegetables, animals that have eaten treated crops, and possibly the water supply. So, while the chemical can be produced in the U.S., it cannot be sold there. Jackson considers all ethical issues related to the situation and shares the USDA report to the Minister of Agriculture; however the Minister is adamant and wants to use the product because he believes that it could help deter crop devastation and more importantly – the devastation of famine. He assures Jackson that they will uphold the stringent specifications of this highly toxic product. The Minister has even read the WHO (World Health Organization) reports that this product could cause health concerns over the long term.

ChemicoSpec's Executive VP and Chief Operating Officer are called into a conference as Jackson discusses the implications. They feel strongly that the order should be placed. Jackson is conflicted about what he has read in both the USDA and WHO reports. Being culturally savvy, he knows how important trust and personal relationships are in this area of the world. Despite the Executive VP telling Jackson to "do what you think is right – you make the ultimate decision", Jackson is conflicted.

1. What issues of group collectivity will come into play with this situation?
2. Is Darren Jackson dealing with a culture that is inwardly or outwardly focused regarding their environment (issues of acceptance or control of nature)? How will this affect his dealings?
3. If Darren were to ask you for advice, what would you say?
4. What options are open to him?
5. What advice should he give to the Minister of Agriculture?

Adapted from: Gesteland, Richard R. (2005). Cross-cultural business behavior: Negotiating, selling, sourcing and managing across cultures. Copenhagen, Denmark: Copenhagen Business School Press.

INTRODUCTION

An ancient Greek proverb says, "A society grows great when old men plant trees whose shade they know they shall never sit in." Consider the Korean proverb, "If you congregate, you live. If you scatter, you die." Proverbs have been used throughout the centuries to illustrate great truths through metaphors. While such proverbs are succinct, they pack quite a punch because their simplicity and cogency provide a wealth of information to the reader (or listener) who takes the time to ponder their meaning. If we know something about cultures of the Mediterranean or East Asia, we might interpret these proverbs as this: People who cooperate for the common good are more likely to survive than those who strive only for individual gain. Contrast this with the thinking of German poet, playwright, novelist, and scientist Johann Wolfgang von Goethe, who saw "individuality of expression [as] the beginning and end of all art." This wisdom reflects a general Western European view that places emphasis on self-actualization as an important element of human socialization. Consider the thinking of U.S. American poet Henry David Thoreau, who wrote in 1854, "If a man does not keep pace with his companions, perhaps it is because he hears a different drummer. Let him step to the music he hears, however measured or far away." Or author Mark Twain, "A man cannot be comfortable without his own approval." Based on these contrasting views of how people live in society either collectively or individually, we will divide this chapter into two sections.

First, we will look at our *inward orientations*, how an individual expresses himself or herself. By looking at our self-identity, we can examine culture's effects on each of us in three ways: First, how do we tend to interact with others in individual or collective ways? Second, how does culture influence learning and cognitive orientation? Finally, how does culture influence learning, problem-solving, and reasoning?

As we examine the universe we live in, our focus will be on a number of important cultural differences between the more traditional Eastern and Western perspectives. How do people react to and interact with the environment? Do we see ourselves as in harmony with nature or do we hope to control it? How do people deal with ambiguity and change? Do those from certain cultures avoid it or accept it as an inevitable part of life? How do cultures view time? Is there a great deal of it, or is it scarce? And finally, how do people use the space around them? What does culture dictate regarding proxemics?

We will continue to distinguish among cultural norms by using the continua that demonstrate opposing poles of attitude and behavior. As we discuss cultural distinctions, one of the most notable features you will observe is the difference between individualism and collectivism, documented by years of research performed by anthropologists, sociologists, and psychologists. Such experts have found that it is easiest to contrast these dimensions of culture by generalizing into larger geographical areas, such as East and West.[2] Eastern cultures tend toward the collectivist end of the continuum and Western cultures toward the individualist end.

Keep in mind that how we analyze these differences (primarily from a Western perspective) is culture-bound and that no two cultures, whether Eastern or Western, are the same. For example, we tend to say *Asian* to represent the broad range of Chinese, Japanese, Korean, Vietnamese, Cambodian, Laotian, and more. But each of these Asian cultures is *not* identical. Most bear distinctive characteristics that make them different from their neighbors. Throughout this chapter we will take care to distinguish among the various Asian cultures so that we steer clear of assuming that they are all the same. To say that the Vietnamese have precisely the same cultural outlook as Koreans would be like saying people from the United States are the same as people from Britain. They are not. But, people from the United States and Britain do have a Judeo-Christian background, which influences the cultural perspectives derived from these religions. Vietnamese and Koreans have a common denominator in Confucian, Taoist, and Buddhist philosophies. It may be enough for our purposes to say that these very different beliefs have shaped the values, attitudes, and behaviors of their people and how they understand themselves in relation to the universe.

National, regional, social, organizational, and generational factors all affect our sense of identity. Culture is learned, not inherited. Layers of "mental programming" are implanted in childhood and influence the actions and interactions of people throughout their lives. These layers, or influences, might include people's wealth, social class, geographic mobility, cultural background of their parents, their socialization, education, and cultural tastes.[3] In the next section we will explore how people view themselves in relation to the societies in which they live. We will focus, in particular, on individualism versus collectivism and their influence on society.

THE SELF

INDIVIDUALISM AND COLLECTIVISM

Dutch interculturalist Geert Hofstede is perhaps best-known for his extensive research on cultural differences in organizations. Like Edward T. Hall, he believes people have cultural orientations that are subconscious and which affect them in their occupations. He defines these orientations as dimensions, which are "an aspect of a culture that can be measured relative to other cultures."[4] To arrive at this definition, Hofstede performed empirical research at a large multinational corporation (plus its subsidiaries in more than fifty different countries) by studying employee values. This helped him to identify several cultural dimensions that affect how we do business and how we interact with others who are different from us. These included: expressions of individualism and collectivism; long-term/short-term orientation; dealing with uncertainty and change; expressions of power; as well as masculinity and femininity. Hofstede, of course, is not the only researcher to write and speak about such cultural dimensions, and throughout the text we will identify a number of others. In this chapter, we will focus on three of these dimensions.

According to Hofstede, individualism means that a person is emotionally independent from group membership.[5] This doesn't mean that the individual doesn't belong to any social or family groups, but that *self-actualization* is at the forefront of identity. Western cultures, such as Canada, the United States, Britain, Australia, New Zealand, and many European countries, place importance on what the individual thinks of herself or himself apart from anyone else; personal autonomy and self-actualization are central to how a person will adjust and find a place in society. This means that what the individual thinks is decidedly more important than what his or her social circles think or expect. (See Figure 3.1)

For example, in some nations such as the United States, once young people graduate from high school or college, they must find their own way in life and depend, to a large extent, on themselves alone. Living at home and being dependent on parents once they have become adults are seen as forms of abnormal dependency. In the United States, once you become an adult, you are expected to take care of yourself, make your own decisions, and be responsible for finding and advancing your own career. But in other societies (e.g., Singapore, Qatar, and Brazil) young people are expected to live at home until they marry. To leave the nest prematurely would embarrass the family and cause them to lose face. A tight social circle keeps them close to home until they can form their own family—a new social structure. For someone from an individualistic society, however, in which young people are expected to find work and live on their own, failing to find employment and gain independence may cause their *parents* to lose face.

Identity: Collective or Individualistic

Do people act collectively for the good of the group identity or individually for the good of one person.

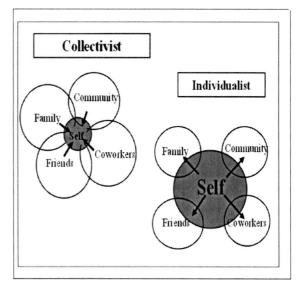

FIGURE 3.1: Identity: Individualism and Collectivism
In individualistic cultures, self-autonomy is at the center with family, friends, and community on the periphery. In collectivist cultures, the self is greatly affected by family, friends and community.

On the job, individualism influences actions. Often, but not always, managers can emphasize task over relationship, meaning that productivity of workers is more important than their satisfaction. This is apparent in the way many Western cultures focus on time as a limited resource, immediately wanting to get down to business rather than taking the time for small pleasantries. This is also evident when employees appear to act in their self-interest. For example, if one team member isn't contributing a satisfactory amount of work to a project, group members might proceed without that person, thinking that they can get just as much or more done without him or her. If the participating team members decide that the slacker needs to "shape up," the way they communicate their displeasure could be direct and confrontational. [6]

Did you know that it was Benjamin Franklin who said, "Time is money."

Characteristics of Individualism and Collectivism

INDIVIDUALISM	COLLECTIVISM
Family/Relationships	**Family/Relationships**
-Set out on own	-Loyalty to group; earnings to help
-Independence	-Interdependence
-Nuclear family	-Extended family
-Speak one's mind (tell honest truth)	-Consider effect of honesty on others
Communication	**Communication**
-Meanings are in words	-Meanings are in actions
-Silence is abnormal	-Silence is normal
-Direct confrontation accepted	-Direct confrontation considered rude
-Freedom to say no	-Must say, "We will think about it"
-Express personal opinions	-Personal opinions do not exist
Work	**Work**
-Act according to self-interest	Act according to group's interest
-Task over relationship	Relationship over task
-Think in terms of "I"	Think in terms of "we"
-Guilt (one's own conscience)	Shame (group conscience)
-Self-respect (point of view of individual)	Face (point of view of society)

Adapted from G. Hofstede, *Cultures and Organizations: Software of the Mind: Intercultural Cooperation and Its Importance for Survival* (New York, NY: 1997), 67.

TABLE 3.1: Characteristics of Individualism and Collectivism

The opposite of individualism is collectivism. (See Table 3.1) We'll define collectivism as *connection with the power of the group*,[7] where people are integrated into some form of group membership. Obligation and loyalty to one's group are paramount when people expect to share resources. For example, employees in a collectivist society who work together on a project view their success as the result of a cooperative effort, not as the product of any one individual's expertise. A classic example is found in the Japanese saying, "*Deru kui wa utareru*" which, translated in English, means "*The nail that sticks up gets hammered down.*" In the collectivistic perspective of the Japanese, it would mean "losing face" to accept personal praise for a job well done. To accept such recognition would bring shame on an individual, because he or she is closely connected to the work group within the larger context of the company. To do a good job means to bring praise to the company and not the individual. Thus, harmony and interconnectedness are extremely important.

Buddhist, Confucian, and Taoist world views have contributed to this sort of interconnectedness and harmony, which are grounded in a philosophy that places high esteem on social relationships.[8] *Buddhism* favors a psychological rather than religious approach to the self and focuses on the idea of a "selfless being," in which an individual is not the center of the universe, but rather must find reality by displaying empathy toward others and seeking awareness through meditation.[9] *Confucianism* is a moral philosophy that aims to build and then maintain strong social relationships among its followers and emphasizes reciprocity. It is built upon four principles: *jen* (humanism), *i* (faithfulness), *li* (propriety), and *chih* (wisdom). Creating warm interactions with people and respect for reciprocity (not doing to others what you wouldn't want them to do to you) are basic tenets of this philosophy.[10] *Taoism* focuses on being virtuous by striving to balance both what is good *and* bad, rather than just conquering what is bad. The ultimate goal is not to find peace through elimination of all that is painful, ugly, or sad, but to transcend it. One must find ways to balance the tension between good and bad—to do away with the bad leaves an imbalance with the good. It is the tension created between the two that keeps interconnectedness in play. So, in life one must experience pleasure and pain, joy and sorrow, life and death in tandem. The good and the bad are merely two sides of the same reality (See Figure 3.2).[11]

One realizes that good and bad, pleasure and pain, life and death, winning and losing, light and dark are not absolute experiences belonging to different categories, but are merely two sides of the same reality—extreme aspects of a single whole. This point has been emphasized most extensively by the Chinese sages in their symbolism of the archetypal poles, yin and yang. And the opposites cease to be opposites in the very essence of Tao. To know the Tao—the illustrious way of the universe—is the ultimate purpose of human learning.[13]

FIGURE 3.2: Understanding the Tao

In collectivist societies, the concepts of identity and self are rooted in what cross-cultural psychologists call "personhood." Personhood is best defined by the Asian concept of *jen*, which defines the self only in relationship to others.[12] Typically in Asian cultures (Chinese, Korean, Japanese, etc.) the concept of *individual* is always defined in relation to a group—the family, the clan, the community, the complicated social system that connects people to one another. A person is defined by his or her place in society, and there are social rules that guide behavior according to what is expected from the group. The expectation as a whole is that a person cannot function apart from a group connection and that it is better to be connected to those who are older and wiser.[14] This concept of group is also exhibited in the language of certain cultures. For example, Japanese culture exhibits general patterns of collectivist behavior by using contextual concepts, such as *wa* (harmony), *amae* (dependency), and *enryo* (reserve or restraint), which all focus on interdependency and preservation of group.[15]

In the scenario that follows, examine how *wa, amae,* and *enryo* were disrupted in the interaction between Mr. Miller and Mr. Choshi. What cross-cultural dimensions were at work in this interaction?

What Went Wrong?

Brad Miller is in the middle of discussing a strategic alliance between his small satellite technology company and a counterpart in Singapore. His previous meeting the week before had been postponed because his wife was expecting, and since it was a false alarm, he rescheduled as quickly as possible. After all, this was a potentially big deal for his struggling company, and he didn't want to be rude to Mr. Katsuo Choshi, so he took the equivalent of a California red-eye flight and arrived in Singapore with just enough time to catch a taxi and get to the meeting.

Brad got very little sleep on the plane, worrying about his wife at home. But the meeting was important so he focused his attention on the task at hand. Mr. Choshi greeted Brad pleasantly but formally, "Good day, Mr. Miller. We are glad that you could meet with us to discuss business opportunities." Brad responded, "I'm glad to meet you, Katsuo; please call me Brad." Aside from the formality of a lavish luncheon where Brad met Mr. Choshi's associates and the many distractions of greetings and various other social pleasantries, the meeting seemed to get off to a good start.

During the afternoon his cell phone rang. Brad was so excited and also anxious so in mid-sentence, he interrupted Mr. Choshi, "Excuse me, but I have to take this; it could be my wife. . . ." With that, Brad jumped up from the table, flipping open the cell phone while turning his back to talk with whoever was on the line. Surely no one would mind that this personal concern had interrupted the meeting. Brad did not notice that Mr. Choshi sat there silently, actually rigidly, indignant that Mr. Miller could have so little respect for their meeting. Brad turned around, grinning broadly and motioning that his wife had just had the baby. Brad was relieved that Mr. Choshi smiled pleasantly and nodded.

When the meeting ended, Brad sensed that there was a bit more distance between Mr. Choshi and him than at the start of the day. Brad asked Mr. Choshi if they could meet again at a future date so that he could discuss matters further with his boss. Mr. Choshi was polite and agreed to meet with him again, but Brad left feeling that something was off-center. Two weeks went by and Brad still had not heard from Mr. Choshi.

1. What happened here? From Brad's (Western) perspective? From Mr. Choshi's (Eastern) perspective?
2. What cultural values and attitudes might be attached to each?
3. How might a culture's collectivity come into play here?
4. How was harmony disrupted? Why? What would Brad's response be to this?

In Latin American cultures, the collective concept is underscored by the importance placed on the family and one's social network. Relationships within the nuclear family, the extended family, and close ties with the community provide protection, structure, and stability that help to maintain family and cultural traditions. Some demographers estimate that a substantial majority of Mexicans, (perhaps as many as 90 percent) still live in their nuclear families.[16] This is revealed in the use of complex surnames that include both sides of the family. Most Latinos have two surnames: the one listed first comes from the father and the second is from the mother. This demonstrates how an individual is linked to both sides of a nuclear family, which implicitly includes extended family. When an individual is addressed using only the first of his two surnames (the father's), a close connection to the rest of the family still remains. For example, if a man's name were Señor Juan Antonio Martínez García, he would be addressed as Señor Martínez (Martínez is the father's surname and García the mother's). If a woman named Señorita María Angeles Gutiérrez Herrera should marry Señor Martínez, she would probably adhere to tradition by taking her husband's name and would subsequently be called Señora María Angeles Gutiérrez Herrera de Martínez.[17].

To people from an individualistic culture who have adopted the more modern practice of women keeping their maiden names, this may appear to be a very complicated way of addressing someone. But knowing about some of the cultural dimensions of collective societies can eliminate some awkwardness in business transactions because they will help you to understand how to correctly address someone and avoid unnecessary misperceptions. The Latin tradition of naming people reveals more than a quaint cultural custom: It signifies the reality of how a culture thinks and behaves because of its people's interdependence on one another.

This emphasis on interdependency and interconnectedness among nuclear family, extended family, and community can create special challenges for global managers working in a Latin American host nation. In a culture in which organizations often hire relatives and friends because of long-standing and trusted relationships, managers from the outside may find it difficult to establish rapport with employees because they are not insiders. This can have complicated ramifications for employee productivity and satisfaction. Trust must be cultivated through strong relationships, which always take time. But a manager from another culture may find it difficult to work through the intricacies of such connections to establish trust in the Latin world. In Colombia, for example, there is a cultural principle called *palanca* that dictates how interpersonal relationships should be managed in the workplace. *Palanca* means a "lever" and translates into interpersonal connections that people use as a form of barter between a provider and a beneficiary.[18] Its tacit rules and subtle ways of translating inferences into action make this form of interpersonal communication near-mythical throughout South America.

The following true story about the development of relationships, told by Geert Hofstede, demonstrates how the concepts of individualism and collectivism affect how people do business.

I, We, and They – Who is in Charge?

Hofstede tells the story of a Swedish high tech company and a potential partner who had close ties in Saudi Arabia. The Swedish company sent one of their engineers (Anders) to Riyadh to work with an engineering firm there. This firm was run by two thirty-something brothers, (we will call them Mahed and Faik) who were British-educated. The potential partner was to help the Saudi government create a relationship with the Swedish company. Anders spent two years developing the relationship between the brothers with at least six visits back and forth. But Anders grew impatient because he felt that the initial Swedish contact was always there to babysit with him and the brothers. He also had suspicions that perhaps this intermediary also did business with the competitors. Moreover, the meetings never seemed to 'get off the ground' and into business – they often discussed art and theater and things that Mahed and Faik favored.

The senior leadership at the Swiss company thought that progress was too slow and considered cancelling any future meetings since they were getting nowhere – and besides, it was too costly to spend money for nothing. However, just before they severed the ties, they received word that the Saudis wanted to meet with them immediately. They were ready to sign a multi-million dollar deal.

Upon arriving, Anders was surprised at how the 'temperature' had changed – they didn't need the intermediary and their Saudi counterparts seemed more relaxed and jovial. The deal went through and Anders was promoted and advanced in the company. He ensured a competent successor and even personally introduced him to the brothers. Not long after, he received an email that shocked him – the brothers threatened to pull out of the deal because of a minor issue. Sanders had to then fly back to Riyadh and deal with the issue. He discovered that it was not really about the minor detail, but the fact that the brothers wanted to do business with him and not with the new person (even though he had substantial experience). Ander's superiors were wise to allow him to stay on the account.

Adapted from: Hofstede, cited in R. L. Wiseman and R. Shuter, *Communicating in Multinational Organizations* (Thousand Oaks, CA: Sage Publications, 1994), 85.

RECOGNITION AND PRAISE

To better understand individualism and collectivism, consider an example of how giving recognition and praise in the workplace may be viewed differently based on a person's individual or collective viewpoint.

To Compliment or Not to Compliment: That Is the Question

Sam Sheppard was recently promoted to the position of Senior Communication Specialist in a large pharmaceutical company in the Midwestern United States that had international subsidiaries in the United States, Europe, and Asia. His primary function was to oversee cross-functional teams that maintained close links with team members at various sites around the world and to ensure that their communications transmitted consistent and appropriate messages for the organization.

Teams in each of the global areas were a mixture of people from different cultures. The U.S. team of communication specialists consisted of three U.S. citizens (two men and one woman), one British woman, and one Japanese man who was new to the organization. After an unusually long and difficult project, Sheppard determined that the team needed a break and organized a company dinner at the completion of the project which, despite all of the setbacks, actually ended on schedule.

It was important as a new director for him to show his sincere appreciation as well as maintain the morale of the group. Team members were encouraged to bring along their spouses. The stress of the past few months appeared to evaporate as team members and guests laughed and conversed freely. Toward the end of the dinner celebration, Sheppard stood up to make a toast to the group and singled out the team member from Japan, Yusaku Futaba, saying that if he hadn't joined the team at just the right time to offer his technical expertise, the group would not have succeeded.

Sam thought it a bit awkward when Mr. Futaba simply nodded his head but didn't smile despite the laughter and good wishes from the other team members, one of whom gave him a good natured slap on the back, claiming that "he saved the day." Mr. Futaba's wife seemed embarrassed and lowered her eyes. With glasses raised high by all of the guests seated at the table, some glanced nervously at each other until one of the team members broke the silence by expressing his gratitude to the group. Others joined in, the conversations resumed and the evening ended well despite this awkward moment. Sam was disappointed, nevertheless, with the unexpected reaction of Mr. Futaba.

1. What happened here?
2. What were Mr. Shepard's expectations? Mr. Futaba's?
3. What does Mr. Shepard need to know about group harmony?
4. What does Mr. Futaba need to understand about individualism?
5. How can the two see eye-to-eye?

This is an example of differing cultural norms at work. What is perfectly appropriate and acceptable to a person from one culture is unacceptable to another. What Sam Shepard had created was a situation in which he praised one member of the team at the expense of the others. He made that individual stand out rather than praising the collective *whole*. Since Yusaku Futaba was enculturated in a collective society, he most likely viewed their success as a cooperative effort and not the result any one individual's expertise. Regardless of expertise, rank, years in service to the company, or loyalty to the team, all had participated in the group effort and that meant all should have been praised as a group. So rather than feeling honored, which by individualistic standards would make one be proud to be singled out, Futaba most likely felt embarrassed at such a lavish and public display of praise. In Sam Shepard's culture, if he had not praised his employee, that person might have felt slighted, so it was only natural (according to his tacit and subconscious cultural norms) that he act the way he did.

As we have seen, a culture of individualism affects how people will seek individual identity, rights, and achievement while a culture of collectivism will focus on group needs over individual needs and desires. Cultures that tend to have high individualistic values are found in the United States, Australia, Great Britain, Canada, the Netherlands, and New Zealand. Cultures that display high collectivistic values include Pakistan, Indonesia, Colombia, Venezuela, Panama, Ecuador, and Guatemala.

Other societies with strong collectivistic cultures are China, Taiwan, Korea, Japan, Mexico, the Philippines, as well as East and West African, and Arab nations.[20]

LEARNING

Individualist and collectivist dimensions also have a profound effect on learning. Individualist cultures approach learning as action-oriented with the purpose of attaining knowledge. Self-actualization, pride in individual accomplishment, and an emphasis on competition are important for learners as they "seize the day." In the United States, for example, individual mastery of learning is essential. Students are rewarded for risk-taking and creativity, for trial-and-error methods of learning. Often, low-context cultures such as the United States value impulsivity, rewarding students who are able to make quick guesses and assertions.[21] Learning is student-centered with an emphasis on personal discovery. The goal is to learn *how* to learn.[22] Translated to the workplace, such learners prefer to work by themselves, focus on a task without input from "the boss," and expect to be praised and rewarded individually for their hard work. While individualist cultures participate in group work, the value of an individual's contribution to completing a task is essential. One may not merely be in a group, but is expected to do his or her fair share of whatever needs to be done.

At the opposite end of this pole is the collectivist approach where people are viewed as the recipients of wisdom. This view is tied directly to respect of elders (teachers, managers, superiors, etc.) who hold knowledge because of seasoned wisdom and experience, and who have the responsibility to share such wisdom with those who are younger. The goal is to *learn how to do* with guidance from the respected teacher.[23] Collectivist societies emphasize cooperation among learners because people from such cultures are highly integrated. Cooperative cultures, such as the Chinese, Mexican, and Arabic societies, prefer cooperation over competition.[24] They are more reflective and take more time to make a decision. The rationale is that if you act too quickly and make a mistake, then you will inevitably lose face. So, in order not to bring shame upon your family, co-workers, or community, you must consider background variables (e.g., historical influences), emotions, and feelings. Translated to the workplace, workers will feel more comfortable collaborating with others, require feedback and approval from authorities, and most likely will only appreciate their success in relation to their membership in the group. See once again the Table 3.1 that lists many of the more important characteristics of individualism and collectivism.

Speaking of Culture

The Japanese have very high anxiety about life because of the need to save face. There are constant pressures to conform. A very strong work ethic and strong group relationships give structure and stability to life. Emotional restraints are developed in childhood, and all behaviors are situation-bound. This makes it extremely difficult for a foreigner to understand the culture.

—Terry Morrison, Wayne A. Conaway, and George A. Borden,
Kiss, Bow, or Shake Hands [25]

COGNITIVE ORIENTATION

Cultural conditioning affects how people orient their thoughts, and influences how they learn. As we saw in the previous section, people from Western cultures generally are conditioned to believe that there is truth to be discovered through logical and scientific methods, by taking action or asking questions to "find it." People from Eastern cultures, rooted in transcendent philosophies, are conditioned to believe that one allows truth to make itself known, if it does at all. One is a recipient rather than a seeker of wisdom.[2]

Cognition is basically the process of "knowing" that includes both awareness and judgment. Cognitive processes are universal: All humans from all walks of life have the capacity to think and reason. And because we are social creatures, our culture shapes both awareness and judgment and how we approach our process of reasoning.[27] Swiss psychologist Jean Piaget, who first articulated the Theory of Cognitive Development, believed that each individual is primarily responsible for his or her own cognitive development, and that people react to their environment and construct their own cognitive world through a dynamic process. Russian psychologist Lev Vygotsky believed that such development was affected by social interaction, and it was he who articulated the Sociocultural Theory of Development. Vygotsky promoted the social constructivist view that each person's development is shaped by how a society's members perceive or construct their reality, and that both language and culture play a big part in our cognitive development.[28]

Two of the cultural differences we have already discussed that have the greatest effect on problem-solving and cognitive patterns are the *high-context/low-context* distinctions and the *individualist/collectivist* dimensions of culture. The U.S. notion of problem-solving looks at the concept of rational order, which is rooted in the assumption that the world is mechanistic. If there is a problem, something needs to be fixed; we can do this by applying logic and rationality as part of the solution. Using facts, data, and knowledge can help the problem-solver overcome just about any obstacle, and we do this by devising strategy, taking action, and implementing plans, policies, and procedures. U.S. Americans are doers.[29]

PROBLEM SOLVING AND REASONING

Culture also influences problem-solving approaches and patterns of thought. Studies have shown that English-speaking people from the United States prefer a more linear and direct problem-solving approach than do speakers of Asian, Romance, and Russian languages. People who speak Chinese, Japanese, and Taiwanese use a more circular approach; the French and Spanish and Italians are circuitous; and Russians are both direct and circuitous.[30] For example, a dominant thought pattern for U.S. Americans is called the *factual-inductive* approach, which means that they first determine the facts and then draw a conclusion. Russian cultures use a pattern of *axiomatic deduction*, in which they reason from general principles to specific applications. Arab cultures use an *intuitive-affective* pattern, in which emotions and subjectivity are preferred to facts. Just because a co-worker comes from France (identified by a more circuitous approach), however, does not mean that he or she will always be thinking in what appears to be a tangential manner, nor will all Asian speakers be circular in their thought patterns. Such patterns of thinking and problem-solving vary with individuals, situations and context; these general patterns, however, are linked to cultural conditioning.[31] It is useful to understand that culture can influence logic and reasoning, which, in turn, can affect individual thought and behavior. This awareness may offer some insight into the puzzling circumstances that can arise unexpectedly in the workplace and that may seem inexplicable.

As you interact with clients, co-workers, supervisors, and subordinates from different cultures, you'll want to think about what is considered reasonable in their cultures.[32] Do they tend to be more factual, linear, or circular in their thinking? Does their orientation to the world mean that they take action to gain knowledge, or are they more inclined to receive wisdom, if it should come their way? The examples that follow will provide some helpful ways to identify how other cultures view reality. The point is simple: It is helpful to be aware of these patterns of thinking and to realize that a person's culture has most likely shaped how he or she both presents data and approaches solving problems.

Factual evidence may be important in one culture (low-context) but have little value in another. Low-context cultures will say, "Just give me the facts," and may define terms such as *facts* and *evidence* as statistical and empirical data that are independently verifiable. High-context cultures, on the other hand, may value chance, luck, and fate as strong evidence. Another distinction in reasoning centers on how low-context cultures favor certain patterns of *rhetorical style*: for example, U.S. Americans favor sets of three. In Japan you can't find things in sets of four because the number four is unlucky. The word for four (*shi*) means death. In the United States, rhetorical patterns use either/or approaches, such as sink or swim, fish or cut bait, it's now or never. These often represent false dichotomies because of the existence of many other options.[33]

Speaking of Culture

Japanese thought patterns are clusters or webs; language patterns also move from one idea or cluster to another and another, but the idea clusters may not have an obvious relationship. They are related more by association than by cause and effect, like stepping-stones that lead to a destination but are spaced out from each other and not in a straight line.

—Louise Damen, *Culture Learning* [34]

The phrase "let me set you straight" is a Western way of thinking, called a universalistic pattern of reasoning. Such reasoning stems from the belief that truth can be known, based upon a logical process of reasoning that includes facts and empirical evidence. An excellent contrast to U.S. linear thinking is that of the Japanese, known as point-dot-space orientation. This pattern of thinking is said to resemble the stepping-stones that adorn the exterior courtyards of temples and shrines. Each stone is strategically placed to ensure harmony and balance. Symbolic of a high-context culture in which meaning is derived from vocal and visual codes versus verbal, the listener is responsible for "bridging the gaps" between the stones by choosing how he or she will "step" from one stone to another.[35] This form of spatial logic can be quite foreign to someone who wants the facts lined up "in order." What constitutes "in order" to the cognitive orientation of one (as influenced by culture) may not look (or sound) the same to another. It is all a matter of whether one perceives that stepping-stones (ideas) should be in a direct path to make logical sense, or if they should be fashioned in relationship to one another. (See Table 3.2)

Differences in Thought and Speaking Patterns of U.S. Americans and Japanese

	U.S. Americans	Japanese
Thought Patterns	-Analytical	-Synthetic
	-Absolute	-Relative
	-Facts	-Subjective ideas
	-Linear	-Point/dot/space
Speaking Styles	-Confront	-Harmony
	-Persuade	-Consensus
	-Linear form of argument	-Circular form of argument
Organizing Ideas	-Show balance between general and supporting details	-Can use general or specific
	-Explore the "how" or "why"	-Explore the "what"
Logic	-Logical proof	-Ambiguity
	-Facts	-Paraphrase
Style and Tone	-Use explicit words ("finally")	-Use ambiguous ("perhaps," "it may be so")
	-Low context (verbalize)	-High context (silence, nonverbal)
	-Speaker as agent of change	-Speaker as perceiver
	-Find answers	-Gather alternatives

Adapted from Roichi Okabe, "Cultural Assumptions of East and West: Japan and the U.S.," in W.B. Gudykunst (ed.) *Intercultural Communication Theory: Current Perspectives* (Beverly Hills, CA: Sage, 1983), pp. 27–39.

TABLE 3.2: Differences in Thought and Speaking Patterns of U.S. Americans and Japanese

RHETORICAL STYLES

Comparing Arab and U.S. American Persuasion Strategies

Few cultures are further apart in rhetorical terms than are Arabs and U.S. Americans. It isn't that the two cultures reason differently; it's that they are worlds apart on what constitutes reasonable evidence and persuasive procedure. Although mass-media reports on events in the Middle East translate the words used by Arab leaders, the reports seldom explain the different cultural standards in Arab societies for evaluating what is reasonable. "We can say," wrote communication scholars Condon and Yousef, "that what is 'reasonable' is not fully separable from cultural assumptions."[36] As spokespeople for Arab and U.S. American viewpoints have stepped forward over the years to articulate their viewpoints on everything from oil production quotas to an independent Palestinian state or the role of democracy in Iraq, they each have employed radically different rhetorical tactics to accomplish similar objectives.

"While only a small percentage (about 10 percent) of present-day Arabs are Bedouins," explain Gudykunst and Kim, "contemporary Arab culture holds the Bedouin ethos as an idea to which, in theory at least, it would like to measure up." While values such as materialism, success, activity, progress, and rationality are important features of U.S. American culture, Arab societies revolve around the core values of hospitality, generosity, courage, honor, and self-respect.[37] U.S. Americans, on the one hand, have a profound respect for empirical data, for the "facts of the case," as objectively determined by unbiased observers, while Arabs are far more respectful of storytelling, metaphor, and a bardic tradition. One person's fact can be another person's lie in the Bedouin world, while the power of storytelling is simply "policy by anecdote" in the West.

In Arab cultures, inspired language and religion are inseparably connected, largely because of the role Arabic plays in Islamic societies. All Muslims must use Arabic in their daily prayers and, in a remarkable and pervasive way, the Qur'an itself serves as the "ultimate book of style and grammar for Arabs."[38] By contrast, rhetorical language in North America focuses exclusively on evidence and the argument itself. Rarely, if ever, does figurative, religious, or divine reference find its way into persuasive argumentation. That is problematic for U.S. Americans because, as one professor of logic put it, "I can't accept as evidence any argument that requires an act of faith."

The Arab's appreciation for the persuasive power of the rhythm and sound of words inevitably leads to a style that relies heavily on devices that heighten the emotional impact of a message. Certain words are used in Arab discourse that have no denotative meaning. "These are 'firm' words," says Hamod, "because the audience knows the purpose behind their use and the words are taken as a seal of definiteness and sincerity of the part of the speaker."[39] Other forms of assertion, such as repetition and antithesis are also common. In the end, for an Arab, eloquence trumps evidence. "He who speaks well is educated," explains Hamod. "He who is well-educated is more qualified to render judgments and it is his advice we should follow." Eloquence and effectiveness are inseparable.[40] An Arab writer establishes credibility by displaying ability and artistry with the language. By contrast, U.S. Americans are more than willing to sacrifice eloquence for evidence.

Thus, culture unquestionably influences what a society believes is persuasive and what is not. Issues such as individualism and collectivism, how we learn (attaining knowledge versus receiving wisdom), and high- and low-context modes of communication will clearly affect the ways we solve problems and organize our thoughts. Each person's way of reasoning can be as valid to that individual as it is foreign and unconvincing to another. So the potential for misunderstanding is high unless we understand this particular dimension of culture.

DISCUSSION

Compare notes with fellow classmates regarding their specific preferences for learning and organizing information.

1. How are these thought or speaking patterns dictated by culture?
2. What is similar or different regarding their thought or speaking patterns?
3. When you give a business presentation, how do your organize your message content?
4. Are you more factual or more subjective?
5. What is your usual delivery style?
6. How does this compare/contrast with others'?

OUTLOOK ON THE WORLD

We have seen how different cultural perspectives shape the way we view both our self and our identity and have also briefly examined the philosophical and religious underpinnings associated with cultural orientations. We will now turn our focus to how people react to and interact with their environment. We will look specifically at harmony, ambiguity and change, time, and spatial orientations so that we can make direct applications to global business interactions.

ENVIRONMENT

An important distinction between Eastern and Western cultures is our perceived relationship with the environment. Do you feel the need to conquer nature or live in harmony with it? We can best separate these two world views by thinking in terms of orientation: inner-directed and outer-directed. Each of these views of the environment is closely correlated with individualism and collectivism, with individualist cultures being inner-directed (controlling the environment). and collectivist cultures being outer-directed (let it take its own course).[41] Inner-directed cultures tend to describe or define organizational culture as mechanisms that function systematically as dictated by their "operators." The basic norm is that humans will, under all circumstances, seek to control their surroundings. Outer-directed cultures, by contrast, view the organization as more organic than systemic, seeing it as a product of its surroundings. It absorbs what it needs from the environment and, therefore, blends harmoniously with it. Earlier in this chapter we looked at the philosophy of Eastern culture as rooted in Confucius, Buddhist, and Taoist ideologies to understand the nature of collectivism. The discussion of Western thought that follows will examine how people from cultures such as the U.S., Canada, Europe, Britain, and Australia interact with their environments.

While contemporary Western thought originated with the ancient Greeks, much has changed since the time of Socrates, Plato, and Aristotle. The ancient Greeks emphasized obligation to the community, and that one could become a decent citizen through sound intellectual reasoning as well as honoring individuals within society. People lived in communal groups and were more connected to nature, which was viewed as a living organism. They subjected themselves to nature and tried to understand their surroundings (both the natural and the supernatural) rather than control them. Medieval scientists searched for God in both the natural world that they could see and the mystical universe, which they could not. Living in harmony with the earth, honoring each other for the sake of community, and searching for the veiled spiritual world were their loftiest goals.[42]

However, things changed dramatically during the Renaissance, which from the literal French translation means "rebirth." Between the fourteenth and sixteenth centuries, this new era of artistic, social, scientific, and political advancement delivered the European world away from the stagnation of the Middle Ages toward a more enlightened, modern form of thinking. The established view of the universe as organic and unknown morphed into a modern system, likened to a machine—a world that could be made known through systematic logic and evidence. Humans now had an even loftier goal: to understand the universe and control it through human reason. If they perceived the universe as a vast machine (as Copernican and Newtonian views of absolute space and time promoted), then they had to learn how to operate it. This was a significant shift in the world view of Western civilization in that nature became objectified while measurement and quantification were the means to establish control of the environment.[43]

Numerous examples of how Western cultures interact with the environment are available each day in the news. This is an interesting phenomenon in the United States, where people are accustomed to fast food, fast commercials, and fast banking. It's 6:15 P.M. and you turn on the evening news to get the weather forecast. The usual jovial, joking weatherman has a serious look on his face. "Wet weather made getting home tonight miserable as heavy rains deluged the highways. Severe thunderstorms will continue throughout the metro area tonight with a flash-flood watch locally until 9:00 P.M. We have a 40-percent chance of hail in the northwest suburbs, with lightning and high winds as the storm front passes through . . . not a good night to be out unless you have to!" His voice carries an end-of-the-world tone when, in fact, it's just raining outside. Since you're already home, you really need to know how the weather will affect your commute tomorrow morning. Impatient for the five-day forecast, you flip to another channel. You become annoyed that there will be more heavy rain throughout the week and possibly into the weekend.

The implicit message here is that we have a need to control our environment. We expect up-to-the-minute, as well as long-range, forecasts so that we can know what to wear, how far we can venture out that day, or when we should return. Bring the umbrella, dress accordingly, and never get stuck outside in weather that wasn't predicted. The same is true, by the way, of traffic reports: "Your outbound commute is a mess this evening if you use the Edens or the Kennedy. It's a 45-minute ride from the Post Office to O'Hare, 38 back in from Lake Cook to the Junction. Outbound Stevenson is stop-and-go all the way to the Tri-State, and the Ryan is now 39 minutes from the Ontario feeder ramp to 95th Street." This attitude is reflected not only in the news media, but in our advertising, our buying habits, and our day-to-day behavior. We now have all-weather, four-wheel-drive sport utility vehicles to drive during dangerous rain and snowstorms (usually on flat, multimillion-dollar highways). Or, if the weather and traffic aren't what we'd like them to be, then we grumble: "Everyone complains about the weather, but no one does anything about it," implying the dream that someone should be able to control it. TV meteorologists show their emotions as they sigh and roll their eyes at yet *another* Labor Day weekend (or any weekend) that wasn't perfect for us to play outdoors.

In a cartoon featuring Sheldon (by Dave Kellett), Sheldon ventures outside only to be confronted by weather that is personified and can't seem to "make up its mind". At first there is hail; then freezing rain; then more hail; then more rain. Sheldon shakes his fist at the weather and says, "Make up your mind already!" Before modern advances in meteorology, explanations for weather phenomena were largely theological. If we can now predict weather patterns, daytime temperatures, precipitation levels, and storm direction seven days in advance, can actual weather control be far behind? General Dwight Eisenhower certainly thought so (or wished it were so). On the eve of his historic D-Day assault on the beaches of France in June of 1944, he ordered the Allied Command Chaplain to pray for good weather. He had done all he could to control every phase of the invasion and was determined to leave nothing to chance. Whether by coincidence or divine intervention, skies above the Normandy coastline on June 6 were mostly clear.

In the Western workplace, leaders now plan for contingencies of every sort—the crisis-management plan contains sections for every emergency from inclement weather to power outages to terrorist attack. Backup plans, alternative work locations, and emergency procedures are now a routine part of most U.S. organizations' approach to business planning. Western cultures are reluctant to admit that there is much in the environment that time, money, and technology cannot influence. Eastern cultures see things differently.

Eastern cultures do not ask how to control their environment, but how to blend into it. They cannot control the universe; they accept that, and ask only to live in harmony with it. Former Sony Corporation Chairman Akio Morita loved classical music and found moments throughout his busy day to listen to his favorite composers. On most days, he would use a Sony Walkman headset and player while commuting to the office. His attitude about listening to music while in the presence of other commuters was that he didn't want to disturb anyone else; if he used earphones, only he would be able to hear the music. Morita became "one" with his environment, respecting the needs of others.[45] A more-Western perspective would be to use the Walkman to drown out the noise of traffic or other people—a way to control privacy. You may have experienced those who seem oblivious to the fact that there are others around—the music pounds away, regardless of taste, style, or volume preference. Others simply have to put up with it or go away. In an Eastern culture, remember, your identity is derived from your oneness with the group or the society. It would be unthinkable *not to care* or to want others to *go away*.

Those who know nothing of foreign languages know nothing of their own.

—Goethe

Fung Shui Land – Disney's Adaptability to Chinese Cultures

Probably one of the most popular icons of the 20th century was Disney's Mickey Mouse. When making plans to expand Disneyland to Hong Kong, its corporate executives had to 'think outside the box' in order to adapt to the local culture. Chinese customs, including food and even mannerisms, as well as the actual park design, both internally and externally, were taken into consideration.

For example, within the many Chinese cultures, luck and good fortune play an important role in one's life. Certain animals, numbers, flowers, and symbols hold powerful influence over the fate of a person. In order to reflect this aspect of Eastern culture, designers created a lucky koi pond, as these golden fish are said to bring a person good fortune. Also, the number 8 is a lucky number, associated with prosperity (unlike the number 4 'sei,' which in Cantonese sounds like the word for 'death'), so the grand ballroom (where many young couples are married) had to be designed to measure 888 square meters. Additionally, to reflect the palate of both Mainland and Hong Kong Chinese, even local 'dim sum' (which literally means 'little bites') is served in restaurants along with other Cantonese delicacies. Finally, Minnie and Mickey are known to bow to guests rather than wave; and during special holidays (such as the Lunar New Year in February), Mickey and Minnie will wear traditional Chinese dress. It will be interesting to see what Disney executives will dream up when the 'Year of the Rat' comes around again in the annual cycle of the ancient zodiac system!

Another example is achieving harmony. Eastern cultures place emphasis on achieving harmony with one's physical environment. Enter the Fung Shui master. This ancient tradition gently manipulates *chi*, or the universe's energy, so that balance and order are achieved in one's surroundings. When planning the theme park's design, Fung Shui masters altered some of the internal floor plans as well as outside designs. For example, unlike the straight pathways found in Florida or California's Main Street U.S.A. theme parks, Disney took the advice from the Fung Shui masters to angle the pathway in order to maintain 'positive' *chi*, keeping that positive energy in the park rather than having it escape into the South China Sea. Other balancing acts were necessary: two of the park's hotels had some alterations – one had its location shifted so that it too was on an angle – therefore encouraging positive chi; another had restaurant decor reflect the five important elements associated with the Fung Shui practice: earth, water, wood, metal and fire.

When doing business and communicating within the global market, it is imperative that we understand how to adapt our own belief and value systems to our business partners, clients, and overall host culture. An ancient Chinese proverb sums up this philosophy by saying, "Enter village, follow customs":

入乡随俗 [rù xiāng suí sú]

For Discussion:

1. What does the practice of Fung Shui say about the nature of culture and identity within Chinese groups?
2. How is this similar or dissimilar to your own cultural identity?
3. What are some other cultural identity issues that Disney should consider? You may want to do some additional research on this topic.

Sources:

-The Fung Shui Kingdom. (2005, April 25). *The New York Times*, pp. C1, C2.

-Gesteland, Richard R. (2005). Cross-cultural business behavior: Negotiating, selling, sourcing and managing across cultures. Copenhagen, Denmark: Copenhagen Business School Press.

AMBIGUITY, CHANGE, AND UNCERTAINTY AVOIDANCE

Another cultural dimension deserving our attention is the way in which cultures react to change or ambiguity. Some cultures have more tolerance for ambiguity than others and readily accept it while other cultures tend to avoid it. This is also known as *uncertainty avoidance* or *ambiguity intolerance*, which is related to open-mindedness about differences and/or contradictions. The term *uncertainty avoidance* is borrowed from organizational sociology in U.S. institutions but has been extended to all forms of human interaction.[46] It means "the extent to which the members of a culture feel threatened by uncertain or unknown situations."[47] The future is uncertain for all of us, but some cultures approach such uncertainty with avoidance and others with acceptance by developing coping mechanisms through technology, law, and religion. The dimension of avoiding uncertainty characterizes people who are less comfortable with unpredictable or unstructured situations. They feel a need for predictability, so they accomplish this by establishing rules and strict codes of behavior in order to plan ahead for any uncertainties that may arise. Their motto might seem to be, "What is different is dangerous." Some of the cultures that seem particularly uncomfortable with change or uncertainty are Greece, Portugal, Belgium, Chile, and Japan.[48]

Speaking of Culture

Latin fatalism looks to destiny as determining a person's, or peoples', fate—they are simply controlled by the forces of nature. This can have an impact when doing business with someone whose cultural norm leads him or her to believe that the individual can control his or her own destiny—even the destiny of others.

For example, in the United States we tend to follow production schedules to a T. It has been noted by expatriates working in Latino environments that such schedules are not as rigid when forces outside of the workers' control disrupt the production. Time commitments are more flexible. Their attitude may be more philosophical rather than be exacting.

This does not mean that people from, say, Mexico will not adhere to international standards and expectations (as dictated by NAFTA, the North American Free Trade Agreement). What it does mean is that foreigners working in Mexico need to understand the more philosophical perspective of their host country so that they don't jump to conclusions at unmet expectations.

—Candace Bancroft McKinnisse and Arthur A. Natella, *Business in Mexico* [49]

Cultures that accept uncertainty, such as Singapore, Denmark, and Sweden, are more comfortable with the unpredictable, are less formal, and have fewer rules.[50] Attitudes adopted by such cultures suggest that they are flexible, adaptable, able to adjust well, and take risks. Their motto might be "What is different is curious."[51] In the United States, people like to take on challenges, support entrepreneurial opportunities, and expand their horizons. This doesn't mean that all U.S. citizens accept ambiguity but that the culture tends to encourage established procedures, consider all angles of potential problems, and gather data to support their decisions. (See Table 3.3) For example, in many U.S. companies (not all) there has been a push to decentralize authority in order to establish a flatter hierarchy. Individuals and work teams are becoming more autonomous in decision making and completing work assignments. Workers in more traditional cultures that tend to have a more typical, pyramid-shaped hierarchy might be intimidated or uncomfortable without clear lines of authority and power, and may feel more stable with structure and procedures.

Acceptance/Avoidance of Uncertainty

Accept Uncertainty	Avoid Uncertainty
Low stress and anxiety	High stress and anxiety
Dissent accepted	Strong desire for consensus
High level of risk-taking	Low level of risk-taking
Few rituals	Many rituals
What is different is curious	What is different is dangerous
Country	**Examples**
Canada	Egypt
Denmark	Argentina
England	Chile
India	France
Jamaica	Greece
Sweden	Japan
United States	Mexico

Adapted from W. B. Gudykunst, *Bridging Differences: Effective Intergroup Communication*, Sage Publications, 1998, 61.

TABLE 3.3: Acceptance/Avoidance of Uncertainty

A simple example of uncertainty avoidance may be found in the ancient ritual of steelmaking and the crafting of Japanese samurai swords. For more than a thousand years, Japanese sword makers developed, rehearsed, and practiced a complicated ritual in which hot metal was pounded thin with an iron mallet, heated, then folded over, pounded again, and folded again. This ritual of pounding, heating, and folding required a specific cadence, assured by the recitation of lines of lyric poetry, over and over and over again. The assumption on the part of the master sword maker was that the words themselves, along with the ritual—which had to be followed exactly each time—were responsible for the strength and durability of the resulting sword blade. Modern steelmakers now know that the actions of their ancient Japanese counterparts were a crude yet effective form of *tempering*—a process known to create some of the hardest, most resilient steel known to man. While modern steelmakers have oxygen-fed furnaces to create very high temperatures, and precise process controls and measuring sensors, the ancient Japanese had only their rituals to rely on. The price for failing to adhere to the process precisely would be death in battle—a significant incentive for avoiding uncertainty.

So, how does all of this affect the global economy in which we now compete? We saw in Chapter 2 the influence of culture on communication, and in this chapter we've examined evidence that shows how dealing with change and uncertainty can affect the ways in which members of a culture communicate. High-uncertainty-avoidance cultures, for example, tend to be cautious about getting to know people outside the group. Since there is a connection between high-uncertainty-avoidance cultures (groups not comfortable with change) and collectivist cultures, this would make sense because such cultures stress the importance of establishing relationships based upon connection within the greater community, status, and family origin. This may mean that integration of new members into an already established work group with a long-standing history will take longer and a manager may have to spend substantial time overseeing the group process. This is most likely because cultures that tend to be more anxious about change depend more on the authority of their leaders and will expect to be shown what to do. They may be less tolerant of risk and will work for consensus in the group since conflict is seen as disruptive to the harmony, which is both valued and necessary for working collectively.

TIME

Attitudes toward time differ from culture to culture, and this is the final dimension we will examine in this chapter. Philosophers have written about the concepts of time and mankind's focus on its passage for as long as there has been writing. Ancient thinkers, from Plutarch to Heraclitus, and moderns from Proust to Einstein, have written of the value of time to a society and the ways in which its members think it about, use it, and are ultimately overtaken by it. While every discipline from biochemistry to theoretical physics has examined the effects of time on mankind, only cultural anthropology has systematically sought to examine how societies define themselves according to their views of time.

Beginning in the 1930s with Edward T. Hall, anthropologists have been examining and classifying social behavior, with time as a variable. Until his work among the Navajo Nation of the American West, the perception was that cultures thought, wrote, and spoke about time in a fairly straightforward way. Unfolding research from a variety of sources indicated that some cultures with a *past orientation* view the traditions of what came before as being more important in many ways than the present. Japan, India, China, and numerous cultures of Eastern Europe have always placed a significant value on past achievement and on honoring the lives and spirits of ancestors. Many cultures throughout Asia and the Latin world have a strong sense of the past and the role that traditional values must play in present-day decisions.[52] Cultures with *present orientation* are focused on the moment, neither invoking the past nor wondering about the future. Societies with simple patterns of organization, fewer rules and norms, and very little outside influence often exhibit such views. The Bedouin tribes of northern Africa, numerous Pacific Islanders, and the Maori of New Zealand see time as a seamless continuum that passes over us—a phenomenon we are neither able to understand or influence. The developed nations of the modern, global economy exhibit still another view of time: They tend to have a strong *future orientation*, focusing on what's ahead, planning for contingencies that may never come about, and anticipating the divisions and demarcations in time that linear, forward-thinkers value.[53]

The concepts of *polychronic* and *monochronic* time come from Edward T. Hall. Monochronic (one-dimensional) societies are those that are punctual, efficient, and like very much to be *on time*. These are mostly linear, rational thinkers who see time as scarce, valuable, something to be saved (or lost), and having a monetary equivalent: "Time is money." Monochronic people feel more comfortable if they are able to stick to the original plans, meet established deadlines, and use their time wisely. In return, they expect others to be prompt, to respect their own use of time, and to adapt quickly to make the most of the time they've been given. They also prefer to focus on one task at a time.[54]

For example, global business specialist Richard Gesteland shares this advice, "In Germany, Switzerland, or Sweden, you can expect to start off with a few minutes of small talk and then proceed in linear fashion from item number 1 to the last item on the agenda with no major digressions."[55] A Swiss friend was once asked whether people in his hometown were all so punctual because they had such good watches. "No," he replied, "we have such good watches because *we are on time*." In most monochronic societies, you could gather up all the clocks and watches, and people would *still* show up on time for work, school, dinner, or the theater. That's simply how they've been enculturated. Nations with a monochronic view of time are usually among the more individualistic cultures, such as the U.S., Canada, and those in northern Europe, but other collectivistic cultures, such as Japanese (largely because of global economic development), also fall into this category. Keeping to schedule and completing tasks in a timely fashion demonstrate respect for the larger group. (Table 3.4 shows the varying degrees of countries and time orientation.)

Varying Degrees of Dimensions in Business Cultures

Very Monochronic Business Cultures
Nordic and Germanic Europe
North America
Japan

Moderate Monochronic Business Cultures
Australia/New Zealand
Russia and most of East-Central Europe
Southern Europe
Singapore, Hong Kong, Taiwan, China
South Korea

Polychronic Business Cultures
Arab countries
Africa
India
Latin America
South and Southeast Asia

Source: Richard R. Gesteland, *Cross-Cultural Business Behavior: Marketing, Negotiating, Sourcing, and Managing Across Cultures* (Copenhagen, Denmark: Copenhagen Business School Press, 2002), 57.

TABLE 3.4: Varying Degrees of Dimensions in Business Cultures [57]

In polychronic (multidimensional) societies, people are more relaxed about time because relationships are more important than schedules.[56] Relationships are crucial to developing trust, which evolves through those relationships and ultimately makes for good business. Hurrying any proposition is considered superficial and deadlines are never missed (they're simply adjusted), but that is part of the process. Usually the more collectivistic cultures see time this way, such as cultures from Asia, Latin America, and the Middle East. Other European cultures, such as French, Spanish, and Irish, also fall into this category. They don't want to rush through life—they'd much rather spend time over a meal or having a drink with friends. The Arabic saying *Insh'allah*, which translated means "God willing," is a demonstration of how strong religious belief shapes Arabic thinking. People simply do not carry the pretense of knowing what will happen in the future. In Indonesian, the saying *jam karet* literally means "rubber time," and refers to a relaxed attitude toward time. Only a true emergency, such as a death or serious illness, makes people rush.[57] In traditional Mexican culture, *mañana*, translated as "tomorrow," is often taken to mean "at some point, the work will get done," but rarely is there a fixed deadline that cannot be adjusted. In many developing nations, traditional notions of time have come into conflict with more modern, monochronic concepts. Still, nations such as India, Brazil, Mexico, and Vietnam are learning to let those two concepts live side-by-side: one time for business (usually with foreigners), and another time for the things in life that really matter.

Speaking of Culture

Understanding the differences in the cultural measure of time is an important factor in communication between the people of the United States and Mexico. In Mexico, the informal measure of time more often prevails over formal time, and activities, rather than the measurement of time by the abstract symbols on a clock, dictate how time is used. Mexicans live not by the abstract dates on a calendar, but by the liturgical year. Life progresses by the feasts and rituals (the activities) that mark time's progress, the year going from Advent and Nativity to Lent and from the Passion to Pentecost.

In Mexico, nothing that is being enjoyed now is worth cutting short in order to do something else. If discussions at hand are not finished, Mexicans consider it senseless to terminate a meeting because time as abstractly measured by the clock is up, nor are meetings strictly scheduled as to order and content.

Many U.S. Americans find it difficult to understand or tolerate the unstructured measurement of time by activity rather than by the abstract and more exact measure of the clock.

—Tracy Novinger, *Intercultural Communication: A Practical Guide* [58]

In polychronic societies, there are literally many kinds of time, such as time for business, time for family, time for friends, and time for food or sleep. This simple illustration may help: Roberto has a 10:00 A.M. meeting (the business day tends to start a bit later in such cultures) with a customer, but enroute to the meeting he sees a friend on the street. He stops to talk with his old friend, Juan, knowing that he hasn't seen him in quite a while. During the conversation, he discovers that Juan's father is very ill. Roberto cannot simply stop the conversation, declare that he has a meeting to attend, and rush off. The rituals and customs of his culture—to stay and talk with Juan, to enquire about his father, and to assure Juan that he will pray for him and call back very soon—obligate him. That chance encounter may take 20 minutes, but it's not a decision that Roberto will regret. If his customer is from the same culture, he or she will understand perfectly. The first 20 minutes of their business meeting will, no doubt, involve a story about Juan and his father, and a series of inquiries about the health and well-being of the customer, his employees, and his family. To a monochronic businessperson, such rituals seem wasteful, unpredictable, and maddeningly inefficient. Perhaps they are. But they serve to cement personal bonds that are so important to business relationships and to reinforce the norms of the culture. To make up for being late to the meeting, Roberto may offer to take his customer out for a two-hour lunch, just to show that his customer and his business are important to him.

Whether they are clock-watchers or clock-ignorers, people of each culture demonstrate their own variations. (See Table 3.5) For example, people in different regions will react differently to time. Getting to your meeting on time for an appointment in New York City may be important, but it may not be as imperative in a small rural town in upstate New York. Another interesting phenomenon common to polychronic societies is the "one among many" philosophy of business meetings. You may schedule a meeting that you believe is reserved solely for you, and be surprised when you arrive. Often, people in such societies will be multitasking while they are meeting with you—an administrative assistant may interrupt to ask a question, another employee may enter and ask for a brief micro-meeting on the spot, or the person running the meeting may step out for a while only to return and expect you to still be there.

Richard Gesteland contrasts the agendas of polychronic and monochronic societies, and writes, "In France or Italy the 'warm up' chat is likely to last several times as long. And if there is any agenda at all, you may start with Item #5, proceed to Item #2 and then wander off in several different directions at once. Polychronic meetings tend to follow their own inner logic rather than a fixed outline. The important thing is that everyone has his or her say. Such digressions can lead to creative problem solving." In monochronic societies, such digressions often lead to frustration and stern e-mail messages about "following the agenda."[59]

Tips for Doing Business According to the Clock	
Past-/Present-oriented	**Future-oriented**
Emphasize the history, tradition, and rich cultural heritage of those you deal with as evidence of their great potential.	Emphasize the freedom, opportunity, and limitless scope for that company and its people in the future.
Discover whether internal relationships will sanction the kind of changes you seek to encourage.	Discover what core competence or continuity the company intends to carry with it into the envisioned future.
Agree to future meetings in principle but do not fix deadlines for completion.	Agree to specific deadlines and do not expect work to be complete unless you
Do your homework on the history traditions, and past glories of the company; consider what re-enactments you might propose.	Do your homework on the future, the prospects, and the technological potentials of the company; consider mounting a sizeable challenge.

Source: Fons Trompenaars and Charles Hampden-Turner, Riding the Waves of Culture: Understanding Cultural Diversity in Global Business (New York: McGraw-Hill, 1998), 143.

TABLE 3.5: Tips for Doing Business According to the Clock

After twenty-six years as a global manager working in Germany, Austria, Italy, India, and Singapore, Gesteland's advice on communication and differing perspectives of time is threefold: plan ahead, stay in close contact, and be patient. First, he says, plan ahead, whether it means adding extra hours to a journey across town in a foreign city or months ahead for project development. If you are from a monochromic culture and expect that a July 15 deadline actually means July 15, consider how a business client from a polychronic culture might plan, so add extra time. Second, stay in close contact with your client. Remember that, for the most part, polychronic cultures are also collectivistic cultures, which focus more on the relationship than on the deal or contract. If at all possible, stay in touch via face-to-face interactions. Third, be patient. Just because the culture you're dealing with doesn't seem to value promptness or meeting agendas the way you do, this doesn't mean that time-relaxed cultures aren't proficient at getting the job done. Time may be scarce to you, but plentiful to others. Consider their ways and perhaps you'll learn something.

To navigate successfully in the global marketplace, managers should examine their assumptions and expectations about how they use time. Do they view time as *sequential* (a series of passing events) or as *synchronic* (with past, present, and future all interrelated), in which all things past affect the present? In monochronic or time-rigid cultures, people will adhere to the original plan, expect promptness, and meet deadlines at all costs. Focus on history and past events as well as the establishment of strong relationships for the present and future are primary goals. In polychronic or time-relaxed cultures, plans can change without notice, meetings are expected to begin late and only after social pleasantries have been offered, and deadlines may simply evaporate. The focus is on the present and how that will affect future success; tasks are favored over relationships, which can come and go without recourse. Knowing about these cultural distinctions will mean fewer surprises, disappointments, and misunderstandings for managers doing business in a global economy.

Waiting in New Delhi

Richard was a 30-year-old American sent by his Chicago-based company to set up a buying office in India. The new office's main mission was to source large quantities of consumer goods in India: cotton piece goods, garments, accessories, and shoes, as well as industrial products such as tent fabrics and cast iron components.

India's Ministry of Foreign Trade had invited Richard's company to open this buying office because they knew it would promote exports, bring in badly-needed foreign exchange, and provide manufacturing know-how to Indian factories.

Richard's was in fact the first international sourcing office to be located anywhere in South Asia. The MFT wanted it to succeed so that other Western and Japanese companies could be persuaded to establish similar procurement offices.

The expatriate manager decided to set up the office in the capital, New Delhi, because he knew he would have to meet frequently with senior government officials. Since the Indian government closely regulated all trade and industry, Richard often found it necessary to help his suppliers obtain import licenses for the semi-manufactures and components they required to produce the finished goods his company had ordered.

Richard found these government meetings frustrating. Even though he always phoned to make firm appointments, the bureaucrats usually kept him waiting for half an hour or more. Not only that, his meetings would be continuously interrupted by phone calls and unannounced visitors, as well as by clerks bringing in stacks of letters and documents to be signed. Because of all the waiting and the constant interruptions, it regularly took him half a day or more to accomplish something that could have been done back home in twenty minutes.

Three months into this assignment, Richard began to think about requesting a transfer to a more congenial part of the world—"somewhere where things work." He just could not understand why the Indian officials were being so rude. Why did they keep him waiting? Why didn't the bureaucrats hold their incoming calls and sign those papers after the meeting so as to avoid the constant interruptions?

After all, the government of India had actually invited his company to open this buying office. So, didn't he have the right to expect reasonably courteous treatment from the officials in the various ministries and agencies he had to deal with?[60]

1.   What does Richard need to learn about the East Indian culture?
2.   How do you think he should obtain this information (e.g., should he talk to one of the people from New Delhi and, if so, should it be someone of higher or lower rank, etc.)?

3. How can Richard realistically adjust his expectations?
4. Have you been in a similar workplace situation and what did *you* do?

Adapted from: Gesteland, Richard R. (2005). Cross-cultural business behavior: Negotiating, selling, sourcing and managing across cultures. Copenhagen, Denmark: Copenhagen Business School Press.

SPACE

Yet another issue relevant to the global businessperson is the concept of proxemics, or personal space. Think about the last time you were in an elevator. In a typical U.S. office building, people enter, avoid eye contact, and move to find "their space." The more people that fill the elevator (or "lift" in Britain), the more rigid they each become. This is because, in the U.S. culture, it is considered taboo to occupy someone else's space. No so in Japan. A visit to the Mitsukoshi Department Store in the Ginza section of Tokyo will reveal what most people would expect: lots of people. They're all well-mannered, polite, respectful people who will nod and say "*sumimasen*," or "excuse me," if they bump into you or wish to pass by. Space is at a premium everywhere, but nowhere is it more precious than in an elevator. Polite young women in bright yellow blazers and straw hats guide visitors into a "holding area" near the elevator doors, and then gently force as many people as possible onto industrial-strength freight elevators using small wooden batons. Nothing in the Western experience is comparable to that two-and-a-half-minute ride to the twentieth floor. You could have dinner, drinks, and several dates with people who would never come as close to you as those shoppers in Tokyo do.

Cultural anthropologist Edward T. Hall has observed and classified four categories of distance, each of which helps to define the relationship between communicators. (See Figure 3.3)

Silence is a source of great strength.

—Lao Tzu

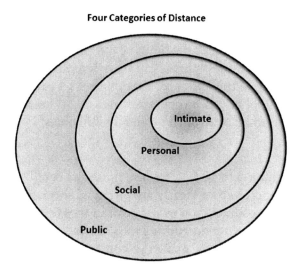

Four Categories of Distance

FIGURE 3.3: Four Categories of Distance [44]

INTIMATE

This ranges from actual touching to a distance of about 18 inches. At this distance, the presence of other individuals is unmistakable: each individual experiences the sound, smell, even the other's breath. To be given permission to position yourself so closely to another implies a personal relationship involving considerable trust. Often, though, we are forced to stand or sit next to someone, perhaps actually touching them, without really wanting to do so—in an elevator, a subway car, or an airline seat. Most North Americans feel some level of discomfort at such closeness when they don't really know the other person. People try to avoid eye contact at this distance, focusing instead on distant or nearby objects. While most people feel uncomfortable at this distance from strangers or casual acquaintances, most are willing to briefly tolerate such closeness in order to get what they need—a trip to the top floor in an elevator, transportation to the next subway stop, or lunch in a crowded café.

PERSONAL

Each of us, according to Dr. Hall, carries a protective bubble defining our personal distance that allows us to stay protected and untouched by others. In the close phase of personal distance, about 18 to 30 inches, we can still hold or grasp each other, but only by extending our arms. In the far phase (about 30 inches to 4 feet), two people can touch each other only if they both extend their arms. This far phase, according to Professor Joseph DeVito, is "the extent to which we can physically get our hands on things; hence, it defines, in one sense, the limits of our physical control over others."[61] The common business phrase "an arm's-length relationship" comes from the definition of this distance, meaning that a proper relationship with customers, suppliers, or business partners might be one in which we are not so close as to be controlled or unduly influenced by them.

SOCIAL

At a distance of about 4 to 12 feet, we lose the visual detail we could see in the personal distance, yet we clearly are aware of another's presence and can easily make eye contact. You would have to step forward, however, in order to shake hands. Note that during most business introductions, people do just that: step forward, make eye contact, shake hands, then step back. The near phase of social distance (4 to 7 feet) is the range at which most North American business conversations and interactions are conducted. In the far phase (7 to 12 feet), business transactions have a more formal tone and voices are raised just slightly. Many office furniture arrangements in the United States and G7 nations ensure this distance for senior managers and executives, while providing the opportunity for closer contact, if participants deem it necessary.[62] Most Latin, Mediterranean, and Arab nations would choose to conduct business at much closer distances, with voices lowered, and a heightened sense of mutual trust evident in the conversation patterns.

PUBLIC

In the close phase of public distance, about 12 to 15 feet, we feel more protected by space. We can still see people, observing their actions and movements, but we lose much of the detail visible at closer distances. We can move quickly enough to avoid someone and are not forced to make eye contact with people we do not know. In the far phase, more than 25 feet, we see people not as separate individuals, but as part of the landscape or scene in the room. Communication at this distance is difficult, if not impossible, without shouting or exaggerated body movement.[63]

Our use of space varies greatly, depending on where we live and how we were raised, but it varies even more from one culture to another and is a frequent source of difficulty for people who move to another culture as adults. Even within cultures, our use of space will vary according to status, rank, age, and custom. Spacious, private offices are the rule in many industries (the legal profession, for example), while micro-efficient cubicles are the norm in others (information technology comes to mind). The culture of some businesses is to share space and work in a more open atmosphere, while others emphasize the privilege of privacy. At Dell Corporation, the computer manufacturer in Round Rock, Texas, everyone, including founder and CEO Michael Dell, operates from a cubicle. Michael's office is a double-wide, but it's still a "cube."

In other societies, proxemics, perhaps more than any other behavior, will vary significantly, leaving outsiders, businesspeople, and tourists confused and uncertain about how to react. A conversational encounter with an Arab colleague whose communication habits are guided by Bedouin traditions will resemble an odd, step-by-step tango as the Westerner backs off and the Middle Easterner continues to close in. Local rules, with some exceptions made for close friends, are your best guide.

Speaking of Culture

Imagine a conversation between a U.S. American, a Middle East-erner, and a Latin American. The U.S. American is generally comfortable in the social distance of an "arm's length" in conversations. The Latin American, as well as a southern European and a Middle Easterner, would be comfortable at a much closer distance for that conversation. The U.S. American, to ease the discomfort, will take a step back to make the distance greater. Sensing a bit of coldness or rejection, the Latin American or Middle Easterner will step forward. The dance will continue until the U.S. American is literally backed against the wall, or in an extreme case, puts his hands up to push the other away.

—Michael B. Goodman, *Working in a Global Environment* [65]

CHAPTER SUMMARY

We have examined the role of the self as we seek to establish our identity, acquire and process information, solve problems, and learn to be productive members of our society. We have also explored how people interact with their environment, and react to change, time, and space. While individualistic cultures put themselves at the center of their world (with family, community, friends, and coworkers on the periphery) collectivistic cultures tend to see themselves as one with their world (family, community, tribe, or clan). Individualistic societies tend more often than not to think in linear fashion and are focused on keeping time under control in order to get today's work done so that they can focus on the future. In contrast, collectivistic societies are more circular and cyclical in their thinking.

They see themselves as being connected with the universe, with nature, and with time in a way that encompasses the past, the present, and the future simultaneously. Some cultures adhere strictly to time, and value linear order, while others are less rigid and find order in flexibility.

Social psychologist Kurt Lewin has said, "Generally, in every situation, the person seems to know what group he belongs to and to what group he does not belong. He knows more or less clearly where he stands, and this position largely determines his behavior."[66] Such differences in the way people identify with self and the environment, as we have discussed in this chapter, clearly affect how they interact in the workplace. As global managers, we must work even harder to understand these particular hidden dimensions of culture in order to be more effective at work and at home when we are overseas or in conversation with those whose cultural traditions are much different from our own. Remember, *culture is not value-neutral*. You need not embrace or praise the practices of another culture, but you certainly must try to understand and appreciate them. Complete acceptance may come later, or not at all.

APPLICATIONS IN THE GLOBAL MARKETPLACE

The following section is a summary of the dimensions (or categories) of culture we have discussed throughout this chapter. After each definition we offer several questions and then an example, which demonstrates at least one specific way (among innumerable ways) to handle the intercultural encounter. As you read through each, picture that iceberg that we talked about at the beginning of the book. It's easy enough to identify the behaviors above the waterline, but as the cliché makes clear, what you see is only the tip of the iceberg. Once you identify either your behaviors or those of others regarding these questions, take some time to consider what supports them from below: what are the values, beliefs, and attitudes that give meaning to the behaviors we can readily see? For this dimension you may also consider discussing your responses with people in your learning team or work team.

IDENTITY: INDIVIDUAL OR COLLECTIVE

In intercultural communication, the term *identity* refers to how a group is conditioned to live and work together. Is there a tendency to be more individual or more collective? Individualistic cultures emphasize personal rights, and focus on personal achievement and success as measures of one's potential or merit. Collective cultures emphasize group rights and the success of an entire group, regardless of position or level of participation.

Helpful Tips

Before you begin an employee performance appraisal take a few moments to think from your subordinate's perspective about how he or she might respond. When you want to give praise to your team members, think before you single out any one person and try to forecast how he or she will receive your words of appreciation.

Be aware of the importance of roles as related to task and relationships. Remember that other cultures may place a higher emphasis on developing trust and maintaining harmony and cooperation within groups.

Questions to Ask Yourself Regarding Cultural Identity

What are the norms (accepted and expected ways of behaving) or hidden rules that influence the way you interact with others? Think back to the way things were done in your home while growing up. Who had the authority? Who ran the household? What role did your father and mother play? What roles did the children play? What traditions or rituals did you observe? What were the rules regarding privacy? Independence? Interacting with unfamiliar people or situations? What were the attitudes toward work and play? It may be easier to determine these if you think about what happened when one of these norms was violated.

Now apply this to your interactions with others at work. Better yet, apply them to an intercultural interaction that you have experienced.

- What are the most important norms of your workplace?
- Who establishes and enforces them (which person or organization)?
- How does your group work: independently or cooperatively?
- Is the focus on the task or the relationship?

Think of a particular situation at work regarding how your identity and how it affects your behavior. Do you lean more toward being individualistic or collective? Do you prefer to work alone or with others? Who do you expect to give you praise or recognition for a job well done?

Final Thought

When interacting with people from other cultures, be aware of whether they come from a more individualistic frame of reference or are more collective. Again, please remember that the statements we make about a culture in general are not necessarily statements about individuals.

LEARNING: ACTION OR OBSERVATION

We each gather and organize information differently, and each of us has culturally biased ideas of what is reasonable and rational. Some cultures focus on active learning and rely heavily on the use of data, evidence, facts and figures. Experimentation that encourages trial and error is the focus. This means that active learners ask questions, pose challenges, and are comfortable with speaking up and being heard during the learning process. In a more reflective culture, the norm is to favor concepts and principles, relying more on intuitive hunches and subjective reasoning. This could translate into an employee or manager who may be quick of mind but not quick to project theories, ideas, or opinions until they have been thought through carefully and patiently.

Helpful Tips

Make sure that you are not too quick to judge an employee as incapable of performing a task. An employee may delay a decision or defer completing a task because he or she needs time to think or mull over the possible consequences of decisions and actions.

If you ask an employee, "Do you have any questions?" you may only receive silence if your subordinates are from a country such as China. More appropriately, you should ask a clarification question, such as, "Have I explained this information clearly?" The first question will probably not get any response because no one wants to lose face by admitting that they do not know something. An employee, however, will be more likely to respond to the second question because the boss is implying that he or she may not have been clear.

Questions to Ask Yourself Regarding Action and Observation

How is information shared in this organization? How do members of this culture approach problem-solving? How do they organize and process information? How do they approach decision making? Who makes decisions? Are decisions decentralized or centrally made? Are decisions the product of a group or team effort, or are they the province of a particular individual? How do members of this culture negotiate during business transactions? Are they focused on the task at hand or on the relationships among those participating?

Questions to Ask Yourself Regarding Learning

Observe and make note of your preferences for acquiring knowledge. Ask yourself whether you are more likely to learn through observation and reflection or by actively seeking out information. Are you quick to act or do you prefer to spend time thinking and waiting until it seems right?

Do you tend to ask inquisitive questions and challenge your boss or instructor or do you think it is more a sign of respect to take in the information and not question your superior's knowledge? Do you tend to think in a linear fashion or in a more circular manner?

Do you form deductive arguments in which you present the major premise first and then support your assertion (e.g., "We need to cut costs in our division. We will do it by reducing overhead, relying on in-house resources, and curbing all unnecessary expenditures.")? Or do you form inductive arguments in which you give the evidence first and then your support ("We have discovered that we are over budget and have too much overhead, we out-source for services too much, and we have some unnecessary expenses that cannot be explained. Therefore, we must cut costs in our division.")?

Final Thought

When interacting with people from other cultures, be aware of whether they may be conditioned to accept information without questioning (out of respect and deference to authority and status), rather than assertively seeking answers. Keep in mind that the statements made about a culture in general are not necessarily true of any particular individual.

ENVIRONMENT: CONTROL OR HARMONY

Each of us has a perspective regarding our environment. That perspective lies along a continuum in which we either believe that we control nature and the universe, or that we live in harmony with it. Those cultures that believe they are in control see life as the result of human perseverance, whereas those who live in harmony see life as the result of fate, with their destiny unfolding bit by bit. These perspectives are often driven by the history and geography of a culture.

Helpful Tips

If your co-worker seems nonchalant about not receiving the bid for the contract that you had worked many months on, it doesn't necessarily mean that she doesn't care. She may be of the view that "what happens will happen" (*que será será*) and may see it as her personal destiny, or perhaps the company's destiny, *not* to obtain the contract.

Questions to Ask Yourself Regarding Environment

Are problems in the workplace resolved through sheer willpower and determination, or are other factors at work? Is technology coveted and revered as the doorway to opportunity and knowledge? Or is doing things "the old way" more commonplace and accepted? Is destiny in your own hands or in the hands of some unknown force?

Final Thought

As we interact with people from other cultures, we must be aware of whether their outlook on life favors control or destiny. Do they take charge of a situation, assuming they can influence the outcome, or are they more content to let "fate take its course?" Remember that the statements made about a culture in general are not necessarily true about individuals.

CHANGE: AVOIDANCE OR ACCEPTANCE

How we react to change or deal with ambiguity is culturally conditioned. In cultures that avoid ambiguity, people are uncomfortable with uncertainty and will do what they can to reduce it. Stability is more important than opportunity, so structure and consistency become the safe choices. In cultures that accept uncertainty, people are not afraid of conflict or challenges that affect change. Taking risks and adapting to change are all part of the excitement of living in a dynamic, ever-changing world that is unpredictable, yet full of opportunities still to be discovered.

Helpful Tips

Checking and rechecking our assumptions are crucial to effective intercultural communication. In any business venture, it may first be useful to separate fact from assumption—that is, to segregate what you know for sure (and can prove) from what you assume to be true but for which you have no direct proof.

Additionally, you may wish to begin a list not only of what you know, but what you might like to know. Will there be a cost associated with gathering such information or proving one or more of your assumptions? On the other hand, it may be equally useful for you to list those issues that you are not only uncertain about, but may never know for sure. Accepting that some things are simply unknowable comes more readily in some cultures than others.

Think about how you view risk-taking. Can you try new things even though you may be uncomfortable? If visitors should adapt to and observe local customs, then trying to use some of the language or eating different types of food can be great ways to show that you are interested in your host's ways of living. Keeping an open mind and being receptive to new ideas and ways of thinking as well as acting can also help you adjust to change.

Questions to Ask Yourself Regarding Change

How do you react to change? Are you comfortable or uncomfortable with it? Do you see the prospect of change in the status quo as a threat or an opportunity? Do you need clear goals as well as structure and security from your employer? Do your employees need well-delineated instructions or can they function autonomously? Are you uncomfortable with unpredictable outcomes? Is your co-worker shying away from a possible promotion because he or she is afraid of the unknown?

What measures do people in your organization take to avoid uncertainty? What steps have management taken to reduce ambiguity and reduce fear in the face of uncertainty? Does the organization you work for reward those who take chances or operate under uncertain conditions? If you were to deal with people from a culture that seemed to avoid uncertainty, how would you go about creating greater levels of comfort and confidence?

Final Thought

When interacting with people from other cultures, be aware of whether they see change as an opportunity or whether change is viewed as disrupting stability. Remember that the statements made about a culture in general are not necessarily statements about individuals.

TIME: FIXED OR FLUID

Through a cross-cultural lens, time can be seen as fixed or fluid. Cultures that are fixated on time (*monochronic* cultures) are constantly creating schedules, adhering to agendas, starting and stopping appointments at a particular moment. These cultures see the chronology of time in an objective fashion: time functions in precisely the same way for everyone. By contrast, cultures with a more subjective view of time (*polychromic* cultures) will see time cyclically. Such cultures are more flexible and fluid in their use of time and certainly don't see time as money. Time, to a polychromic culture, has many uses depending on the individual. Tasks will get done . . . eventually . . . but relationships come first, and taking the time to work on the relationship takes precedence over completing the task at hand.

Helpful Tips

Take some time to check out the cultural practices relating to time of the person you are paying a visit. Determine ahead of time if he or she most likely be focused on monochronic time or polychronic. Understand when to arrive, how long you should be expected to wait (if at all), and how the agenda will be handled. You may also want to consider whether *you* are expected to be on time but whether your *associate* may not.

Questions to Ask Yourself Regarding Time

Is time in your organization viewed as linear, in which one thing happens after another with precision and consistency, or is time more circular where people are not so concerned about rigid order but rather with the flow of nature?

When should you arrive? Early? Late? Will you be expected to wait or be seen right away? Will you begin with small talk? Will you even talk business on the first visit? Will agendas be strictly adhered to or will they be more flexible? Will your host multitask and expect you to wait while he or she attends to other business that suddenly comes up?

What are your expectations regarding the timeline for negotiating a deal, signing a contract, and delivering the goods or services you have promised? What are the expectations of those with whom you're doing business?

Final Thought

When you interact with people from other cultures, observe whether they adhere to schedules with an eye on the clock or whether they prefer to carry on and "go with the flow." Remember that the statements made about a culture in general are not necessarily true of any particular individuals.

A CASE STUDY

COCA-COLA AND THE EUROPEAN CONTAMINATION CRISIS

Doug Ivester, CEO of The Coca-Cola Company, thanked James Burke for his time and returned the phone to the handset. On June 18, 1999, four weeks after the first report was filed in Europe citing adverse health effects suffered following the consumption of Coca-Cola products, Ivester sought to reformulate his communication strategy. Ivester called Burke, the former CEO of Johnson & Johnson who successfully managed the Tylenol scare in the 1980s, to discuss how Coke could regain its reputation and credibility. He hoped it was not too late to mend Coke's relationship with the European consumers.

KEY FACTS IN THE CRISIS COCA-COLA FACED IN EUROPE

During May and June of 1999, hundreds of consumers in Europe became ill after consuming Coca-Cola products. In the biggest recall in Coca-Cola history, Coke products, including *Coke, Coke Light, Fanta,* and *Sprite,* were pulled off the shelves in Belgium, France, Luxembourg, the Netherlands, and Germany. Here is a time line of the specific events that took place from mid-May through the end of June, 1999:

> **May 12:** *A bar in Belgium reports to the Belgian Health Ministry and to Coca-Cola that four people who drank Coke products have become ill. Samples of Coke from the same batch are sent for analysis at a government-licensed laboratory in Belgium. Results prove inconclusive and no poison is found. The incident is not widely reported and no public safety warnings are issued.*
>
> **June 8:** *Schoolchildren in Bornem, Belgium reportedly experience dizziness, nausea, and other symptoms after drinking Coke. Forty-two people are hospitalized during the next 24 hours.*
>
> **June 10:** *Eight children are hospitalized in Bruges, Belgium after drinking Coke and Fanta.*
>
> **June 11:** *The German Health Ministry summons Coca-Cola officials for a meeting regarding the reported illnesses. Thirteen children are hospitalized in Harelbeke, Belgium.*
>
> **June 12–14:** *The Belgian government establishes a telephone hotline for health complaints about Coca-Cola products and receives more than 200 calls.*

June 14: *Forty-two children are taken to a hospital in Lochristi. The Belgian government orders all Coca-Cola products off the market and halts production at bottling plants in Antwerp and Ghent.*

June 15: *Eight children are reported sick in Kortrijk, Belgium. Luxembourg bans Coca-Cola products. Health authorities in France close a bottling plant in Dunkirk. The Netherlands bans all Coca-Cola products shipped through Belgium. At the same time, Coca-Cola Enterprises (CCE) holds a press conference in Brussels to provide an explanation for the cause of the illnesses.*

June 16: *Germany bans Coca-Cola products produced at the Dunkirk plant. Coca-Cola issues its first apology to European consumers in the form of a written release under Doug Ivester's name. German officials empty store shelves of Coke products.*

June 17: *The ban on products is eased in Belgium with the exception of thousands of Coca-Cola vending machines.*

June 18: *M. Douglas Ivester, chairman and CEO of Coca-Cola, arrives in Belgium to oversee management of the crisis.*

Coinciding with the negative responses from the Belgian and French governments, Coca-Cola's sales and reputation suffer well beyond these borders. Following the product bans issued by these two governments, the Netherlands and Luxembourg restrict sales of certain Coca-Cola products until possible health risks are fully identified. There are also reports that Saudi Arabia and Germany have banned imports of all Coca-Cola beverages produced in Belgium and that the Spanish government had stopped a shipment of Belgian-bottled Coca-Cola and other brands for fear of contamination.

Even the health minister of the Central African Republic takes a stand on the issue, saying citizens of that country shouldn't drink Coke "until further notice" because of the health questions. Sweden's *Svenska Dagbladet* runs a headline on June 16 claiming, "200 Poisoned by Coca-Cola." An Italian newspaper's front page headline reports "Alarm Across Europe for Coca-Cola Products." *Wall Street Journal* reporters James Hagerty and Amy Barrett describe the rapid proliferation of news of the crisis across international borders:

> *It amounted to a harsh lesson for Coke in the perils of global marketing in the electronic age. No one has been better than Coke at creating an enticing image and sending it flashing around the world. Now Coke is learning that an image can come unraveled in an instant (Hagerty).*

The outbreaks appeared to be caused by two sources: contaminated carbon dioxide and fungicide sprayed on wooden pallets used to transport the product. The contaminated carbon dioxide found its way into the product at a bottler in Belgium. The company was unable to determine whether the carbon dioxide was already contaminated when the bottler received it or whether contamination occurred later at the bottling facility.

In an interview with *The Wall Street Journal*, Anton Amon, Coca-Cola's chief scientist, said that, "contrary to Coke procedure, the plant wasn't receiving certificates of analysis from the supplier of the gas, Aga Gas AB of Sweden. This certificate vouches for the purity of the CO_2." A CCE spokesman confirmed this statement and acknowledged that the company did not test the CO_2 batch at the Antwerp plant. In either case, key quality-control procedures were not followed.

At the Coca-Cola bottling facility in Dunkirk, France, the plant received wooden pallets that had been sprayed with a fungicide that left a medicinal odor on a number of cans. Jennifer McCollum, a spokeswoman for Coca-Cola, described the substance as p-chloro-m-cresol or PCMC, "a chemical commonly found in wood preservatives and cleaning fluids." The Environmental Chemicals Data and Information Network (ECDIN) states that PCMC can be absorbed through the skin and cause redness, burning sensation, pain and skin burns. If inhaled, the chemical can cause symptoms such as cough, sore throat, shortness of breath, headache, dizziness, nausea, vomiting, unconsciousness, and may cause effects on the central nervous system, liver, and kidneys. These more-severe conditions are said to require large doses or chronic exposure to the chemical.

Coca-Cola said that the substance was sprayed on approximately 800 pallets used to transport cans produced in Dunkirk to Belgium. The supplier of the pallets was said to be Dutch. The company, however, declined to name the company, stating only that it was not one of their regular suppliers. The foul odor is believed to have caused numerous symptoms, including upset stomachs, headaches, and nausea after drinking the product.

Dr. Hugo Botinck, medical director at St. Joseph's Clinic in Belgium and one of the first physicians to see these patients, stated in an interview that affected persons were treated for, "headaches, dizziness, nausea and muscular vibration." He added that, "some of them were vomiting, but there was no fever."

COMPANY PROFILE

The Coca-Cola Company is the global leader in the soft-drink industry, with world headquarters located in Atlanta, Georgia. Coca-Cola and its subsidiaries employ nearly 30,000 people worldwide. Syrups, concentrates, and beverage bases for Coca-Cola, the company's flagship brand, and more than 160 other soft-drink brands, are manufactured and sold by Coca-Cola and its subsidiaries in nearly 200 countries around the world. Approximately 70 percent of volume sales and 80 percent of profit come from outside the United States. The European market provides 26 percent of the company's US$18B in revenues. Coca-Cola owns a 49-percent share of the European soft drink market, compared to Pepsi-Co's 5 percent.

Coca-Cola's Corporate Mission Statement

We exist to create value for our share owners on a long-term basis by building a business that enhances The Coca-Cola Company's trademarks. This also is our ultimate commitment.

As the world's largest beverage company, we refresh that world. We do this by developing superior soft drinks, both carbonated and non-carbonated, and profitable nonalcoholic beverage systems that create value for our Company, our bottling partners, our customers, our share owners and the communities in which we do business.

In creating value, we succeed or fail based on our ability to perform as worthy stewards of several key assets:

1. Coca-Cola, the world's most recognized trademark, and other highly valuable trademarks.
2. The world's most effective and pervasive distribution system.
3. Satisfied customers, from whom we earn a good profit selling our products.
4. Our people, who are ultimately responsible for building this enterprise.
5. Our abundant resources, which must be intelligently allocated.
6. Our strong global leadership in the beverage industry in particular and in the business world in general.

Additionally, Coca-Cola has a stated commitment to social responsibility through philanthropy and good citizenship. The company's reputation for good corporate citizenship results from charitable donations, employee volunteerism, technical assistance and other demonstrations of support in thousands of communities worldwide. The Coca-Cola Foundation, the company's philanthropic arm, contributed more than $100 million to education during the 1990s, supporting mentoring programs and scholarships at more than 400 schools, colleges and associations around the world. On a local level, Coca-Cola offices and bottlers around the world support community activities. From supporting the arts in Russia to building schools in rural areas of China and the Philippines to funding a class for entrepreneurs at the University of Zimbabwe, The Coca-Cola Company is an active corporate citizen.

The company has said repeatedly that honesty and integrity have always been cornerstone values of The Coca-Cola Company. Coca-Cola feels that all company representatives have a responsibility to act in every situation according to the highest standards of ethical conduct.

COCA-COLA MANAGEMENT

From 1984 to 1997, Robert Goizueta ran Coca-Cola like a ship in calm waters. In his 13 years at the helm of Coke as CEO, Goizueta transformed Coke from an Atlanta cola company to an international brand phenomenon. Analysts and employees alike viewed Goizueta like a god. In 1997, Doug Ivester succeeded Roberto Goizueta as CEO of Coke following Goizueta's death from lung cancer. Ivester, an employee of the company since 1979, had previously been Goizueta's right hand financial engineer and later his chief operating officer. On the face of it, the transition would appear seamless.

Doug Ivester was often been described as a very "rational" man with a "bulldog" leadership style. James Chestnut, Coca-Cola's chief financial officer, said Ivester was a "terribly rational" manager. He states, "Doug believes everything should go through a logical sequence. He's fixed on where he wants the company to be." Ivester's recent focus had been on two potential acquisitions to increase Coca-Cola's presence in Europe: Orangina in France and Cadbury Schweppes in England. The tactics Ivestor pursued to acquire Orangina and Schweppes, however, were met with much criticism, especially by Europeans.

A July article in *Fortune* magazine summarized the conventional wisdom this way: "the way Coke went about the acquisitions—arrogantly, urgently, intensely—absolutely reflects Ivester's personality. And it's not working." Other analysts who have followed Coca-Cola for years believe that if Goizueta still had been running the company, controversy surrounding the recall in Europe would not have festered as it did under Ivester.

One of Coke's greatest strengths lies in its ability to conduct business on a global scale while maintaining a "multilocal" approach. At the heart of this approach is the bottler system. Bottling companies are, with only a few exceptions, locally owned and operated by independent business people, native to the nations in which they are located, who are contractually authorized to sell products of The Coca-Cola Company. These facilities package and sell the company's soft drinks within certain territorial boundaries and under conditions that ensure the highest standards of product quality and uniformity. Coca-Cola Enterprises (CCE) manages most of the European bottlers. The Coca-Cola Company controls a 40-percent interest in CCE.

Coca-Cola Belgium

Belgium was introduced to Coca-Cola in 1927. Today Belgium is among the world's top 20 countries in terms of per capita consumption of Coca-Cola products. The Coca-Cola Company currently employs close to 2,000 people and serves up to 30,000 restaurants, supermarkets, and other customers in that country.

Coca-Cola France

Coca-Cola was introduced in France in 1933. Coke has been the number-one soft drink in France since 1966 with total sales doubling over the past eight years. Coca-Cola France employs more than 1,000 French citizens and has invested more than 3 billion francs in local economy since 1989. Today, French consumers drink an average of 88 servings of Coca-Cola products each year.

External Factors Involved

In May and June of 1999, it is fair to say that Coca-Cola executives vastly underestimated the sensitivity of European consumers to food contamination issues in light of the existing social and political environment. Contributing to the anxiety was the "mad-cow" crisis that had taken place three years earlier. Additionally, the Coke incident coincided with a recent governmental ban on the slaughter of pork and poultry in Belgium. Earlier in June, cancer-causing dioxin was found in a large shipment of meat, which was believed to have originated through contaminated animal feed. In the end, this scandal forced the resignation of Belgian Prime Minister Jean-Luc Dahaene as well as the country's health minister. With the Belgian government facing elections on June 13, all political platforms were under scrutiny.

In the wake of the Coke crisis, European government agencies were scrambling to protect their reputations as watchdogs, taking a high-profile role in contamination issues. Consumers had previously considered Coke invulnerable to contamination concerns due to the artificial, manufactured nature of the product.

In addition to its proximity to other food scares in Europe, the crisis also occurred at a time when Coke was looked upon unfavorably by the European Commission. Earlier in 1999, Coke had made plans to acquire Cadbury Schweppes brands around the world. The European Commission was opposed to this acquisition, viewing Coca-Cola as excessively dominant. The company was forced to scale back its acquisition plans.

Coca-Cola's Response

By the time the recall was completed, 249 cases of Coke-related sicknesses were reported throughout Europe, concentrated primarily in Belgium. A total of 15 million cases of product were recalled costing the bottler, Coca-Cola Enterprises (CCE), an estimated $103 million dollars. When the outbreak began, Coca-Cola executives waited several days to take action. Viewing the issue as low-priority, an apology to consumers was not issued until more than a week after the first public reports of illness. Top company officials did not arrive in Belgium until June 18, ten days after the first incident was reported.

The company's casual and muted approach to the crisis was first made evident in its neglect to mention the May 12 incident—in which affected consumers suffered similar symptoms—once the other cases were reported, beginning in June. Ivester remained largely silent, at least publicly, throughout the crisis. He admitted that he happened to be in Coke's Paris office on June 11, shortly after the first wave of illness reports surfaced, and was briefed in person on the Belgian situation. Ivester and Belgian Coke executives attributed the problem to a bad batch of carbon dioxide and "hardly a health hazard." The next day Ivester boarded a plane back to Atlanta, as planned.

On June 14, the Belgium government ordered all Coca-Cola products off the market and halted production at bottling plants in Antwerp and Ghent. The government took the lead to protect consumers from the health scare, rather than Coca-Cola management. Coca-Cola issued a statement on June 15 from Atlanta refuting the contamination claims. On June 16, Ivester released a statement under his name expressing regret for the problems, but he mostly left the public side of the damage-control campaign to company spokesmen and CCE.

On June 18, Ivester realized the magnitude and impact of the crisis and arrived in Belgium for the first time to manage the crisis. Ivester's mission to Europe was his most visible step during the crisis and came only after the number of reported cases had ballooned to more than 200. Coca-Cola officials avoided the media, however, stating afterward that this decision was in response to a request from the Belgian Minister of Health, Luc van den Brossche, asking that the crisis be handled out of the public eye.

Many faulted Ivester's personality as "too rational" to initially consider the European contamination scare a "crisis." The media criticized Ivester's lack of responsiveness for allowing the health scare to spin out of control.

DISCUSSION QUESTIONS

1. Recognizing that the company had lost valuable time for action due to its lack of response until June 18, what should the company's strategy have done moving forward?
2. What audiences should Coca-Cola have considered in the development of a communications strategy to address the crisis?
3. What efforts could Coca-Cola have employed to rebuild its reputation and restore consumer confidence in Europe?

SOURCES

Li, L.H., "Origin of Coke Crisis in Europe Is Termed Psychosomatic," *The Wall Street Journal*, April 2, 2000, p. A-21.

McKay, B. and Deogun, N., "After Short, Stormy Tenure, Coke's Ivester to Retire," *The Wall Street Journal*, December 7, 1999, pp. B-1, B-4.

"Coca-Cola Tests Find No Problem," *The New York Times*, October 26, 1999, p. C-1.

Hagerty, J. R. and Carreyrou, J., "Coke Drinks' Safety Arises Again as Children in Belgium Feel Ill," *The Wall Street Journal*, October 25, 2999, p. A-4.

"European Report Doubts Explanation by Coke," *The New York Times*, August 18, 2999, p. C-4.

Mitchener, B. and McKay, P. A., "EU Warns Coke Not to Use Rebates to Give Sales a Pop,"

The Wall Street Journal, July 23, 1999, p. A5.

Hayes, C. L., "Pepsi Acknowledges Role in Putting Coca-Cola Under Inquiry," *The New York Times*, July 23, 1999, p. C-4.

Hayes, C. L., "Coca-Cola Bottler Reports Surprisingly Big Slide in Sales," *The New York Times*, July 14, 1999, p. C-3.

Hayes, C. L., "Recall to Cost Coke Bottler $103 Million," *The New York Times*, July 13, 1999, p. C-7.

"Belgium Re-Opens Coca-Cola Vending Machines," *Reuters News Service*, July 8, 1999, http://famulus.msnbc.com.

Hayes, C. L., "Coca-Cola Recalls Water in Poland After Bacteria Are Found," July 3, 1999, p. B-2.

Sellers, P., "Crunch Time for Coke," *Fortune*, July 19, 1999, pp. 72-78.

Sewell, D., "A Tough Year for Coke," *The South Bend Tribune*, July 1, 1999, p. B9.

"Coke's Hard Lesson in Crisis Management," *Business Week*, July 5, 1999, p. 102.

Hagerty, J. R.; Barrett, A., "France, Belgium Reject Pleas to Lift Ban," *The Wall Street Journal*, June 18, 1999, p. B-1.

CHAPTER 4

Culture and Power

He who is able to conquer others is powerful;
he who is able to conquer himself is more powerful.[1]

—Lao-tzu

W e have considered ways that culture influences perception of identity and how people react to and interact with their environment. Let's focus now on the final two dimensions of culture—power and achievement—by contemplating a few questions: What do we mean by power and control? How do people get what they want from each other? How are societies organized in terms of task and social orientation? What sort of emphasis do we put on achievement? How important is respect in any given culture? These are some of the issues we will consider in this chapter.

Consider the following scenario and determine what you would do in this situation. You may want to think back on the previous chapters in which we discussed cultural dimensions such as values, context, identity, and environment. Then read on to learn more about how power is affected by cultural norms.

Negotiating a Sale in Latin America

John Todd is now the Director of Purchasing at Reliant Automotive Company, which is a British-owned and top supplier in the global automotive industry. The company specializes in precision engine and transmission components (cars, small trucks, and SUVs). John is stationed in a manufacturing plant in Latin America with a customer base of assembly plants primarily in Latin America and Mexico, but also in the U.S. and Europe.

John has just gotten his MBA and has a BS in Engineering. The head of a local metal specialties firm, Sr. Roberto Garza-García, recently responded to a request from John's firm and has offered to supply precision-milled ball bearings. While these ball bearings may be small, they are nevertheless a key ingredient in many of Reliant's products.

John does his due diligence and checks out the company, Group Omega, S.A. It is definitely a well-connected and respectable company that has been around for quite some time – research shows that it started making these precision parts in 1949.
Sr. Garza-García also wants the business and is willing to charge the same price as other regional competitors, and guarantees on-time deliveries. In turn, John wants to uphold Reliant's longstanding policy to support local suppliers whenever possible (with the criteria of industry-set standards of quality and on-time delivery).

John is pleased to think of having both quality and on-time delivery from a local supplier because he is well-aware of the issues related to previous vendors who couldn't meet the standards or the schedule. When suppliers fell through, it was more costly to have to shift transport of the ball bearings from the U.S. or even Europe.

To sweeten the deal, Sr. Garza-García proposes an even more enticing prospect with a personal offer – his company, Grupo Omega, would like a long-term contract with Reliant Automotive. He offers a "facilitation payment" of USD equivalent of $50,000 to be paid directly to John, but privately, so that the payment would be 'off the books'.

This is tempting because John has had some family related medical issues and bills from his business school loans are piling up. He knows that payments such as this are fairly common throughout Latin America. Reflecting back on a conversation he had with a predecessor over one too many beers, he was almost certain that this person had responded to off the record deals. After all, John read Reliant Automotive's code of business conduct and it didn't specifically address any "facilitation payments."

John turns to you, a trusted friend, because you too have had substantial international business experience abroad. He calls you, "I need your help." He explains his point of view – Reliant 'turns the other way' regarding facilitation payments, but he also realizes that there is the FCPA (Foreign Corrupt Policy Act) that holds North American companies to task. John's persuasive strategy is – "I could use the money to get out of debt, and I surely don't want to offend Sr. Garza-García…..What do *you* think?" he asks.

1. What issues of power are at work in this scenario?
2. What issues involving authority do you see?
3. What is John Todd's company policy regarding facilitation payments?
4. What cultural norms is Sr. Garza-García most concerned with in offering the facilitation payments to John Todd?
5. How should Todd proceed? What advice would you give him?

Adapted from: Gesteland, Richard R. (2005). Cross-cultural business behavior: Negotiating, selling, sourcing and managing across cultures. Copenhagen, Denmark: Copenhagen Business School Press.

INTRODUCTION

Which of the following nonverbal gestures signals power to you? Bowing. Shaking hands. Addressing someone as Mr. or Ms., rather than by a first name. Standing when a colleague enters the room. Sitting at the head of the table. Entering second even when a door is opened for you. Perhaps you think these nonverbal actions more accurately signal respect, and you would be correct. However, respect is linked to power, in that those who are in higher positions naturally should be granted a higher level of respect. These actions are actually symbols of power, and include greetings such as addressing someone according to professional or educational title. Included in such symbols of power are also family connections, age, gender, and language.

We can also add how spatial relationships demonstrate power: how office suites are arranged by size, location, and degree of privacy. Status is awarded to those who get the office with a window. The type of furniture in an office, the type and value of décor, and the way in which chairs and desks are positioned also measures status. For example, is there a large desk in the center of the room facing the door? Are the chairs for visitors lower than the chair the officeholder sits in? If so, the officeholder is perceived to have greater power than associates and visitors. Japanese managers will typically sit at desks alongside their subordinates, and often find it difficult to understand why U.S. business counterparts would want individual offices, separate from their employees. To the Japanese, being close to their employees is seen as a symbol of both status and respect. An emphasis on harmony means that the manger can be in frequent contact with subordinates—and it is an honor for employees to sit near their respected boss. In U.S. culture, however, sitting among lower-ranking employees would be considered an insult because management is traditionally set apart from the staff. North American offices also display a clear hierarchy of office space: Having an office with a door that closes is clearly preferable to having a cubicle with no door, no ceiling, and no privacy. An office that has no windows (or no view) typically goes to a new or junior member of a team while the same protocol dictates that an office with a window would go to someone with more experience or power. Corner offices (with windows) are seen as the epitome of having "arrived" in a career. [2]

In this chapter we will examine the concept of control as it relates to culture. Power in the workplace is demonstrated in ways both tangible and intangible, through explicit symbols (such as a title on a sign outside an office door) or implicit symbols (having office furniture made of wood or a specialty chair upholstered in leather). We will look at the concept of power distance, which helps to explain whether a culture favors equality and egalitarian attitudes toward its people. Organizational structure reflects the level of power distance in a business, with flatter structures prevalent where power is decentralized and distributed among many people, and more-hierarchical structures evident where an organization favors a paternalistic and authoritarian approach. We will consider how businesses view authority: Is it earned or is it granted? How do organizations think about achievement? Do they tend to favor internal competition— you against a co-worker—or do they promote collaboration and affiliation? Finally, we will look at how respect contributes to power and authority and social stability. These concepts will help us to formulate some sense of how culture influences power (and vice-versa), and how organizations are shaped by those influences.

Speaking of Culture

In the 1983 movie Local Hero, actor Peter Riegert plays a charac-
ter called Mac MacIntyre, a fast-paced, aggressive New York con-
tract negotiator working for a U.S. American oil company. His
assignment is to go to a remote seaside village in Scotland to buy
up the entire town in order to build an oil refinery. They choose
McIntyre, thinking that he is Scottish because of his surname. In
the scene before MacIntyre is called into the CEO's office, he con-
fidently brags to a fellow colleague about his negotiating abili-
ties—he is confident and competent.

When he is summoned to the top floor executive suite, however,
his reaction changes. As he makes his way up to the inner sanc-
tum, he timidly opens the floor-to-ceiling glass door, timidly whis-
pers his name to the receptionist, and then gingerly ascends a
winding staircase as he gapes wide-eyed at the crystal chandelier,
the spectacular aquarium filled with exotic tropical fish, and
other accoutrements that clearly distinguish this important space
as outside of MacIntyre's realm of position and authority in the
offices "below."

Such a scene, with barely any dialogue, makes a tacit, yet impor-
tant statement about power and authority through the physical
arrangement of the office suite.[2]

You may be familiar with leadership principles such as *coercive power*, *legitimate power*, and *democratic* versus *autocratic power*. Similar to our other discussions of how culture influences values, communication, identity, and control, we will examine some of the hidden dimensions of culture that dictate how people interact with power and authority. Power may be defined as how people get what they want from each other (socially, polit- ically, and economically)—how people fulfill their needs, goals, and val- ues.[3] Conflict and misunderstanding occur when a group's needs, goals, or values are incongruous with the individuals who are members of the group. As a result, issues of influence based on power and authority come into play.

POWER: ASCRIBED OR EARNED

HIGH POWER DISTANCE

Power (or authority) is another cultural dimension that we will address. Hofstede has chosen the term power distance to describe an important cultural relationship among people in a society, an industry, or a business organization. Power distance, from his perspective, measures the degree of inequality within a society and how people accept or reject it.[4] Inequality exists in every society. There are always those who have and those who have not—whether this means material possession, wealth, intellectual abilities, political power, or position in society. A high power distance means that the culture is hierarchical, usually more traditional and paternalistic, while a low power distance reflects greater equality and fairness for all, regardless of race, religion, gender, or social status. A high-power-distance society has been compared to the shape of the Eiffel Tower, which symbolizes a formal bureaucracy. Its incline is steep and narrow at the top; its base is broad and solid at the bottom. All societies demonstrate some aspects of both high and low power distance (whether inequality is accepted or challenged) but, as we have seen with each cultural dimension we have discussed, all cultures tend to exhibit a preference for one or the other (with varying degrees along the continuum).

Speaking of Culture

Level of education along with family background and wealth determine status in France. Graduates of the select Grandes Écoles hold high positions in government and industry. Three out of four top managers of the 200 largest French companies come from wealthy families, whereas in Germany the figure is one out of four, and in the United States it's one out of ten.

French executives tend to run their companies in an authoritarian style. Managers are expected to be highly competent and to know the answer to virtually every question that arises. They are often reluctant to delegate authority. Fraternization with the rank and file of French workers is not common.

—Richard R. Gesteland, *Cross-Cultural Business Behavior* [5]

Cultures exhibiting high power distance tend to view work life as decidedly unequal and hierarchical; power is centralized in the hands of just a few who determine the rules and procedures for others to follow. A wide gap exists between superiors and subordinates, all of whom view those in a higher position as people who both control and are responsible for them.[6] This arrangement can create an expectation among the less powerful that those in control will take care of them. Those who hold less power are dependent on those who hold more power. This structure is found in mostly agricultural societies that do not rely on modern technology, that do not have strong public educational systems, and that feature lower income per capita. Countries positioned toward the high end of the power distance spectrum include Mexico, the Philippines, Peru, Indonesia, Japan, and those in West Africa. Among these, only Japan is considered to be a first-world nation with a highly developed economy. But, as we will see, the Japanese view of power distance may actually imperil their developed-nation status. High power distance in all national cultures is demonstrated in four specific ways: politically, socially, relationally, and professionally.

Politically, high-power-distance cultures often accommodate change by removing and replacing people in positions of power—sometimes by decree or appointment, sometimes by force. Governmental transitions of power in Africa, Latin America, South Asia, and Eastern Europe frequently follow this pattern. In such hierarchical and traditional societies, these inequalities have existed for centuries and are understood (if not tolerated) by the broad majority of people, usually out of economic and political necessity. They must accept and obey a political system that controls them, their government, and their economy in a top-down fashion, making power of all sorts less accessible to its people.[7] Often the power of governmental figures goes unchecked or unchallenged, resulting in oppression and both economic and social instability.

The *nomenklatura* or bureaucratic ruling class of the Communist regime is a relatively recent example of how certain Eastern and Central European governments (and the former Soviet Union) went unchecked for decades, while controlling every aspect of those societies.[8] Such rigid control stifled creativity and individual expression for seventy years during a totalitarian reign. Beginning in 1989 with the fall of the Berlin Wall and the collapse of the Soviet Socialist Republics, people not accustomed to having choices or making their own decisions were suddenly free. Many of them, many years later, are still acclimating to new economic and social systems as democratic reforms continue to make progress. Just because the governmental forms in those nations have changed, however, doesn't mean that the cultures have changed overnight.

A visit to the eastern region of Germany reveals that young people in their teens, 20s, and 30s have adopted many of the customs and aspirations of their western neighbors, but many of the older residents of the former communist society still cling to old ways. Hotel clerks and waiters in Dresden, Leipzig, and Potsdam regard management as "them," and hourly workers as "us." Customer service is a complete mystery to most, including management. Western notions of entrepreneurship and upward mobility in society are not yet well-known or understood. Some former eastern bloc nations have adapted more quickly, including Hungary, Poland, and the Czech Republic, perhaps because they never really bought into the Soviet system to begin with. Other nations, including Bulgaria, Albania, and Slovakia, have been slow to reform, perhaps as much because of geographic and technological isolation as cultural tradition.

A significant aspect of the high-power-distance culture found in post-Soviet Russia is how all forms of communication during business deals must be channeled through government ministers as part of the state-run system. This creates a cumbersome and formidable bureaucracy, forcing foreign and transnational organizations to do business with the assigned Russian officials (usually in Moscow), rather than deal directly with contacts at the actual business location. Going through an intermediary not directly associated with the company or firm can be maddening, but trying to deal directly with your business contacts at the actual site would yield few results since most do not have the authority to make decisions. Business decisions, including purchase and construction contracts, are still centralized with state planners, ministers, and officials who have significant influence over commercial enterprise, even in the twenty-first century. This steep hierarchy of power makes business deals more complicated and drawn out because the contacts with the most useful knowledge are frequently not key decision makers.[9] Key decision makers frequently do not have a particular firm's best interests in mind; often their own political ambitions come first.

A failure to play by local rules can be dangerous for businesspeople of all sorts, including those who come from high-power-distance to low-power-distance societies to do business. Bribing a state clerk or minor official is commonplace in Russia (and elsewhere throughout Eastern Europe). In Russia, if someone is pulled over by a police officer for speeding, the fastest way to resolve the problem is to provide a small bribe of 15 or 20 rubles, and the violator is free to go. Russians, unthinkingly handing a twenty-dollar bill to a U.S. police officer who has just pulled them over for a minor speeding violation, may find themselves in jail with more than one charge pending. The same goes for paying income taxes in western nations. Russians accustomed to a notoriously corrupt system of taxation at home often try to pay very small amounts of taxes owed in the United States and have ended up in a serious mess with the Internal Revenue Service. A young Russian businessman who recently immigrated to the United

States says, "It is very common for rich Russians to 'buy a situation' by giving out bribes, buying witnesses, judges, state officials, and so on. These wheeler-dealers come to the U.S.," he says, "with the same mentality, not realizing that bribing in this country is much more sophisticated and expensive, and sometimes even impossible. If they underestimate the cost or feasibility of 'buying a situation,' they often begin the process and run out of money on the way. They are almost guaranteed to end up in jail and broke."[10]

While systems set in place by the government may reveal hierarchical pressures and structures, contradictions do exist. One value of the Russian people is known as *uravnilovka*, which translated means "egalitarianism." Russians would prefer that everyone had similar opportunities for material wealth, advancement in the workplace, and health. Contrasts such as this abound all over the world and are part of the complexities of understanding intercultural differences.[11] For example, the Japanese model of decision-making, or consensus, might lead us to think that Japanese culture is generally low power distance because of their emphasis on social harmony. Japan, however, tends to be more closely related to high-power-distance values. While consensus must be achieved and the group will take credit (rather than an individual) for any success, someone in the hierarchical chain of command will ultimately make the decision—after an extensive discussion process has been completed.[12]

The Importance of Rank

Many Asians and some Westerners are highly sensitive to status and rank. That means that you should not only use a person's correct title in your communication but also acknowledge the high position of a senior official. The latter can often be accomplished by a reference to the person's "busy schedule" or "extensive responsibilities." Conversely, you should avoid communications that purport to pair a junior executive with a senior executive.

Speaking of Culture

An American consultant recently complained that he was having difficulty getting several Japanese-American joint ventures off the ground because the CEOs of the American companies kept sending junior executives to Japan to meet with the CEOs of the Japanese companies. This was insulting to the Japanese, who responded by sending their own junior executives to the meetings, and nothing was getting achieved.

-David L. James, *The Executive Guide to Asia-Pacific Communications*[13]

Socially, high-power-distance cultures assign importance to a person's position in society, as in the ancient Hindu caste system of India. While the word *caste* comes from the Portuguese word for color, *casta*, this tradition is more about separating people socially than by color. This 3,000-year-old system of separation began with a classification of people into four categories of work groups: priests, rulers, businesspeople and farmers, and artisans and laborers.[14] According to this highly complex and ancient system of organizing society called *jati*, a person's place in society is based upon birth. Hindus are born into a place within the social hierarchy and this rank can never be changed. While Indian law did away with the caste system in the mid-twentieth century, the effects of this hierarchy of society still linger today. One major implication of permanent hierarchy is that people from different castes (such as managers and laborers) cannot communicate with each other directly, and people from the skilled laborer category cannot advance through the ranks as they develop certain skills. This creates difficulty in communicating crucial information when no clear channels for such communication exist.[15]

Relationally, power distance exerts its influence within a culture by affecting everything from structure to customs in the family. Certain traditional cultures, in Italy and Latin America, for example, have what is called the *patrón* system, in which a senior male figure plays the role of a "godfather." Strong ties are associated with the internal structure of the nuclear family and its extended members. For example, while all cultures change, Latin American societies maintain their historical roots as agrarian cultures from the structure of colonialism which has left a lasting cultural legacy on the way that people view authority. Even though Latin cultures are still primarily agrarian, few of the people dependent on the land actually own any. Land ownership is the privilege of a few who live in the *hacienda*, run the ranch, and employ many lower-status people. This relationship between owner and employee is more than a work arrangement, however. For centuries, a reciprocal relationship has existed in which the landowner, or *patrón* (translated as "protector"), is responsible for taking care of or protecting his people. In return, the hired hands are loyal to the boss.

Workers in such cultures have generally stayed with their *patrón* for life and worked the farm or ranch in return for modest housing, food, and even protection for legal problems. The *patrón* remains involved in the lives of his workers and even is godfather to their children. Such social structures in the Latin American culture of the *hacienda* became known for the loyal, paternalistic sponsorship of a landowner and his people, and this tradition has carried over to this day. Even in the modern workplace, employees know their "place" relative to their superiors and are fiercely loyal. Decision-making is centralized and authoritarian. As long as subordinates comply with rules, complete their work on time, and get along with co-workers, they expect (as did workers under the *patrón* system) to be taken care of and be granted favors.[16]

Professionally, a hierarchy of power is demonstrated in the workplace when a superior or "boss" is granted both power and privilege, which carry over to other aspects of life. Such people customarily benefit from living in a better neighborhood, attending better schools, and socializing with more "important" people. One's position in society is usually based upon status, knowledge, age, and profession, and is ascribed rather than learned. It is to the employees' advantage to make sure that they have good relationships with their superiors, since the superior may be able to grant favors and pave the way for future gain. While the employer expects to be obeyed in return, the employee expects to be taken care of. This is an age-old reciprocal relationship based on respect, favors, and (occasionally) fear. As you might expect, a system based on favors and connections plays a big role in relationship-focused markets. If you want to get something done, you need to tap into your network of resources and connections. Russians have a term for such reciprocal relationships, called *blat*; Asians call it *guanxi*; Latin Americans, *palanca*; and Egyptians, *wastah*.[17] In cultures where people place emphasis on position, power, and status, the more powerful the resource, the better your chances for getting what you need.

The Economic Power of a Neglected Resource

In today's business environment it's easy to think that gender equality is the same around the globe. However, professional women in Japan are still challenged in the workplace. For example, even if you are a high ranking employee, it is still common to be asked who your boss is – especially if you have been out front with a presentation or in charge of negotiating an important contract.

One story in the New York Times talked about a woman who owned her own company and had to constantly prove herself to male customers. Rather than get discouraged, she employed a clever strategy – she hired a man to accompany her because even having a male counterpart increased her chances of closing deals. The woman interviewed said, "If I brought a man along, the customers would only establish eye contact with him, even though I was the representative of the company, and doing the talking."

According to the office of the Prime Minister, "Japan is still a developing country in terms of gender equality." In fact, in 2003 Japan ranked 69 out of 75 in terms of a nation that empowers its women (World Economic Forum). According the Forum, 40% of Japanese women work (compared to 45% of women in the U.S.), which is only 9% of all managerial position held and wages for women are only 65% of men – this makes for one of the widest gaps in the industrialized world.

—Howard W. French, *The New York Times*[18]

High-power-distance cultures have a clear separation of superiors and subordinates with distinctive roles for each, and huge pay gaps between them. Workers are generally unskilled and uneducated, and the special privileges that accrue to superiors are just one more cultural aspect that separates the worker from the boss. Referent power is widely and regularly used because a person's status is derived from his or her background and experience. Organizations are usually tall structures within a rigid hierarchy, in which power is centralized and information is controlled. Deep-rooted cultural traditions and customs have lasting effects on how power is distributed and maintained. Cultures with high-power-distance include Malaysia, Guatemala, Panama, the Philippines, Mexico, Greece, Japan, France, Venezuela, Arab countries, Ecuador, Indonesia, India, and West African countries.

Here are a few questions you might consider when dealing with high-power-distance cultures:

1. Will your business contact expect to be granted appropriate respect based on his or her position in the organization, or will he or she downplay his or her position, opting for a more egalitarian approach?
2. Who will make the final decision: the senior ranking official, or his or her associates?

3. What are the different levels of authority within your organization and your business contacts? Can people of differing ranks interact and negotiate directly, or must a higher authority review their offers?
4. How will certain verbal and nonverbal cues differ in such cultures? How can you tell for sure when someone is really saying no?

How to Make a Big Insult by a Simple Misunderstanding

Richard Gesteland tells this interesting story about how misunderstandings can occur so easily, yet have a huge impact on business relationships:

José García Lopez, a Mexican importer, had been negotiating with a Danish manufacturing company for several months when he decided to visit Copenhagen to finalize a purchase contract. The business meetings went smoothly, so on the last day of his visit, Sr. García confided that he looked forward to signing the contract after his return to Mexico.

That evening, the Danes invited Sr. García out for an evening on the town. Mr. Flemming, the 40-year-old export manager and his 21-year-old assistant, Margrethe, hosted an excellent dinner and then took their Mexican prospect on a tour of Copenhagen nightspots. Around midnight, Flemming glanced at his watch.

"Sr. García, as I mentioned to you when we discussed your visit, I have an early flight tomorrow to Tokyo. So you'll forgive me if I leave you now. Margrethe will make sure you get back to your hotel all right and then drive you to the airport tomorrow morning. I wish you a good flight!"

Next morning in the car on the way to the airport, José García was uncharacteristically silent. Then he turned to the young assistant, "Margrethe, would you please tell your boss I have decided not to sign that contract after all. It is not your fault, of course. If you think about what happened last evening I believe you will understand why I no longer wish to do business with your company."[19]

1. From your perspective, what went wrong here?
2. What cultural dimensions may have affected this interaction?
3. Had you been in Sr. García's position (from your own cultural perspective), what would this interaction have meant to you?
4. What if Mr. Flemming had simply told Sr. García in advance that he would be leaving for Tokyo early in the morning after their meeting? Would that have sufficed? What is the risk in doing that?
5. What basic rule of intercultural communication did Mr. Flemming violate?
6. Looking at this from another angle, was Sr. Garcia rather harsh in making his decision based on an unintentional miscommunication? Why? Why not?

From: Gesteland, Richard R. (2005). Cross-cultural business behavior: Negotiating, selling, sourcing and managing across cultures. Copenhagen, Denmark: Copenhagen Business School Press, p. 48.

LOW POWER DISTANCE

National cultures with low power distance expect each person to enjoy fundamental personal liberties. This means systemically decentralized control, putting more decision-making power into the hands of ordinary people. Unlike the Eiffel Tower analogy (triangle with a sloping, steep incline), this type of society would be a flatter pyramid with a broader base, signifying a greater distribution of power toward the middle and bottom. Some have even suggested an inverted pyramid. While there will always be inequalities among people in terms of status, social class, intelligence, education, and wealth, people from low-power-distance cultures believe that such inequalities should be minimized.[20] In cultures like in the United States, Canada, Great Britain, the Netherlands, Australia, and New Zealand, power and authority are generally earned rather than ascribed, and virtually anyone is able to improve his or her education, status, social class, or wealth. Low power distance is demonstrated in national cultures in four ways: politically, socially, relationally, and professionally.

Politically, in low-power-distance cultures, change is made within government through a democratic process, in which people are free to vote and voice their opinions. Great Britain (known formally as the United Kingdom) is a constitutional monarchy with a Prime Minister and a Parliament. Switzerland is a confederation of cantons known for its neutrality. Israel is a parliamentary, multiparty democracy. And the United States is a federal republic in which individual states control their own local governments and a constitution ensures the liberties of its people. The U.S. Civil War (1860–1864) and the Civil Rights Movement following a century later were manifestations of people rising up in response to structural inequalities within society. These national events of enormous importance tested the very concepts of the U. S. Constitution and Declaration of Independence. A motto familiar to all U.S. Americans, penned by Emma Lazarus and engraved in stone at the base of the Statue of Liberty in New York Harbor, supports the human longing for freedom: "Give me your tired, your poor, your huddled masses yearning to breathe free."

Socially, low-power-distance cultures are concerned about narrowing the gap between wealthy and poor, educated and uneducated. In the United States, for example, recent political campaigns have focused on issues of welfare reform, public education, universal health insurance, and medical care for the elderly and less fortunate. The aim of such a society is to reduce or lower the power distance that separates its people. Such gaps can never be entirely closed to form a utopian society, but the goal in such societies is to acknowledge the obligation to provide aid and assistance where possible. Governmental programs such as public assistance for the unemployed, medical care for the elderly, and charitable agencies for numerous causes are an important part of these societies. High-power-distance societies have such programs, too, but the cultural gaps remain enormous, largely because of the absence of social mobility. Moving from one social class to another is simply not an option in a high-power-distance society.

Relationally, low-power-distance cultures are less formal regarding how subordinates may address their superiors. In the United States (depending on the organization's internal culture), subordinates are often on a first-name basis with their bosses. In some (though not many) academic institutions, graduate students even may call their professors by first name. One's status is believed already solidified because of a degree or a job title, and it is not always necessary to reinforce it through formal address. For example, recognition of individual achievement might be more important than recognition of age. A senior vice president may not care that you call her by her first name as long as you know what her position is. However, high-power-distance cultures, such as in Japan, often use language as a symbol of authority. For example, a manager addressing a male subordinate would use the suffix *kun* at the end of his name (e.g., *Mr. Takaki* would become *Takakikun*) but the employee would use the more respectful suffix *san* tagged onto the end of his supervisor's name (e.g., *Mr. Futaba* would become *Futabasan*).[21] Trends such as Japanese formality are changing as more students educated in the informal United States return to the more formal Japanese culture.

A Discernable Shift in Japanese Formality

The NYT reported that a Tokyo based semiconductor company, Elpida Memory, was changing its policy of formality – people at the factory would no longer use their titles, but call each other by their names with the traditional Japanese suffix "san".

In the past, an employee would need to address her or his boss as "Department Chief Sato" or Senior Director Takamoshi. Now, rather than use such a formality, you would say "Takamoshi-san". But the CEO and president, Yukiko Sakamoto, thinks that using such formality impedes decision making...and even innovation.

There is a definite shift in Japanese formality – a recent departure from what has traditionally been a hierarchical society. Rather than having authority ascribed to a person – that person has the ability to 'rise to the top'. Japanese companies are using fewer titles in favor of a more casual view on 'who's the boss'. Now, performance trumps seniority and the traditional order has been turned upside down, causing confusion with the young and the old.

The custom of honorific language is changing within the home as less traditionally minded parents use this form of address to elders less. This creates a shift in how school children address their teachers, university professors, and eventually their employers.

Honorifics has its origins with the nobility who ruled Japan more than a thousand years ago and were considered the social elite. Post World War II found Japan creating a more democratic society so the meaning of honorific titles shifted to use between close friends and family members. With the younger generation, this intimacy is dissolving. According to Fumio Inoue, a linguistics professor at Tokyo University, "the decline of the honorific form represents a loss of the beauty of their language and a coarsening of the social culture." He explains that Japanese has traditionally used language to indicate a person's social place.

Japanese, perhaps more than any other language, has used language to delineate social status. Professor Inoue explains, "While French speakers must decide between the familiar *tu* and the formal *vous* in addressing someone in the second person, in Japanese, there are many ways to say "I" or "you," calibrated by age, circumstance, gender, social position, and other factors. Verb endings, adjectives, and entire words also shift according to the situation."

With the shifting tide of generations to come, CEO Yukiko Sakamoto is hoping that using "san" will lessen the age and rank barriers between people allowing them to talk and share ideas freely.[22]

Adapted from: Norimitsu Onishi, "Japanese Workers Told From on High: Drop the Formality," The NYT, (October 30, 2003), A1, A6.

Professionally, low-power-distance cultures display a different view of life within an organization. Supervisors are often seen as resources rather than autocrats. Employees are encouraged to interact with superiors by asking questions, receiving feedback, and even soliciting personal advice at times. Subordinates also expect to have their opinions taken into consideration, even if the organizational makeup is more formal. There are many ways to do this: through frontline supervisors, through formal feedback solicitation systems, or even through the organization's ombudsperson, if a problem arises. Subordinates in low-power-distance cultures are less dependent on their superiors and often interact more freely with them, even if this means voicing criticism of an issue or decision. Figure 4.1 shows one way to visualize various national cultures and their views of power orientation and collectivism.

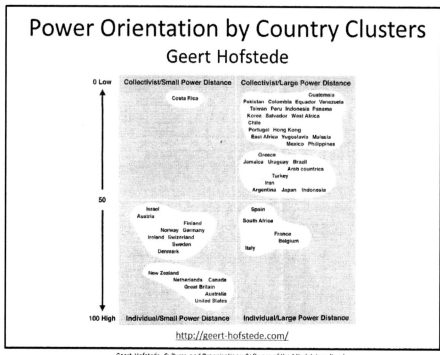

Power Orientation by Country Clusters
Geert Hofstede

Geert Hofstede, *Cultures and Organizations: Software of the Mind: Intercultural Cooperation and Its Importance for Survival* (New York: NY, McGraw-Hill, 1997), 54.

Figure 4.1: Power Orientation by Country [23]

Procter & Gamble has long been regarded as a major power of the marketing world and a prime training ground for marketing managers. By the summer of 2000, however, with half of P&G's top 15 brands losing market share and employee morale in ruins, company executives realized that the firm was in trouble. "In a global, multitiered marketing firm, it's not unusual for senior management to become emotionally detached from its people," according to P&G marketing chief James Stengel and University of Cincinnati professors Chris Allen and Andrea Dixon. "The best way to avoid such detachment," they say, "is to actively seek employee feedback and to listen to the feelings and folklore in the organization." It's equally important to recognize that "listening to employees isn't something you do once and then go back to business as usual." For Procter & Gamble, and other large firms hoping to compete in a global economy, it's a matter of facilitating cultural change—from high to low power distance—to meet the changing needs of their customers and the challenge of the marketplace.[24]

Low-power-distance cultures have a more egalitarian perspective about superiors and subordinates. There is less separation of the two and less formality regarding titles and use of names. Legitimate power is respected because people earn their titles through achievement. Salary differentials between a manager and direct reports may not be as steep as in high-power-distance cultures, which can spread the decision-making process among lower-level employees. Organizations are usually characterized by flatter structures with a decentralization of power, and information often flows much more freely throughout all levels. Countries with cultures of low power distance include Austria, Israel, Denmark, New Zealand, Ireland, Scandinavian countries, Switzerland, Great Britain, Germany, Australia, Canada, and the United States. Figure 4.2 categorizes various characteristics of high- and low-power-distance cultures, using the work of Dutch interculturalist Geert Hofstede.

Here are a few questions you might consider when dealing with low-power-distance cultures:

- If your business contact plays down his or her status or role, how should you proceed? Should you interact on a more familiar level or more respectful level?
- Is it ever appropriate to use a superior's first name? Should you make any distinction about private and public use of such names?
- When doing business with a low-power-distance organization, will the senior ranking official make the final decision or delegate the decision-making authority to someone else (possibly of lower status)? How will you know?
- Should you dress in a manner that is customary for your organization, or should you plan to look like those you are hoping to do business with?

In some South Pacific cultures, a speaker holds a conch shell as a symbol of temporary position of authority. Leaders must understand that who holds the conch is who should be listened to and when.

—Max DePree

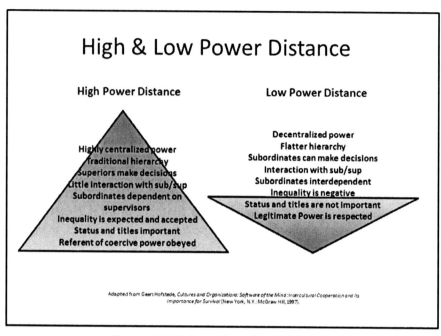

Figure 4.2: High and Low Power Distance

The Origins of Power Distance

Professor Geert Hofstede has analyzed cultural dimensions in some unique ways – such as the correlation of language areas (national countries) and power.

His research shows that countries where Romance languages are spoken (Spain, Portugal, Italy, France) tend to score high in Power Distance. Yet, countries that speak Germanic languages (Germany, England, Netherlands, Denmark, Norway and Sweden) score low on the Power Distance dimension.

He explains that a country is 'rooted' in the connection of its history and language. "The fact that a country belongs to a language area is rooted in history: Romance languages all derive from Low-Latin, and were adopted in countries once part of the Roman Empire, or, in the case of Latin America, in countries colonized by Spain and Portugal which themselves were former colonies of Rome."

He further elaborates, "Germanic languages are spoken either in countries which remained "barbaric" in Roman days, or in areas once under Roman rule but re-conquered by barbarians (like England). Thus, some roots of the mental program called power distance go back at least to Roman times—2000 years ago. Countries with a Chinese (Confucian) cultural inheritance also cluster on the medium-to-high side of the power distance scale, and here is a culture at least 4000 years old."

People groups such as under the Chinese rule of Emperors or under the Roman empire had centralized power that commanded its people. However, in Germanic Europe, power was distributed among small tribal groups ruled by local lords. His conclusion: "It seems a reasonable assumption that early statehood experiences helped to develop in these peoples the common mental programs necessary for the survival of their political and social system."

—Geert Hofstede, *Cultures and Organizations* [25]

We have made the distinction between cultures that tend to maintain a clear separation of power and those that tend to relax the boundaries. In all cultures, power is played out to varying degrees politically, socially, relationally, and professionally, based on how the norms determine those who earn authority and those to whom it is ascribed. The main difference between high and low power distance is people in positions of superiority in high-power-distance (vertical-hierarchy) societies tend to view themselves as something separate or different than those in lower positions. Authority is something that is ascribed. People coming from low-power-distance (flatter-hierarchy) societies will acknowledge inequality, but they do not see it as ascribed. They aren't limited by a caste system, as in India, or as submissive as women in some West African countries or in traditional Arab cultures. Some cultures condition people to view their place in society as ascribed—a fact of life—while others believe they can change their place through achievement.[26] The next type of cultural control deals with how a society differentiates the roles of men and women.

MASCULINITY AND FEMININITY

In his landmark study of IBM employees, Geert Hofstede identified another aspect of cultural variability that demonstrates the difference of gender roles in a culture: *masculinity* and *femininity*. This is another way a society taps into its sources of power. Masculine cultures draw clear divisions between male and female roles. Traditionally, men are more assertive, achieving status and material gain for the family, while women are the nurturers assigned to a clear role as caregiver for the family. Feminine cultures accept that both men and women can be ambitious and are comfortable with overlapping gender roles that include both those of provider and those of the empathic caregiver.[28] While the terms *masculinity* and *femininity* may be awkward to ascribe to a culture such as in the United States, they nevertheless help us to identify how cultures determine the roles of men and women in a given society.

Masculine cultures are noted as performance-oriented, while feminine cultures are noted as supportive and nurturing. This doesn't mean that masculine cultures are cold, harsh, or uncaring about their people. On the contrary, these terms simply reveal some of the implicit social norms of such societies. Hofstede is careful to point out that such differences are relative rather than absolute: men and women can both be either more masculine or more feminine. The distinction relates to socially and culturally determined roles.[29] As we examine this aspect of culture, both in its general and specific applications, we must remember that all cultures change and evolve over time—some more quickly than others. For example, a phenomenon in the United States just over the last couple of decades is the rise of women as chief breadwinners and husbands who attend to the house and children. This role-reversal is possible in a culture that blurs the divisions among traditional roles of men and women. The countries with cultures that emphasize distinct differences in gender roles and are considered high on the masculinity scale include Arab countries, Mexico, Japan, Switzerland, Great Britain, and Germany. Such cultures value power, control, and assertiveness.

The following excerpt from a *Fortune* magazine article exemplifies aspects of a more feminine culture, which demonstrates equality between both men and women concerning professional achievement as well as overlapping gender roles regarding who provides for the family.

The New Age of Trophy Husbands

We've all heard of the 'trophy wife' – it has even been made into a reality T.V. Show. Originally, the term had a positive connotation – that a man was lucky enough to have both a successful career *and* a successful wife – she had her own career as well. However, over time the connotation came to mean 'gold digger'.

Well, an article in Fortune, "The New Age of the Trophy Husbands" has flipped the original stereotype to describe a fast growing demographic of men who reverse roles – rather than become the bread-winners they become the bread-makers. "Call him what you will: househusband, stay-at-home dad, domestic engineer. But credit him with setting aside his own career by dropping out, retiring early, or going part-time so that his wife's career might flourish and their family might thrive. Behind a great woman at work, there is often a great man at home. He is the new trophy husband."

Betsy Morris, "Trophy Husbands, "*Fortune* (October 14, 2002) 31

Hofstede devised the masculinity-femininity term to draw an important and clear distinction between assertive, independent, and achievement-oriented behavior (masculine) and the more modest, cooperative, and nurturing behavior (feminine). His own personal story helps to shed some light on these different perspectives.

Speaking of Culture

*As a young Dutch engineer I once applied for a junior manage-
ment job with an American engineering company which had
recently settled in Flanders, the Dutch-speaking part of Belgium.
I felt well qualified: with a degree from the senior technical university of the country, good grades, a record of active participation in student associations, and three years' experience as an
engineer with a well-known, although somewhat sleepy Dutch
company. I had written a short letter indicating my interest and
providing some vital personal data.*

*I was invited to appear in person, and after a long train ride I sat
facing the American plant manager. I behaved politely and mod-
estly, as I knew an applicant should, and waited for the other man
to ask the usual questions which would enable him to find out
how qualified I was. To my surprise he asked very few of the
things that I thought should be discussed.*

*Instead he wanted to know some highly detailed facts about my
experience in tool design, using English words I did not know, and
the relevance of which escaped me. Those were the things I could
learn within a week once I worked there. After half an hour of
painful misunderstandings he said, "Sorry. We need a first-class
man." And I was out on the street.*

—Geert Hofstede, *Culture and Organizations* [31]

Years later, Hofstede found himself in the position of the hiring agent (of
both Dutch and American prospective candidates) and realized what had happened in his interview years earlier. U.S. Americans tend to "sell themselves"
by listing every award, honor, and outstanding quality in order to impress a
potential employer. During the interview they are talkative and keep emphasizing their ability to do things. Dutch candidates, however are the opposite:
they "sell themselves short" by U.S. American standards. To list all of one's
accomplishments on a long and detailed résumé is considered bragging and,
therefore, immodest. The Dutch candidate expects to eventually dialog about
his or her important qualities when asked. This is yet another example of how
culture can influence a person's perspective on how to behave.

A higher masculinity rating for a country usually means there are
fewer women in the workforce. Women in the workplace are often not

able to climb the ladder as easily as men, and you will see few women elected to political positions. This is often reflected in a dominant religion or philosophy that stresses the authority of the male in relation to the female. However, in a country with a higher femininity rating, you will typically see many women in elective offices, women who have successfully "climbed the corporate ladder" in the workplace, and an emphasis on promoting work-life balance. A list of high-feminine countries would include Chile, Portugal, Thailand, Sweden, Norway, Iceland, the Netherlands, Denmark, and Finland.[32] It has also been noted that these cultures most likely have a dominant religion that stresses the "complementarity of the sexes."[33]

As we have seen, the concept of masculinity and femininity is a way of characterizing cultural values towards assertiveness and nurturance in the roles of men and women. In masculine-oriented cultures, managers would be expected to be assertive in making decisions, while in feminine-oriented cultures, managers would be expected to use consensus. Masculine-oriented cultures would focus on performance and expect competition among peers; feminine-oriented cultures would focus on both equality and the quality of interpersonal relationships. While masculine-oriented cultures might resolve conflict through the use of authority and position power, feminine-oriented cultures might try to reach an equitable compromise through negotiation.[34] These are just a few of the ways that these cultural differences might play out in the workplace, and awareness of them may help intercultural communicators identify potential problems before they escalate.

ACHIEVEMENT

Our examination of masculine and feminine values in culture leads directly to a consideration of how a society defines success or achievement. We have talked about how masculine-oriented societies have a clear role distinction between men and women and define success in terms of status, material gain, and provisions for the family. Feminine-oriented cultures, on the other hand, seek rewards that are less tangible; they are rewarded with strong relationships with people in the community and family, and in the use of quality time spent in those relationships. We will use these concepts of masculinity and femininity as a backdrop for talking about how a society views achievement.

The final cultural dimension that we will examine is the notion of achievement, whether a culture focuses more on *doing* or *being*. This is a fundamental perspective related to how we view work: Do we work to live or live to work?[35] Achievement may be defined as the act of accomplishing or finishing something successfully, especially if it is by means of exertion, skill, practice, or perseverance. While it's obvious that people in every culture and all walks of life seek to achieve, the key point here is that part of the definition, "especially if it is by means of *exertion*." Along with the masculine-oriented attributes we have previously discussed (assertive, achievement-oriented, seeking material gain), we can connect this idea of *how* a culture may perceive achievement with the idea that achievement-oriented cultures live to work. These are *doing* cultures.

Doing cultures tend to be active, always in a hurry, on the go, and up to something. Such cultures reflect monochronic time values. If you're always in a hurry and consistently value activity over reflection, then you tend to think of time as lost, scarce, and of value if not used properly. In the fast-paced business culture of the United States, hard work, productivity, ability to get along with co-workers, dedication to the task at hand, and commitment to the company are seen as the important indicators of who will receive monetary-based rewards, promotions, and recognition.

All cultures change over time and humans adapt to the ways in which their societies change. People in the United States are working harder and longer hours, taking their children to sports, music, and school activities, caring for aging parents, volunteering in the community, and participating in activities and service at places of worship. As the perception that "there are so few hours in the day" has become the standard, numerous 24/7 facilities have been created. From gas stations to copy centers to convenience stores to fast-food establishments, people in the United States are constantly on the go and always in a hurry. Microwaved meals, shopping-mall food courts, and supermarket delis with fully prepared dinners now compete with quick service and convenience dining restaurant chains on nearly every corner. Home delivery services; on-demand maid and concierge service; Internet banking, shopping, and news retrieval now meet the need for people in "doing" cultures such as in the United States to manage their frenetic lifestyles. Advertising campaigns have clearly targeted the overextended person. For example, the iconic golden arches of McDonalds have tempted us in the past with that catchy jingle, "You deserve a break today . . . so get out and get away . . . to McDonald's." U.S. Americans are so busy as a society, and so preoccupied with living to work that exhaustion and stress-related illnesses are common. The drive for success would seem to have a price.

While U.S. Americans may be action-oriented and love the saying, "Don't just sit there, do something!" a completely different view would come from the Zen perspective, which might say, "Don't just do something, sit there."[36] The opposite of the fast-paced life is one of serenity, contemplation, and stillness. These cultures focus on being rather than doing; they revere reflection over action and the goal, as we have seen before, is to try to find harmony with the environment, people, and the world. Such cultures mark time not by the clock, but by natural events. Waiting in a reception area for a business meeting to begin is not necessarily unproductive; like silence, time spent sitting quietly is an opportunity for quiet reflection, not an inconvenience.[37]

Still other cultures have a different view of achievement and prefer to work to live, focusing their priorities on enjoying the good things in life (as well as hard work). For example, European cafés are an integral part of social life for people who go to meet and talk and debate politics and social issues. The cafés of Europe have served a different purpose than those in the United States. Until the last decade or so, coffee shops were places to go first thing in the morning to grab a cup and head off to work. Now, as specialty shops such as Starbucks and Seattle's Best seem to have appeared on just about every city corner in the United States, they have become more of a place where people can stop to chat and meet with friends and colleagues, rather than a quick stop for a caffeine fix before you rush to the next event. Contrast that with the Mexican, Spanish, and Latin American tradition of closing the office at midday so people can return home for an extended lunch and a much-needed afternoon siesta. People return refreshed to finish out their day's work and meet friends or family for late-night *tapas* (snacks) and a glass of wine or beer before retiring.

U.S. Americans, who are often characterized as people who live to work, complain regularly about not having enough free time and having little time off from work. Compared to other developed, industrial nations, they may have a point. A Chicago-based research group recently compared time off from work in nine countries: six in Europe plus Japan, Canada, and the United States. All of the nations are similar in approach to time off for public holidays, with totals ranging from eight days in the Netherlands and the Great Britain to fourteen in Japan. The United States has nine.[38]

It's in the category of "required vacation at full pay" that we see a big difference. Outside the United States, mandatory vacation time ranges from ten days in Canada and Japan to twenty days in the Netherlands and Great Britain, 24 days in Germany, 25 in Sweden and France, and 35 days for managers in Italy. The required vacation in the United States? None at all. U.S. firms, however, typically provide their workers with 10 days (two weeks) off in the first year of employment, increasing to 25 days after 20 years. This compares to 21 days after 15 years in Japan, 25 days after 20 years in Canada, and 30 days after the same length of service in Germany.

The French are legally entitled to two and one-half days of vacation per month worked, which means 25 days off after less than a year on the job. Additionally, the French work week is now limited to 35 hours.[39]

You will note that the higher a country is on the "doing" scale, the less vacation time their workers will typically receive. The further a country is toward the "being" end of the same scale, the more time off they will get. Many countries that measure achievement through "being" rather than "doing" will also provide workers with vacation allowances. For example, in Mexico, if you're entitled to 20 days' vacation, your employer must pay you for the 20 days plus another 25 percent, or the equivalent of 25 days' pay. What's more, Mexican employers often give much more than the statutory requirement—typically around 80 percent. Granted, base pay is low, but other nations who value "being" over "doing" will provide the same benefit, even if wage scales are higher. In Belgium, the vacation premium is 85 percent of one month's pay.[40] Figure 4.3 depicts the average number of vacation days earned by full-time employees in the United States.

Paid Vacation for U.S. Workers

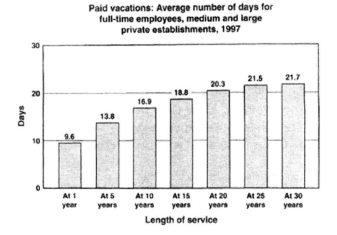

Paid vacations: Average number of days for full-time employees, medium and large private establishments, 1997

Source: U.S. Department of Labor, Bureau of Labor Statistics. Retrieved December 31, 2003, from http://stats.bls.gov/opub/ted/1999/nov/wk2/art02.htm.

FIGURE 4.3: Paid Vacations for U.S. Workers

The U.S. businessperson is expected to be assertive when communicating. This can have repercussions if you are a U.S. American aggressively trying to succeed in negotiations with a business contact from a face-saving society such as China or Japan. International negotiation expert Drew Martin calls international negotiations an "entirely different animal." He notes, "Culture impacts negotiation in four ways: by conditioning one's perception of reality, by blocking out information inconsistent or unfamiliar with culturally grounded assumptions, by projecting meaning onto the other party's words and actions, and impelling the ethnocentric observer to an incorrect attribution of motive. Culture affects the range of strategies that negotiators develop as well as the many ways they are tactically implemented."[42] On the one hand, directness when negotiating (or communicating) can be seen as aggression, while indirectness can be seen as lack of interest. Since we can enter into an intercultural communication interaction with our own biased lenses, we should be aware that we are judging other people by our own standards, rather than theirs. We should proceed with caution and care.

Speaking of Culture

"Filipinos also value a communication style that stresses calmness, equanimity, and interpersonal harmony. One term, amor proprio, translates into English as "harmony" and refers to a very fragile sense of personal worth and self-respect. In interactions with others, it denotes being treated as a person rather than an object. This value makes the Filipino especially vulnerable to negative remarks that may affect his or her standing in society. Consequently, Filipinos seldom criticize others; and if they do, it is in the most polite manner. They see bluntness and frankness as uncivilized, and will speak vaguely and ambiguously in a meeting to avoid a stressful confrontation. They have such high respect for others' feelings that they will always agree and keep their reservations to themselves."

—Larry A. Samovar and Richard E. Porter, *Communication Between Cultures*[41]

In sum, cultures that focus on *doing* are competitive when it comes to achievement. Such cultures are decision-driven, strive for short-term gains, and expect results. Cultures that focus on *being* are more concerned with a cooperative perspective, are generally relationship-driven, consider long-term growth, look for process and not always the product, and try to be collaborative.

RESPECT

Finally, we will examine culture and control in terms of respect. We had suggested that showing respect (a communication behavior) is a conduit for one's power (an expression of values). People from different cultures can show respect in many ways, ranging from eye contact to greetings, to the exchange of a business cards, to their tone of voice, or gifts they choose to give.

The issue of eye contact, for example, can convey many different meanings (intended and unintended). Not making *direct* eye contact is taken as a sign of respect for speakers of Xhosa in South Africa. Speakers of Xhosa, the language spoken in the Eastern and Western Cape, will avoid looking directly into your eyes when speaking because this signals honor and respect. Also, because the Xhosa language has a strong oral as opposed to literary tradition, speakers tend to pace themselves when presenting ideas in a conversation. Meaning is derived from the symbolism within the story that most always accompanies a conversation. If you quickly come to the point, you would be considered rude because the correct way, according to the speakers of this language, is to take your time and engage people either in conversation or in presenting a beautiful background of information.[43]

Taking your time when greeting others can also signify respect. One sure way to insult an international visitor in the United States is to say hello while you continue on your way. U.S. Americans often do things "on the go," eating or talking on their cell phones while walking or driving. Time-conscious U.S. Americans are always in a hurry. International visitors often wonder why is it that when they meet a friend on the street and say, "Good morning, how are you?" the other person simply waves and says, "Hi," but keeps walking. In many other cultures, such as in Latin American and Arab countries, Italy, and Russia, you are expected to stop and inquire about the other person's health and family's well-being. To merely walk past a person with a wave of the hand and a quick hello is considered rude. The ongoing relationship is crucial: Certain obligations of care and concern must be met.

Other forms of respect, such as the Japanese business-card ritual, are important and time-honored. This brief ceremony, called the *meishi*, includes both a respectful way to greet a business contact and a way to show reverence and respect for that contact through the handling of the business card. Normally you shake hands (lightly) and/or give a slight bow. You must only bow to the same depth as you have been bowed to, as this demonstrates the extent of the relationship. Lower your eyes and keep your hands at your side as you bow. You should present your card, holding it in both hands between thumb and forefinger, print side up facing the recipient. You then receive the other person's business card with both hands and are expected to study it for a few seconds before respectfully placing it on the table or putting it in a leather holder. It is considered rude to put the card in your pocket or wallet, and you should never write on it. The manner in which you treat the card demonstrates your respect for the person with whom you are meeting.[45]

Another way people express respect for others is through tone of voice. As in all intercultural encounters, however, what one culture perceives as appropriate and acceptable, another may think is odd. Speakers from Latin American cultures are generally expressive and use a large degree of vocal variety—their pitch rises and falls steeply as well, along with their volume and range, as they emotively express their point of view. They say that they have their heart in the matter because of such expressiveness. People from North America and Northern Europe also have an expressive tone; however, they are not quite as animated as Latin Americans in their expression. The Asian tone of voice is the most neutral and signifies both control and the ability to display deference in conversation to those with whom they come in contact. To the North or South American, such tone would be considered monotonous. To the Asian speaker, it is a sign of respect; often the person at a higher status level is expected to maintain a lower and flatter tone.[47]

How Seating Arrangements in Meetings Convey Meaning

First meetings with Japanese are akin to opening ceremonies. If the first meeting physically takes place in a Japanese office, from an American point of view, it may seem formal to the point of being ritualistic. Nothing is left to chance. From the time that the business visitor arrives at the door and is appropriately greeted to the time that he is seen off from the sidewalk in front of the office building as his car or taxi pulls away, attention will have been given to every detail, including seating arrangement and refreshments and, perhaps even to what artwork is to be hung in the meeting room that day.

Seating arrangements both in private homes, restaurants, and even in offices during meetings are very important to Japanese and are treated with close attention. Who sits where is a genuinely sensitive matter even for relatively small gatherings. Japanese guests feel that they have been treated well when the seating arrangements are done properly in accordance with formal rules.

While informality and casualness are the concrete expression of hospitality in the United States, Japanese feel that they are being treated hospitably if things are done according to form. It is simply a mistake to tell Japanese guests to "sit wherever you like." In Japan, an employee who fouls up the seating arrangements for an important occasion involving upper-level management can actually get demoted.

To arrange the seating of the Japanese guests correctly, it is necessary to know something about traditional Japanese rooms. The principles that apply there are carried over into Western-style rooms and even office conference rooms.

Every formal traditional Japanese room has a *tokonoma*. A *tokonoma* is a discrete area along one wall of a room that is a designated place of honor. The *tokonoma* can be identified by the artwork that is hung there, traditionally a scroll, or where perhaps a flower arrangement or sculpture is placed. It is considered the best spot in the room. The functional equivalent of the *tokonoma* in an office may simply be the wall on which the most expensive painting hangs or simply the location of the best view if the room is in a glass-walled high rise.

In the traditional Japanese seating arrangement, the highest-ranking guest is placed with his back to the center of the *tokonoma*. Lower-ranking guests are positioned on either side of him in order of descending rank. The host group is seated on the guest group's left flank with the highest-ranking member of the host group closest to the guest group. The lower ranking guests sit along the right flank of the higher-ranking guests, that is, facing the hosts. The traditional arrangement described may be modified in international meetings and sometimes must be modified to accommodate positioning of interpreters.

—From: Hiroki Kato and Joan S. Kato, *Understanding and Working with the Japanese Business World* [48]

GIFT OR BRIBE?

Gift-giving (or -withholding) is also a way to extend courtesy and respect; however, you must know the do's and taboos of the culture. For example, giving a gift of white flowers to someone from a Chinese background would be an insult since white carnations symbolize death. You also wouldn't want to give a clock to someone from China for the same reason—not only does it symbolize death, but it can bring bad luck. Generally, you should not give cutlery items because in certain cultures—Asia, for example—knives symbolize severing a relationship. Often in Asian cultures the recipient of the gift will not open it until you have left, but in Europe and North America this would be considered rude since the giver expects to see delight and gratitude expressed by the recipient.

International business consultant David James tells this story from his practical book, *The Executive Guide to Asia-Pacific Communications*. "On a recent visit to Tokyo, an American called on a Japanese executive to whom he had been introduced on an earlier visit. At the meeting the American presented a small gift to the Japanese. Although the meeting had been arranged in advance, the Japanese was not prepared for an exchange of gifts. His face flushed a bright red, and the remainder of the meeting was a shambles of lost face. In Japan, gift-giving is a social ritual of great importance, but it is not always observed for casual office visits, even visits by overseas businesspeople. The lesson for the American was that in arranging the meeting he should have mentioned that he would be 'bringing a small gift.'"[49]

Communicating Through Gifts

In Japan gift-giving is an important part – even a necessity – for establishing and maintaining relationships – especially in business. The Japanese have essentially institutionalized the custom of giving gifts. Kato and Kato in their book, *Understanding and Working with the Japanese Business World,* have said that gift-giving for a Tokyo business person is akin to the business lunch of a New Yorker. It has been noted that the Japanese business person often will keep a record of the gifts that have been given *and* received.

They explain that, "Japanese gift-giving practices express basic Japanese cultural traits. *Wa* is promoted by long-term, stable relationships. Gift giving buttresses these relationships. Who gives what to whom and when is rarely a matter of happenstance, but is entirely predictable by reference to long-standing custom. In other words, like so many other factors in Japanese life, gift giving has been refined and ritualized over a long period of time."

So, it is important to note that when doing business with Japanese counterparts, it's not only enough to extend an invitation to lunch, but that you should also consider giving a gift – it doesn't have to be expensive, but the gesture will demonstrate that you want to develop an ongoing relationship to be built over time.

—Hiroki Kato and Joan S. Kato, *Understanding and Working with the Japanese Business World* [50]

One final caveat about gift-giving: U.S. Americans planning to do business overseas should familiarize themselves with the U.S. Foreign Corrupt Practices Act. This legislation, which applies to all U.S.-based firms and U.S. employees of foreign firms, prohibits the offering or accepting of bribes, gifts of unusual value, or facilitation payments that are of more than nominal value or unusual in nature. For additional information, visit the U.S. Department of Commerce Web site and review their restrictions and stipulations written into the U.S. Code since the 1970s.[51]

WHEN IN ROME ...

The United States is among the very few nations of the world that levies strict fines and imprisonment for its citizens who engage in bribes or illegal facilitation payments. It is interesting to note, however, that societies in which these payments are accepted will share several cultural values.

- They are collective societies (relationship-centered that regard personal connections as paramount).
- They are hierarchical societies (power is limited to a few at the top who control resources and access to advancement).
- They are relaxed about time (strict schedules and adherence to rules are not the norm because rules are meant to be changed according to situation and expediency).[52]

This knowledge can serve the businessperson who is traveling overseas as a reminder that what is acceptable procedure in one culture may not be acceptable in another because of its cultural norms. Be prepared and know your company's policies and procedures *before* you get into an uncomfortable, and potentially illegal, situation.

LONG-TERM/SHORT-TERM ORIENTATION

Respect, trust, and harmony manifest themselves in other ways within culture. As we have seen in previous chapters, much of the research and writing regarding intercultural communication is culture-bound, coming from a Western perspective. Hofstede was well aware of this and found it necessary to add another dimension. A fellow researcher, Michael Bond, worked with Asian businesspeople in Hong Kong and came up with this cultural dimension for long-term orientation, called *Confucian Dynamism.* This dimension relates to a long-term versus short-term focus on life: The long-term focus includes persistence, maintaining order in relationships through status, thrift, and having a sense of shame. The short-term focus includes stability, saving face, respecting tradition, and giving favors and sharing gifts.[53] Table 4.1 lists a few of the more notable characteristics of long-term and short-term orientation societies.

Long-Term and Short-Term Orientation

LONG TERM	SHORT TERM
• Use resources sparingly.	• Keep up with the Joneses.
• Create large savings to invest in future.	• Save little money for investing.
• Be persistent when results are slow.	• Expect quick results.
• Respect what is virtuous.	• Seek what is true.

TABLE 4.1: Long Term Short Term Orientation

Confucian Dynamism can best be remembered by thinking of virtue. The teachings of Confucius (551 B.C.E. – 479 B.C.E.) were philosophical rather than religious. Drawing upon Chinese history, Confucius crafted four pragmatic premises:

- Stability of society based upon hierarchy (ruler-subject; father-son; older brother-younger-brother; husband-wife; senior friend-junior friend).
- Family as center of all social organizations (society is based on interdependence of all members and harmony must be sought).
- Virtuous and benevolent behavior toward others (Chinese Golden Rule: Do not treat others as you would not want to be treated yourself).
- Virtue regarding tasks (work hard, be patient, persevere, be thrifty and do nothing in excess).[54]

Values toward the long-term pole are more future-oriented and dynamic. Countries that tend to be more long-term oriented include China, Hong Kong, Japan, South Korea, Brazil, and India. Values that reflect a more short-term orientation (focus on past and present) are usually more static. Countries with short-term orientation include Pakistan, Nigeria, the Philippines, Canada, Great Britain, the United States, and New Zealand. This is demonstrated in the business world by the notion of reciprocity. As we have already discussed, part of the Asian way of developing and maintaining strong business relationships is through trust and mutual respect. Meetings serve the purpose of establishing the relationship. Taking time to get to know your clients is paramount to Asian ways of thinking; after all, how can you do business (which requires trust) with strangers? The following example highlights this concept of benevolence in establishing relationships. While Confucian philosophy did not originate in Japan, its influence has spread throughout Japan, other Asian countries, and the world.

First Meetings to Establish Harmony

From a Western perspective, business professionals often think that upon the first meeting with someone from the East, they will automatically start to 'talk business'.

This is not the case with many people because of the values and norms of society that place emphasis on establishing relationships first. For example, often it is the highest level executives who begin the connections. To a Western perspective (say you are from Germany and you are meeting with clients from Japan) you would probably want to 'get right down to it' and not 'waste time', after all, your highest ranking people are extremely busy. However, if you expect that the first meeting will focus on business dealings, you may be in for a surprise. The Japanese prefer to be polite and enter into an important business deal by discussing sports – or even your marital status and number of children! Both general and very personal questions help to establish the familiarity upon which they can build mutual respect and trust.

In Kato and Kato's book, *Understanding and Working with the Japanese Business World*, they say, "It is not that Americans do not also enjoy chatting before commencing substantive business discussions, but their attention span is limited to 5 or 10 minutes, after which they want to "get on with it...On the other hand, Japanese believe that they *are* getting on with it—"it" being the mutual establishment of personal credentials, in the absence of which they are extremely reluctant to progress to the next stage of commitment. In other words, what Americans view as collateral to doing business, Japanese view as falling squarely within the business agenda."

For those coming from a Western perspective where time is to be watched carefully and introductions are to be brief, you will need to be aware that it could take many meetings before the discussion of business even comes up – let alone a prospective transaction or contract! If you can be patient and hold back from 'charging ahead' with a business agenda but rather gently slide into a relationship agenda that will develop over time, you might be pleased over the long term to see just how well your business transactions become because of the sturdy foundation you build with your Eastern counterparts.

—Adapted from: Hiroki Kato and Joan S. Kato, *Understanding and Working with the Japanese Business World* [55]

While developing trust and mutual respect are vital to a healthy and successful business relationship in long-term orientation cultures, so is respect. To that end, meetings can often be formal and ritualistic with the purpose of demonstrating proper respect. This underscores the Confucian philosophy of maintaining the stability of society based upon hierarchy and through the establishment of solid relationships. Establishing trust and respect along with maintaining order in relationships through status are all essential components of long-term-oriented cultures.

CHAPTER SUMMARY

Whether bowing, shaking hands, grasping someone with a bear hug, or planting kisses on their cheeks, you're likely to encounter many different demonstrations of respect across cultures. This discussion of respect brings us full circle to the beginning of this chapter, where we talked about power and status and their connection to the ways in which we give and receive respect. We have looked at the importance of a culture's use of power in society. Some cultures display a hierarchy of power that is limited to just a few at the top who exercise control, while other cultures feature a flatter structure in which authority is spread out among many who are capable of making decisions. We have looked at how cultures view the roles of men and women and have examined the importance of achievement as a manifestation of doing and being. We have looked at how both long-term and short-term orientation can affect the social stability of a culture group. An understanding of these aspects of culture will provide some insight into cultural perspectives that are different from your own.

APPLICATIONS FOR CULTURAL DIMENSIONS IN THE GLOBAL MARKETPLACE

This section is a summary of the dimensions (or categories) of culture that we have discussed throughout this chapter. After each definition we offer several questions and then an example that demonstrates at least one way (among innumerable ways) to handle the intercultural encounter. As you read through each, picture that iceberg you read about in Chapter 1. It is easy enough to identify the behaviors above the waterline, but as the cliché makes clear, what you see is only the tip of the iceberg. Once you identify either your behaviors or those of others regarding these questions, take some time to consider what supports them from below: What are the values, beliefs, and attitudes that give meaning to the behaviors we can readily see? For these dimensions you may also consider discussing your responses with people in your learning team or work team.

AUTHORITY: ACHIEVED OR ASCRIBED

Authority is a form of power, control, and prestige that is either achieved or ascribed. In many cultures, status, power, and authority are achieved through individual effort and hard work. Organizations operating in cultures that emphasize earned status tend to operate with a flatter hierarchy, with authority and responsibility delegated to lower levels. Equality is valued. In non-egalitarian cultures, people are ascribed power because of social standing, education, wealth, or circumstances of birth. Structure in organizations that operate in such cultures is usually more traditional and hierarchical. Decision-making authority customarily rests on one or a few people at the top of each organizational structure. Inequality is not only accepted but expected as a condition of life.

Helpful Tips

What are your attitudes towards formality or informality in your workplace? Think about formality and informality with respect to status, names, self-disclosure, titles, and recognition of accomplishments. Do the organizations you work for or with expect the use of titles or honorifics (i.e., Dr., Mr., Ms., Director, or Vice President)? Do higher-ranking employees receive special privileges, such as designated parking, a separate dining room, or separate restrooms? Observing how others in the organization address one another can be instructive. Do people use first names in addressing those of higher rank? Observing and abiding by local customs can be helpful in establishing goodwill for newcomers and outsiders.

Questions to Ask Yourself Regarding Authority

Who has the authority and how is it displayed? What roles do people play? Are they formally established or informally observed? What are the workplace traditions that you observe? How should people who have different levels of status power interact with each other? Are they equal or unequal? How do people expect to be shown respect—through gifts, seating arrangements, proper titles, or recognition for hard work or accomplishments?

Final Thought

When you interact with people from other cultures, be aware of whether they expect to be treated with equality (and informality), and whether or not they are more comfortable with making their own decisions or not proceeding until they receive permission from someone in authority. Remember that statements made here about culture in general are not necessarily true for any particular individual.

ACHIEVEMENT: LIVE TO WORK OR WORK TO LIVE

When we think about culture's influence on success and achievement, we think about the importance placed on external (tangible) rewards versus internal (intangible) rewards. Is success measured by material gain and prestige, or is the focus on wealth cast in terms of good relationships with people at work and at home? Achievement-oriented cultures tend to favor competition over cooperation, making relationships in the workplace more difficult to develop and nurture.

Helpful Tips

Assess the importance that you place on your job. Think about the ways that you talk about your work to others and the significance that you place on what you do. Now think about how others view you and the work that you do. Observe your colleagues and discuss the importance of work to them. Ask how they balance professional and personal responsibilities. Not everyone approaches work in the same way you do.

Questions to Ask Yourself Regarding Achievement

- How should genuine achievement be rewarded? How do you define success? Are you more inclined to appreciate tangible rewards (money, position, material possessions) or do you value what is intangible (free time, friends)? Do you live to work or work to live?
- How competitive are you? What are your expectations for yourself and those who work with you? Do you hold others to the same standards you have set for yourself? Why or why not? How might this affect the way people respond to you in the workplace?
- Look for underlying meanings and reasons before passing judgment. Did your subordinate choose to stay home with a sick child rather than attend the important meeting with the Senior VP? Perhaps the decision to stay at home is rooted in a deep commitment to family over work
- Are you perplexed because an employee has family and friends visit them frequently during working hours? Often such behavior is tied to obligation and expectations of how family and friends care for each other.

Final Thought

When you interact with people from other cultures, be aware of whether they are *driven* or *driving*. The driven person may have cultural norms that dictate hard work and perseverance toward the visible attainment of specific goals, whereas the person who is driving may still be a hard worker but have a different perspective on life with a different emphasis on work-life balance. Remember that the statements made here about a culture in general are not necessarily true for particular individuals.

A CASE STUDY

BIG DOG SOFTWARE, INC. (ALSO KNOWN AS LA JOLLA SOFTWARE)

Todd Batey returned from lunch with high hopes for a productive afternoon. Two large, long-term projects had just been completed and this would be his opportunity to dig through that stack of unopened mail, deferred memos, file folders, journals, and magazines he simply hadn't had found time to read.

Among the larger, more important projects Batey had worked on during the past several months was a new product launch in the company's enterprise software division. At the same time, he had been working with Big Dog Software's senior team on a highly confidential and potentially profitable strategic alliance: Big Dog executives were targeting several Japanese firms for a joint venture that would permit the company to distribute its famous "S-4" supply chain management software in Japan and, perhaps, throughout much of Asia.

COMPANY BACKGROUND

Big Dog Software, Inc. is a small but rapidly growing firm located outside of Silicon Valley in LaJolla, California. This quirky back-bedroom start-up had grown from $8 in capital with no revenues just five years ago to a $150 million, publicly-held firm that specialized in enterprise software, customized applications, and innovative thinking in systems integration and supply-chain management. Chad Lucas and his college roommate, Joshua Flynn, had converted an interest in management information systems into a successful business long before most of their classmates had paid off their college loans.

Virtually all of their efforts had been internal, however. Lucas and Flynn hired half-a-dozen of the smartest young programmers and systems engineers in Southern California and began developing a product line. Perhaps their brightest move was to hire Todd Batey, a recent Santa Clara grad who specialized in marketing. Piece by piece, the team of Lucas and Flynn had put together a very strong business, but now things were beginning to move much more quickly. If they were to take advantage of the window of opportunity now open in Asia, they would need more than bright programmers and a young marketing director. They would need a business partner who knew the territory.

OPPORTUNITY KNOCKS

As Batey tossed his soft drink cup in the recycling bin, one of the interns stuck her head in Todd's cubicle. "Chad and Josh need to see you."

"What's up?" he asked.

"No clue," she replied. "I just know something's happening and you're next on the agenda."

Batey grabbed his Palm Pilot and headed down the hallway. With just 75 employees, Big Dog Software didn't take up much space: two floors of a modern office building where Torrey Pines Road meets I-5. On a nice day (and they were almost all nice) you could see Pacific Beach from the windows in Batey's cubicle. Not much privacy, but a great view.

Batey walked into Chad Lucas's office without knocking. Formality was about as common around Big Dog Software as neckties. "You need to see me?" he asked.

"Hey, Todd," came the reply, "have a seat."

"We just got a fax from Masahiro," said Lucas. "Our endless series of trips to Tokyo has finally paid off." The fax in question was from Masahiro Fudaba, a Senior Vice President with Ichi Ban Heavy Industries of Japan.

"Really?" asked Batey.

"Finally," said Flynn. "We're going into partnership with Ichi Ban to form a joint venture. Their shareholders, business partners, bankers, and Keiretsu executives have finally bought off on the deal." He paused for a just a moment. "Looks like the Big Dog is going to Japan."

"First, though, we're going to have some Japanese visitors," said Lucas. "The word from Masahiro is that Kazushi Yakura and a team of eight Japanese managers will be here next week to begin the process of organizing our new, jointly-owned company. Apparently Mr. Yakura will be here for just a few days. The transition team, however, is planning to stay until we have all the details worked out."

"How can I help?" asked Batey.

"Well," said Flynn, "we're engineers. You're the marketing guy, so we figured you would be the logical person to help make these folks feel welcome."

"More to the point," said Lucas, "we need to help the people on Ichi Ban's transition team understand a bit more about us. They know our business, our market, and our industry, but I'm not sure how much these guys know about the U.S., about California, or about doing business with Americans. According to Masahiro," he added, "only Mr. Yakura has been to the United States. Most of the others have never been out of Japan."

"Interesting," said Batey. "What else do we know about them?"

"Here's a list of people they've identified for the visit," said Lucas. "We have ages, job titles, and a little bit of background, including education and prior work experience, but not much else."

"What do you want them to know?" asked Batey.

"It's clear to me that we have to reduce their anxieties, eliminate their fears, and raise the level of mutual trust," said Flynn. "I know that you understand something about intercultural communication, so we'll leave the details up to you." He paused for a moment, and then said. "Let's make it more than a Padres' game and a day at the zoo."

"No problem," said Batey. "I'll have a preliminary plan worked up for you by the close of business tomorrow."

Lucas and Flynn thanked the young marketing manager and expressed complete confidence in his ability to make the Japanese managers' visit productive and successful. Todd left Lucas's office and, heading down the hallway, thought to himself, "No problem? Maybe there is a problem here. What are we gonna' do with these guys?"

QUESTIONS

1. Assume that your cubicle is near Todd Batey's and he has asked you for some advice on this subject. What would you say to him?
2. What objectives or measurable outcomes should Batey specify for his immersion into American culture for these visitors?
3. What American concepts can you safely assume these managers know and understand? What concepts do you think they *absolutely must* understand in order for the joint venture to succeed?
4. How would you go about showing them what the United States is all about? Where would you take them? What would you show them?
5. How can you be sure what your visitors will understand when they're ready to go home?
6. What sort of budget would you need for this program?
7. How much do you suppose other Big Dog employees understand about Japan and Japanese culture? Should any of them be

involved in your effort to introduce North America to your new Asian business partners?

8. Will your business contact expect to be granted appropriate respect based on his or her position in the organization or will he or she downplay his or her position, opting for a more egalitarian approach?

9. Who will make the final decision, the senior ranking official or his or her associates?

10. What are the different levels of authority within your organization and your business contacts? Can people of differing ranks interact and negotiate directly, or must a higher authority review their offers?

11. How will certain verbal and nonverbal cues differ in U.S. and Asian cultures? How can you tell for sure when someone is really saying "no"?

12. What other cross-cultural issues (dimensions) should your team consider in anticipation of their arrival?

Source: This case was prepared by James S. O'Rourke, Concurrent Associate Professor of Management, as the basis for class discussion rather than to illustrate either effective or ineffective handling of an administrative situation. Copyright ©2000. Eugene D. Fanning Center for Business Communication.

CHAPTER 5

Applications for Intercultural Communication

Two iron rules of international business are:
#1 In international business, the seller adapts to the buyer.
#2 In international business, the visitor is expected to
observe local customs. [1]

—Richard R. Gesteland

INTRODUCTION

The purpose of this book has been to provide a series of snapshots about some of the most fundamental dimensions of culture, including context, identity, learning, environment, change, time, authority, and achievement. That's an admittedly long list, but one you must be aware of in order to do business in other cultures. We have talked about the importance of developing an awareness of our own cultural influences and how these values, beliefs, attitudes, and behaviors affect how we communicate in the global marketplace. We have compared some of the contextual differences in how people communicate—whether through primary focus on verbal or nonverbal codes. We have examined how we view our personal identity in relation to group identity and how we, as humans who are part of specific cultural groups, relate and respond to the environment. We have explored some of the norms associated with perception and expression of power.

James Downs once wrote, "One of the greatest stumbling blocks to understanding other peoples within or without a particular culture is the tendency to judge others' behavior by our own standards."[2] As we saw in Chapter 1, it is human nature to harbor an egocentric or ethnocentric view of the world: We accept what is familiar and safe as we mentally process unfamiliar information, make generalizations, and reject what is unfamiliar. If we are to become interculturally competent as businesspeople in a global marketplace, however, we must develop both an awareness of how others perceive and embrace the world, as well as the ability to interact with such people and their differences successfully.

With this awareness comes a responsibility to act and interact appropriately. How do we act appropriately unless we know where to begin? To begin to understand different cultural norms (the accepted and expected ways of behaving), we have outlined some of the intercultural phenomena that distinguish cultures from one another, which we have defined as the "hidden dimensions" (or, what we *don't* see below the waterline). We have talked about how, in order to make sense of different situations, we create schemata or mental images that help us sort out what is confusing. While we may generalize based on these broad categories (which we have defined in the preceding chapters) we should, nevertheless, consider each intercultural interaction as unique. We must consider the complexity of each situation and context, and realize that it is up to us to make what is hidden more visible as we try to understand the people with whom we live and work. In the preceding four chapters we have sought to bring awareness to the surface. This final chapter will focus on some practical applications, putting the ideas and examples we have discussed to work.

Our goal has been to provide you with a framework for thinking about intercultural communication in the global marketplace, starting with several dimensions of culture to build your awareness. The task now is to put this awareness into practice, counteracting the perfectly normal human tendency toward ethnocentric thinking.

This final chapter begins by looking at intercultural communication problems and solutions, including several stumbling blocks to effective communication and how we might reconcile cultural dilemmas. Then, we'll briefly review our dimensions of culture—context, identity, learning, environment, change, time, authority, and power/achievement. This chapter is meant to be reflective—an accumulation of all of the thoughts you've gathered while reading and discussing these intercultural concepts. The cases at the end of this chapter are also meant to be reflective and are composite sketches of many of the dimensions we have discussed. These cases have been selected for their richness and complexity of cross-cultural issues at many different levels and provide useful summaries of the concepts presented throughout this book. We encourage you to use this final chapter as a springboard for more inquiry and discussion, especially as it relates to current or future business interactions across cultures.

CHALLENGES AND SOLUTIONS

STUMBLING BLOCKS TO INTERCULTURAL COMMUNICATION

LaRay Barna, Professor Emerita of Communication at Portland State University, was one of the first pioneers of intercultural communication. She identified a number of stumbling blocks to intercultural communication, which we will examine as we conclude our discussion here. [3] These six stumbling blocks include

- Assumptions of Similarities
- Language Differences
- Nonverbal Misinterpretations
- Preconceptions and Stereotypes
- Tendency to Evaluate
- High Anxiety

We will look first at what these stumbling blocks are and follow with a discussion of Fons Trompenaars' ideas associated with reconciling intercultural differences.

Speaking of Culture

Human beings draw close to one another by their common nature, but habits and customs keep them apart.

—Confucius [4]

ASSUMPTIONS OF SIMILARITIES

Can you remember a time when you encountered a new situation, whether starting a new job, moving to an unfamiliar city or neighborhood, becoming active in a new professional or civic association or even just signing up for a membership in a new gym? Among the things you probably did first was to look for someone familiar to make that initial connection to ease the awkward transition. It is what we do as the "new kid on the block:" We look for people who are most like us. This is human nature because, in order to assuage our nervousness regarding uncertainty, we need to find familiar ground, something like getting our bearings or "sea legs." Although this is a natural part of humanity, when applied to cross-cultural situations, it can prove problematic. One of the most common stumbling blocks to intercultural communication is that we make *assumptions of similarities*. We assume that what we say or do, think or believe, is shared by everyone, which is a form of ethnocentrism. For example, one of the biggest mistakes for English speakers (whether from Canada, the United States, or Australia) is to assume that since English is the most popular and sought-after language of business, everyone naturally speaks English. Another example is the frequent assumption that other countries have the same amenities that we are accustomed to in our homelands. For example, in the United States, U.S. Americans expect to have hotels complete with private bathroom, air-conditioning, television, and popular fast-food restaurant chains readily available with familiar food. This is not the case when traveling abroad. Often hotels will not have private baths, air-conditioning is not standard, and even a Big Mac or a Coke *will* taste different.

For an example that could have more far-reaching consequences than simply not enjoying your room or food "just like home," we could turn to the significant ritual of exchanging business cards with the Japanese. In the United States it is customary to hand out business cards to just about anyone who asks for one. Most people, after shaking hands and greeting someone, will quickly find a place to stash the card—the focus is on the interpersonal interaction and not much thought is given to that small piece of cardstock. Unless you are aware of cultural practices regarding the ritual of business card exchanges in other cultures, you will probably assume that all cultures simply shake (or bow), greet, and put away the card. Not so. As explained in Chapter 4, simply putting the card away would be a big mistake in Asian cultures such as Japan, where the exchange of business cards *(meishi)* is a ritual and demonstrates respect for the status of others. *How* you receive and hold the business card as well as *where* you place it (never in a wallet or back pocket) have significant meanings and are potential stumbling blocks for communicating goodwill. Simply taking the card and placing it in your pocket would be a bad omen and signal a lack of respect for or trust with your Asian counterpart. You would unintentionally insult them, and this faux pas could have negative consequences on any business transaction you are conducting.

You won't find any cookbook of communication recipes that will help you to communicate perfectly in all intercultural encounters by providing you with prescriptive do's and don'ts for the customs and rituals in any given culture. Our goal is to help you be aware of possible differences that will surely occur. We hope that you will learn more about the specifics of the cultures in which you will interact so you put into practice what you have learned.

Language Differences

Another common stumbling block is to assume that similar words have similar meanings in different cultures. George Bernard Shaw (among others) is thought to have said, "England and America are two great nations separated by a common language."[5] He may have been right. In the United States, for example, business leaders will speak about the "exciting changes" happening in their organizations. Using this term with business leaders in Great Britain may bring you some quizzical looks since people use this word in connection with things that children rather than adults might do (e.g., "The children's trip to the zoo was exciting.")[6] Or, in Latin countries, what U.S. Americans call soccer is known as football. If an associate in Great Britain were to say, "A couple of messages, sir. Miss Norris called this morning, saying she'd like to speak with you," a U.S. American would assume that was a phone call. A British subject would more properly assume that Miss Norris appeared in person. Had she phoned in, your associate would have said she "rang." While these particular examples of differences in word usage would not necessarily lead to hard feelings during an intercultural encounter, they do highlight the opportunity for misunderstanding if you are not astute enough to check for clarification of meanings while communicating.

Other mishaps could damage your reputation with advertising campaigns that are not carefully researched. One legendary advertising debacle was the 1965 Pepsi-Cola campaign urging readers to "Come alive with the Pepsi Generation." In the Taiwanese market, however, that slogan translated as, "Pepsi brings your ancestors back from the grave." Since there is a strong following of Shintoistic beliefs where ancestors are revered and worshiped, the meaning in this translation was not only confusing but insulting to many people. Pepsi's competitor, Coca-Cola, has had its share of translation problems as well. Since Chinese is a tonal language, the phonetic equivalent in Chinese / ko-kou-ko-le / is translated as "bite the wax tadpole." A careful review of more than 40,000 Chinese characters with a better phonetic translation produced a better slogan / ke-kou-ke-le /, which more appropriately meant "happiness in the mouth."

Speaking of Culture

Be cautious in asking an Indonesian Chinese a question. English speakers would give a negative answer to the question "Isn't my order ready yet?" by responding, "No." (Meaning, "No, it's not ready."). The Chinese pattern is the opposite: "Yes" (meaning, "Yes, it is not ready.").

—Terry Morrison, Wayne A. Conaway and George A. Borden,
Kiss, Bow, or Shake Hands [7]

We must always be aware that what we say may have different connotations in another language and culture. It is important to obtain expert, local advice; perform clarification checks: asking directly or observing indirectly the reactions of conversation partners. Most importantly, keep your sense of humor and don't be afraid to laugh at yourself (but never at someone else because of the importance of saving face). Don't be reluctant to apologize for a misstatement. Showing humility and a sense of humor can produce goodwill as you use the language and customs of another culture.

NONVERBAL MISINTERPRETATIONS

Nonverbal mishaps are among the most common stumbling blocks to intercultural communication. We are often unaware of our facial expressions or gestures as we use them, especially if we've been raised in a low-context culture. Roger Axtell is a former vice president of worldwide marketing for the Parker Pen Company who spent more than thirty years living and working abroad. He captured his experiences in several best-selling books that illustrate specific differences in cultural behavior around the world. "Gestures pack the power to punctuate, to dramatize, to speak a more colorful language than mere words," he writes. "You may discover that . . . innocent winks and well-meaning nods are anything but universal."[8]

For example, a familiar gesture using the thumb and forefinger to form a circle will mean "OK" in the United States, while in Latin American cultures, along with those in Russia and Arab countries, it is considered an obscene gesture. In Japan it means "money," and in France, "worthless."[9] The most common affect display, the smile, has numerous cultural norms attached to it. In the United States, it can be considered appropriate in many areas of the country to smile and look at someone you do not know (either male-to-female or vice versa). In Asian or Arab cultures, however, a female making eye contact and smiling at a man would hint of innuendo. Another common form of nonverbal confusion is whether to kiss, bow, or shake hands.[10] Naturally, each culture has its own way of demonstrating a welcome, and because touch and personal space come into play, there is great potential for mishaps and misunderstanding. In Western cultures it is customary to shake hands while maintaining a comfortable distance; in Asian cultures one bows (and *how* one does this depends on status and superiority); in Latin cultures one gives an *abrazo*, or strong hug; in French culture it is customary to greet one another with a light kiss on each cheek.

Speaking of Culture

In Moscow, restaurant employees had to be specially trained to smile in the friendly McDonald's way because Russians do not feel comfortable smiling at strangers.

—Richard R. Gesteland, *Cross-Cultural Business Behavior* [11]

To that end, it's good to have an idea of what behavior is most common and how gender, age, and status might affect the reactions you receive. You need not sit on your hands when interacting with people from other cultures, nor is it necessary to know every type of gesture and their variations in meaning. It *is* necessary, however, to understand that the meanings we attach to certain gestures are symbolic and will evoke different meanings in different cultures.[12]

Speaking of Culture

The causes of friction in communication between two cultures lie not in the shortcomings of either culture but rather in their interaction.

—*John C. Condon and Fathi S. Yousef, An Introduction to Intercultural Communication* [13]

PRECONCEPTIONS AND STEREOTYPES

In Chapter 1, we examined a cognitive process known as *stereotyping*, in which we develop mental categories or schemata that help us to make sense of unfamiliar behavior and align it with our own frame of reference. Creating mental categories can be a positive process to help us identify and respond to unfamiliar behavior, but it may become counterproductive if we then judge all members of a group or class by the characteristics or behaviors we observe in just one or a few. Stereotyping is the final stumbling block to intercultural communication.

Our aim all along is to provide broad exposure to various dimensions of culture in order to foster insight and encourage understanding of intercultural communication and interaction, rather than to provide a comprehensive checklist of cultural do's and don'ts. Think of our examples as signposts along the trail as you embark on your journey with intercultural communication. Not all trails have the same signposts. If we visit a national park for a hike, depending on what part of the country and what type of park it is, there inevitably will be different markers along the path. The examples we have used in this chapter will provide the foundation for our discussion of the various stumbling blocks to intercultural communication and will illustrate various negative, neutral, and positive generalizations. For example, while some U.S. Americans might assume that there will be McDonald's or Burger King restaurant in most other countries, others will not. To say that all U.S. Americans are culturally illiterate is a gross generalization and, therefore, a negative stereotype. To say that *all* Japanese will *always* bow and will *certainly* be offended if you don't do so correctly would also be a stereotype—but it's neutral rather than negative, since there are no harmful meanings associated with it. A more positive stereotype would be the assertion that *all* Brazilians will give you a big, squeezing hug, or *abrazo*, upon meeting you. A hug is usually a positive interaction, showing warmth and affection between friends, but not all Brazilians will hug in every circumstance. Keeping an open mind about this and seeking clarification about an *individual*'s expectations and behaviors can turn a potential stumbling block into a stepping stone.

Just Say No To Stereotypes!

At this point as a review, you might want to re-examine Milton Bennett's "Stages for Intercultural Sensitivity" (see Chapter 1) and think of an example for each of those six stages from your own experience. The stages are: denial, defense, minimization, acceptance, adaptation and integration. Now that you are more aware of the hidden dimensions of culture, how might you do things differently next time a similar situation arises?

As you talk with others, analyze what you say and pinpoint the attitudes that motivate your comments. For example, what sort of stereotypes do you find useful? When do you use them? Can you think of a recent incident when you stereotyped someone or something? Remember, stereotypes can be positive, neutral, or negative.

What are your perceptions of others? What behaviors make you uncomfortable? What beliefs or attitudes to do you attach to them? How can you move more toward an understanding of the attitudes that motivate others' behaviors?

Assumptions of similarities, language differences, nonverbal misinterpretations, and stereotypes are just a few of the stumbling blocks that can hinder our journey as we seek to understand the ways and behaviors of people from other cultures. But stumbling blocks are not the end of the road; they *can* be overcome. We have to remain alert to potential potholes and obstacles, and maintain the agility to step over and around them with finesse.

TENDENCY TO EVALUATE

As we have talked about ethnocentrism, as human beings we have the tendency to jump to conclusion and even judge others based upon what is familiar to us and our familiar "in-groups". We approve or disapprove of ideas, values, beliefs, and practices based upon how others act or communicate. If we can work hard at being 'mindful' of our thoughts, then we can catch ourselves when we make hasty generalizations or value judgments of others. It's when we base everyone or everything else on our standards that we can stumble with our intercultural communication.

For example, I once conducted some research in southern Spain. When I arrived in Seville, I found the way to my hotel and being a beautiful day, I immediately wanted to set out and explore. But it was about 4pm in the afternoon and no one was around. I knew that this was typical of countries where the majority of people close shop for the afternoon and spend several hours with family over their main meal of the day and/or take a nap. But I wasn't prepared for *how* deserted it was. I enjoyed my time exploring but it wasn't as fun because there were few people around – I like the hustle and bustle of daily activities and the interaction with others. Later – probably around 8pm-9pm – was when people ventured out to sit in the square and eat dinner, listen to music, or watch their children play football on the sidewalk. If I were not aware of this, I could become frustrated or angry at the shopkeeper who was closed during the afternoon when I needed to buy some bottled water. Why wasn't *she* around? Was she taking a nap and neglecting her duties? And, why is it that people from other cultures do things *backwards*? After all, *we* have business hours during the day (and even into the evening) when people are out and about. If we can resist evaluating someone else or an entire group of people based upon our norms and practices, we will be open to the effectiveness of understanding what time and business and family means to people who are different than us.

HIGH ANXIETY

Also connected to people, places, and customs is anxiety. This is because people and their customs are different and the lack of clarity of what things mean and why people do things the way that they do brings uncertainty. It is natural to want events, interactions, and situations to be certain – to not have uncertainty as Geertz Hofstede calls it. Social psychologists tell us that we develop our sense of self within our families, circles of friends, and communities, yet we develop anxiety with uncertain situations and environments. It simply takes more time and emotional energy to 'figure things out'.

With anxiety comes physiological reactions – we can worry and develop all sorts of ailments in response to our stress. We can become defensive, or withdraw, or even react in hostile ways towards people. If we think about it – using stereotypes is a defensive mechanism that helps us to release the anxiety that we fear of the unknown. When we are defensive, we feel threatened and we find ways to help us cope. Often this anxiety follows a pattern of cultural adaptation called 'culture shock.'

With culture shock, there is a four stage emotional roller coaster that is said to occur upon interaction with difference over a length of time. In the first stage as a sojourner, everything is new and exciting. This is the honeymoon stage where you are positive about the culture and you embrace everything as exotic. However, in the withdrawal stage, you experience cultural differences on a daily basis and what was once exotic and exhilarating becomes frustrating and unpredictable. Under stress you react negatively and begin to dislike the culture. After a time of withdrawal emotionally (and perhaps physically from interacting with people) you become acclimated to your new environment and settle into a daily routine. This is the adjustment stage. Perhaps you've made some friends, become more accustomed to people's behavior and you venture out once again, breaking your isolation. Finally, in the last stage, you have enthusiasm for the culture and its people and you begin to feel like you can function in the environment – and even enjoy it.

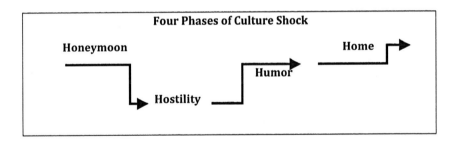

The thing to remember about culture shock is that we all go through it at one point or another. And just because we've gone through it once doesn't mean that we'll be immune to it in the future! It will happen again, and again, and again! Whenever we encounter difference there is ambiguity and uncertainty, and with that often anxiety and/or discomfort. Realizing that this is a natural human occurrence can go a long way in assuring us we are experiencing the natural ebb and flow of human interaction and emotion.

DEVELOPING INTERCULTURAL COMPETENCE

As we move toward intercultural competence by turning stumbling blocks into stepping stones, we must consider three specific skill sets: an awareness of cultural differences, respect for those differences, and the ability to reconcile them.[14]

AWARENESS OF CULTURAL DIFFERENCES

It would be naïve to say that all intercultural misunderstandings could be avoided if only we were aware of the differences. Still, we have to start somewhere. Our discussions have done just this by examining various cultural dimensions and providing examples for each. Understanding the many intricacies of human interaction is difficult, but we can begin with the basics by understanding the *states of mind* [15] or *programming of the mind*.[16] You now understand a number of different cultural dimensions that will permit you to assess how the people of various cultures believe, think, and behave. Understanding the motivation for your own values, beliefs, attitudes, and behaviors will provide you with the ability to compare them with those of people from other cultures. Most of what we believe, and certainly much of what motivates our behavior, is not immediately self-evident. A good deal of it is where we have always said: below the waterline. Awareness is the first step in understanding and reconciling those differences that separate us from the inhabitants of other cultures.

Identifying Values

This exercise is about exploration. It might help to reference a current or previous situation or encounter with someone in your learning team or work team.

Values are the most basic and fundamental, unmovable tenets that make us who we are and which shape all other structures in our attitudinal system, a psychological assessment of the things, those concepts, those ideas we hold dear.

Think about some of the common values shared by members of your culture (e.g., freedom, self-reliance, group consensus, spirituality). Then do the same for another culture. Consider potential points of conflict or discord.

My Cultural Values	Values of Culture A	Values of Culture B	Differences

Now rank the priority of the values across cultures. What does this tell you about yourself? What might this tell you about someone from another culture? Discuss these priorities with your peers/coworkers and talk about what is culturally important to each of you regarding culture. What assumptions have you made? How might these assumptions affect your interaction with someone from a different culture?

RESPECTING CULTURAL DIFFERENCES

As we discussed in Chapter 1, our goal is to move away from a self-centered view of intercultural issues toward an *other*-centered perspective. Rather than *denying* that there are any differences, being *defensive* about the actions and behaviors of others, or trying to *minimize* differences as merely superficial, we must work toward *integrating* or recognizing and understanding differences by being adaptive. The goal is to *empathize* with others as we learn to *accept* and explore the many differences (some good, some not) that exist.[17] It is better to assume differences rather than similarities so that we can proceed cautiously, keeping an open mind, taking in feedback, and seeking understanding. Once we're aware of and have some understanding of fundamental differences, the next step is to demonstrate an openness to learning about the business customs and practices of others. This, in turn, can lead to the establishment of credibility and identification of common ground.

RECONCILING CULTURAL DIFFERENCES

There are many practical ways to reconcile cultural dilemmas. Once we are aware of the differences and have developed both respect and empathy for the ways of others, we can take practical steps to bridge the gap toward better—not perfect or flawless, but better—understanding and more successful interactions. Saint Ambrose's admonition to St. Augustine of Hippo, "When in Rome, do as the Romans do," is basically good advice. If we're genuinely interested in doing business globally, whether we go abroad and become the foreigner, or welcome others who come to us, we should be responsible for taking the initiative to learn about other cultural practices. We can familiarize ourselves with the hidden dimensions of culture and begin to learn even more about specific cultural attributes. We can look inward for those natural ethnocentric perspectives that we each hold and be willing to alter them, trying to put things into perspective from someone else's viewpoint rather than our own. We can look for assumptions and seek clarification about our own communication and behaviors. We can keep an open mind so that we're less evaluative, judging others less by those norms and standards that make sense only to us.

By doing so, we have a much better chance of treating others as individuals and not as stereotypical caricatures of another cultural group. We can reverse the situation and try to put ourselves in *their* shoes, thinking about the assumptions and stereotypes that they may have of *us*. Most importantly, we can be flexible by keeping our sense of humor, even in the midst of ambiguous situations. If we are open-minded, rather than defensive, and seek to understand our business counterparts—sincerely expressing this desire—we can open many doors, developing the potential for trust and healthy intercultural business relationships.

REVIEW: DIMENSIONS OF CULTURE

It is human nature to make assumptions about other people's actions and behaviors based upon what we know or assume to be the "right" way of doing things. Our various cultures dictate the norms of any given group and provide us with our beliefs, values, attitudes, and behaviors. These norms, or unstated rules, are the accepted and expected ways of behaving and interacting with other people. Culture is something that we learn—from infancy on we are conditioned and learn about how people in our "world" do things from watching them, conversing with them, and interacting with them.

The following (Table 5.1) is a summary of the various cultural dimensions that have been discussed in this book. You may want to use these as a springboard for discussion with your peers/coworkers about any personal intercultural encounters that you have experienced. As always, our goal is *not* to make gross overgeneralizations about any one culture or cultures but to merely define key dimensions that every culture possesses. These ideas are supported by leading anthropologists, interculturalists, and sociologists and are placed on a continuum that is intended to allow people to reflect on the degree to which they have experienced these aspects of intercultural encounters.

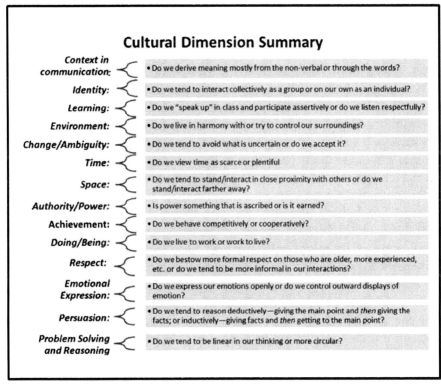

Cultural Dimension Summary

Context in communication:	• Do we derive meaning mostly from the non-verbal or through the words?
Identity:	• Do we tend to interact collectively as a group or on our own as an individual?
Learning:	• Do we "speak up" in class and participate assertively or do we listen respectfully?
Environment:	• Do we live in harmony with or try to control our surroundings?
Change/Ambiguity:	• Do we tend to avoid what is uncertain or do we accept it?
Time:	• Do we view time as scarce or plentiful
Space:	• Do we tend to stand/interact in close proximity with others or do we stand/interact farther away?
Authority/Power:	• Is power something that is ascribed or is it earned?
Achievement:	• Do we behave competitively or cooperatively?
Doing/Being:	• Do we live to work or work to live?
Respect:	• Do we bestow more formal respect on those who are older, more experienced, etc. or do we tend to be more informal in our interactions?
Emotional Expression:	• Do we express our emotions openly or do we control outward displays of emotion?
Persuasion:	• Do we tend to reason deductively—giving the main point and *then* giving the facts; or inductively—giving facts and *then* getting to the main point?
Problem Solving and Reasoning	• Do we tend to be linear in our thinking or more circular?

Table 5.1: Cultural Dimensions Summary

CHAPTER SUMMARY

The quote at the beginning of this chapter, which acknowledges that sellers should adapt to buyers, and visitors should observe local customs in the global marketplace, helps us connect with the central point throughout this text: developing strong intercultural communicative competence means that we have to open our eyes to the tacit differences (hidden dimensions) of intercultural encounters in order to understand *why* we want to say something, *what* to say, *how* to say it, *when* it is an appropriate time to say it, and to *whom* we should say it. If we are to be effective as intercultural communicators, we must first understand ourselves and then act on that understanding as we share similar meanings in our interactions with others. We must be aware of our own cultures: the values, beliefs, attitudes, and behaviors based on our family and social relationships. We must also be aware of the power relationships that exist in national culture. Understanding how our nonverbal behavior can affect our interactions is a first step. People have different ways of processing and organizing information, and we must be open to and patient with these ways of interaction. Finally, we must understand that there are many different views of how we, as humans, should interact with the world and deal with change and uncertainty. Being aware of these differing viewpoints and then *acting* on this knowledge and learning from our experiences can help us to improve our communicative competence.

Culture might well be compared to the Great Wall of China. It is expansive and seemingly goes on forever, far beyond what the human eye can see. There are many parts to it as it twists and winds its way throughout the landscape, and it would surely take many visits for you to feel as if you had grasped even a portion of its magnificence. What we have attempted to do here is to introduce you to the Wall of Culture by taking several snapshots of various important parts that will give you a limited but useful sense of its splendor.[18] Our goal has been to provide you with a framework for thinking about intercultural communication in the global marketplace so that you can place these snapshots together to get the big picture. We have presented a number of pictures from different angles to give you an idea of the major themes and dimensions that characterize intercultural communication in order to build your awareness. The task now is to put this awareness into practice, counteracting the normal human tendency toward ethnocentric thinking. The rest is up to you: to take your own journey to explore other cultures and see where they take you. We encourage you to write your own stories to record, share, and compare with your colleagues as you become more aware of the many hidden dimensions of intercultural communication that lie behind every human interaction.

A CASE STUDY

CANWALL PAPER, LTD.: CANADIAN AND CHINESE NEGOTIATIONS

A Canadian team of two men representing Canwall, a wallpaper printing equipment manufacturer, went to a town north of Shanghai in the province of Jiangsu, China, to negotiate a sale to a new wallpaper production company. Charlie Burton, president of Canwall, traveled with his marketing director, Phil Raines. The company had never before sold its equipment outside Canada, and the two Canadians were delighted with the warm reception they enjoyed in China.

This wasn't the first meeting between the Canadian company and the Chinese wallpaper factory. The manager of the Chinese company, Mr. Li, had been a member of a delegation to Canada. He had met with one of Canwall's senior salespersons and the director of manufacturing. Subsequently, a trade representative from Canada had been in China representing Canwall's interests to the Chinese manager. After these meetings and numerous letters and faxes, Canwall's top people were now ready to negotiate the sale.

The day they arrived they were met at the airport in Shanghai by manager Li himself and transported in a chauffeur-driven car 90 miles to the town. Their accommodation was in a newly built hotel, and while it was not luxurious, it was certainly comfortable. A few hours after their arrival, they were treated to a 12-course banquet given by their host, with several high-level municipal officials present. This red-carpet treatment made them feel optimistic about the sale.

The next day they were taken to see the sights nearby: a large, new port for container ships and several factories that indicted the prosperity of the region. They were eager to begin discussing the sale, but after lunch they were given time to rest. In the late afternoon one of the manager's English-speaking employees came by with the news they would be taken to see a local dance company's performance that night.

The third day they finally sat down to meetings. Progress seemed very slow—each side giving generalizations about itself that seemed unrelated to the sale. The Canadians used an interpreter, supplied by the Chinese, who was eager to please them, so the Canadians felt comfortable with her, but translation slowed down communication. Their interpreter seemed to be unfamiliar with technological terms since she and the interpreter from the factory spent some time discussing the terms between themselves. After listening to various apparently unrelated points, the

Canadians thought, "So what?" The Chinese also spent a lot of time talking about the Canadian trade agent who had been in their town earlier. Burton wasn't able to tell them much about that person, since he had never met him personally.

When the Canadians at last were able to make the presentation they had prepared, they were surprised at the number of people who showed up. There were two of them, but there were ten Chinese facing them across the table. Still, the Chinese frequently nodded and smiled, and said yes. Burton and Raines had prepared sales data and showed—effectively, they thought—that within five years the factory could double its present production. At the end of the day, the jubilant Canadians returned to their hotel rooms confident they had sold the equipment.

The next day they were asked to explain once again things they thought had been covered already to a Chinese team with four new faces in it. They were confused about who their negotiating counterparts really were. Their jubilation began to evaporate. They were asked to explain the technology in minute detail. Neither Burton nor Raines had been involved in the engineering of the high-tech component that was the heart of the equipment. After doing the best they could, they returned to the hotel exhausted.

The next day, the Canwell negotiators were asked again about the technological details of the equipment. This time one member of the first-day team pointed out discrepancies between what they had said and what the manufacturing director, an engineer, had told them in Canada. Burton and Raines were chagrined. The Chinese were reproachful about the discrepancies, as if the Canadians had been caught in a shameful act. At lunchtime the two Canadians quickly faxed Canada for specifications and explanations. The afternoon session was uncomfortable although everyone was polite. Burton and Raines were a bit unsettled when a middle-aged woman suddenly burst into the negotiating room and whispered in the ear of one of the key Chinese speakers, who immediately got up and left the room. The Canadians expected some explanation for the emergency, but none ever came.

The next day, because of the time difference, the Canadians received some of the documentation they needed by fax, and discussions resumed with the same questions being asked yet again. It all went very slowly. The Chinese appreciated the high quality of the Canadian product but worried they wouldn't be able to fix the equipment if it broke down. They suggested (delicately, so as not to imply they *expected* breakdowns) that perhaps the Canadians could give them some help with maintenance training. The Canadians pointed out the expense and difficulty of keeping someone in their city for several weeks or months and expressed confidence that there wouldn't be any problems the manual didn't cover. The Chinese would be able to look after the equipment just fine.

Finally, the technical discussions gave way to the issue central to most negotiations in most countries: price. This proved to be the most difficult of all. The Chinese began by asking for a 20 percent price discount. The Canadians thought this was a simply outrageous negotiating ploy; they stuck to their price, which they knew to be fair, and offered a 3 percent discount on the printing cylinders.

Although Burton and Raines had heard that negotiations took time in China, they had thought a week would be ample. Now time was running out and they were due in Beijing in two days. They already had learned that getting plane tickets wasn't easy, so they were anxious to be on the plane as previously arranged. The Canadians began to ask pointed questions about what the Chinese were unhappy with and in which areas they needed to review issues again. During the last two sessions, the Canadians tried to get the Chinese to focus on the unresolved points, but the Chinese seemed reluctant to do so.

A number of issues remained unresolved when the farewell banquet was held the following noon. The question of price seemed near solution, but not the method of payment. That was the final apparently insurmountable hurdle since the Chinese couldn't guarantee the payment schedule; it seemed tied to deadlines and requirements of the municipal officials. Nevertheless, Manager Li smiled and spoke of mutual cooperation for the future, past Chinese-Canadian relations, and the great amount he and his factory could learn from the Canadians. They signed an expanded version of the letter of intent that had been signed nine months earlier in Canada. The Canadians left with expressions on both sides of willingness to continue to discuss the sale through mail and fax.

The Canadians were stunned to learn two weeks later that the factory had decided to buy from a Japanese equipment manufacturer. They knew their product was good and their price was fair. What had happened to derail their sale?

In discussing what had happened to derail their sale, consider the following cross-cultural dimensions that came into play regarding this transaction:

- Context
- Identity
- Learning
- Environment

- Change/ambiguity
- Time
- Authority
- Achievement
- Other

Adapted from Linda Beamer and Iris Varner, *Intercultural Communication in the Global Workplace* (Boston, MA: McGraw-Hill, 1995). Used with permission.

A CASE STUDY

THE WALT DISNEY COMPANY: LAUNCH OF A HONG KONG THEME PARK

INTRODUCTION

On November 3, 1999, an official announcement by Judson Green, the chairman of Walt Disney Attractions and the executive in charge of development, made Hong Kong Disneyland no longer a much-debated possibility but an inevitable reality, with no less than the Hong Kong government as a business partner. After much negotiation, the parties agreed to a US$3.55 billion collaboration deal to build Hong Kong Disneyland at Penny's Bay, on Lantau Island. This massive project would be Disney's fifth theme park resort and the third outside the U.S.[1]

At the opening ceremony, the Walt Disney Company's CEO Michael Eisner and the Hong Kong Chief Executive Tung Chee-hwa broke ground together with a golden shovel into the reclaimed land of Lantau Island, celebrating the start of construction of the Hong Kong Disney project. Eisner called the joint venture, "the most culturally sensitive theme park ever."[2]

Irene Chan was appointed the Vice President of Public Affairs for the Hong Kong Disneyland Resort. Previously, she was the Regional Director of Corporate Communications for the Asia Pacific region of the Walt Disney Company and was selected for her extensive range and depth of knowledge and experience on the issues and public affairs related to the Hong Kong Special Administrative Region (SAR) and the Greater China mainland. In her position as Regional Director, she was a key driver in significantly increasing foreign investment and business development in Hong Kong, Taiwan, Singapore, Australia, and other parts of the Asia Pacific region.

Chan is the official spokesperson for the Hong Kong Disneyland Resort and responsible for governmental affairs, environmental affairs, community relations, media relations, and publicity.[3] She is instrumental in communicating the vision and story of Disney, its unique, high level of guest service, and the creative content and quality of its family entertainment to the Hong Kong public and the greater Asia Pacific region. She is responsible for the task of assuring the public of the Disney theme park's success, which will feature a traditional American concept and theme, while also reassuring them of Disney's respect and appreciation of the culture and traditions of Hong Kong and China.

A BRIEF HISTORY OF DISNEY THEME PARKS

Founded in 1927 by Walt Disney and his brother Roy, the Walt Disney Company began as a small, unassuming cartoon and animation production company and has since grown to a global entertainment empire that consists of theme parks and resort complexes, motion picture and television production and distribution, publishing and retail, consumer products licensing and various limited entertainment ventures.

Walt Disney Attractions consists of theme parks, retail complexes, hotel and conference facilities and a range of various recreational properties. It is its theme parks, however, that provide Walt Disney Attractions with its most significant and consistent revenues, which are also used to financially support other Disney divisions as needed.

Walt Disney Attractions opened its first theme park, Disneyland, in 1955 in Anaheim, a city near Los Angeles, California. In 1971, Disney opened its largest property, the Walt Disney Resort, which spans 29,000 acres near Orlando, Florida, and is comprised of three separate theme parks: the Magic Kingdom, Disney-MGM, and the EPCOT Center.[4]

In 1983, the company launched its first international theme park, Tokyo Disneyland, located in the metropolitan city of Tokyo, Japan. The theme park was designed by Disney but owned and operated by the Oriental Land Company, a well-established Japanese management company. The park spans over 114 acres, more than twice the size of the Disneyland in Anaheim, but is substantially similar in concept, design and delivery.[5]

When Michael Eisner became CEO of the Walt Disney Company, he was struck by the enormous success of Tokyo Disneyland, which seemed to prove the appeal and success of the Disney theme park experience in international markets. In 1992, Euro Disney, located in the outskirts of Paris, France, officially opened to the public amidst worldwide anticipation and speculation. Eisner had envisioned a Disney theme park with a distinctly European and French atmosphere. The company made a great effort to adjust and incorporate aspects of the local culture in the theme park design and marketing, departing much more from the classic Disney brand formula and approach than in any of its other theme parks. Euro Disney opened to great fanfare but tepid response from the French public. Disney encountered numerous complications and difficulties in launching and operating Euro Disney (now called, Disneyland Resort Paris), which is only recently showing marked improvement in performance.

TOKYO DISNEYLAND

BACKGROUND

The Tokyo Disneyland project was not initiated by Disney; a Japanese company, the Oriental Land Company, Ltd. (OLC), a railway and development joint venture, approached Disney with the idea of an international theme park. Disney was not particularly interested and was reluctant to open discussions on this, as the company was focused on completing the Epcot Center project at the Disney World Resort in Florida, which had encountered numerous difficulties and challenges. They were particularly reluctant to direct strained funds toward an international theme park in Asia, where sales of Disney movies and products were not strong.[6]

The Oriental Land Company's proposal was to obtain a license from Disney to construct and operate the theme park. The company already had a location in mind in Urayasu-City in the Chiba Prefecture, located near the nation's capital, Tokyo.

ISSUES AND CHALLENGES

The current CEO of Disney at the time, Cardon Walker, later reconsidered the proposal as he needed additional funds to complete the Epcot Center project and believed the project with OLC could be done without taking substantial risk.[7] From his perspective, if Disney could convince OLC to accept a franchise agreement that substantially favored Disney without requiring much of its own capital outlay, Walker would accept their proposal for the Tokyo Disneyland project.

After protracted and difficult negotiations, Walker and OLC reached an agreement in 1979. The OLC agreed to pay 10% of admissions revenues and 5% of food and souvenir revenues as the royalty for Disney Productions. Disney Productions did not take any ownership and also did not contribute any financial support to the OLC in the development of the theme park project. Although Disney Productions didn't take substantial risk, if this project didn't work, it could deteriorate the Disney's brand equity. Moreover, this was the first offshore and the first franchise theme park. Thus, what they could do to guide this situation was limited from the beginning.

The biggest challenge faced by the OLC as the sole owner and operator of such a huge facility was to implement Disney's theme park concept successfully in a completely different culture and context. Other challenges were the higher than average costs and the climate. Tokyo is as hot as Orlando in summer and as cold as Paris in winter, and also has rainy season in early summer.[8]

A Successful Formula: Japanese Ethos, Location, Entertainment, and Merchandise

Unlike the some other European and Asian societies, Japanese people generally do not consider foreign culture as a form of cultural contamination. Although Japan has a long history and its own original culture, at the same time, the Japanese are fond of enjoying foreign culture very much.

In doing business overseas, one of the most important points is to adjust a company's own culture to a specific region while respecting local culture. Doing so is obviously easier for a local company. Basically, OLC did just copy Magic Kingdom of Disney World and then pasted it in Tokyo. However, at the same time, they successfully made some adjustments especially in marketing, food, and souvenir goods.

Site selection was another important aspect of success. "Tokyo Disneyland has approximately a population of 30 million within a 50 kilometer radius. Households in this area have higher income."[9] It is also conveniently connected to central Tokyo, just 15 minutes by commuter train from Tokyo Central Station.

One of the unexpected good results was the high percentage of repeat visitors. OLC estimated 75% of guests were repeat visitors in 1988. That is well above 50% of Disney's theme parks in the U.S. The first time visitor ratio was continuously decreasing, on the other hand, more than 30 times visitor ratio was continuously increasing. About 65% of visitors come from the neighboring Kanto region. Thus, repeat visitors from neighboring areas have been the key to attendance.

Another unanticipated positive outcome was the greater than expected amount of money spent by visitors in the park. Revenue per visitor has been averaging $90. That is also well above that of other Disney theme parks. In 1988, food and souvenir revenues, $569 million, were larger than that of admission revenues, $470 million.

EVALUATION OF TOKYO DISNEYLAND AND THE NEXT STEP

Tokyo Disneyland itself was generally regarded as a huge success for both Disney Productions and OLC. It is a reasonable assessment because Disney Productions successfully made money, "$80 million royalty fee in 1988," without taking substantial risk or making significant efforts on cultural adjustment.[10] Moreover, regardless of the disadvantageous climate, the park realized consistent attendance figures throughout the year. Some, however, took a contrarian view.

According to Tetsuo Anima, "Michael Eisner, who took over [as] new CEO in 1984, considered Disney's passive commitment to Tokyo Disneyland as a big mistake."[11] He decided to become more involved in the next offshore venture, Euro Disney, now known as Disneyland Resort Paris. Then, the company decided to take a 49% ownership position. Disney's final alternatives were Paris, for its central location in Europe, and Barcelona, Spain, for its warmer climate. Tokyo Disneyland's success under similar unfavorable weather conditions was reportedly the tipping factor toward France over Spain.

EURO DISNEY

BACKGROUND

Disney's tradition and successful formula of innovative park design, the rich history of its cartoon characters, the unique role that visitors play in the theme park, and its renowned service quality and delivery were brought to work on the European continent. Would such an American concept be viable in Europe? What else might convince the European visitors who flock to the Walt Disney World Resort in Florida to instead choose Euro Disney? Many complex questions and issues faced Disney executives as they officially opened Euro Disney in April 1992, only to be met with a cool reception by the French.

ISSUES AND CHALLENGES

Euro Disney was based on the U.S. model, but localized and adjusted to suit the European location. This is a different strategy from Tokyo Disneyland, where the full American Disneyland experience is provided down to the cast members' use of English and American mannerisms. In contrast, Euro Disney's rides, attractions, foods, language and other elements were "localized" to better suit the French and European preferences, and the Disney culture was adjusted much more for the local culture.

One of the greatest challenges for Disney when it was starting the Euro Disney business in 1992 was to recruit more than 10,000 employees in six months.[12] Disney held to its usual U.S. recruitment process and criteria but found resistance from the French public due to a combination of its strict dress and grooming rules[13] and the dismissal of Disney as unsophisticated and a symbol of American cultural imperialism.[14]

Ultimately, Disney used a combination of recruiting Europeans who had worked in North America and local Europeans as well as relaxing their strict dress codes to address the criticism that it faced.[15] However, more than 1,000 employees left Disney employment during the first nine weeks following Euro Disney's opening,[16] with some employees claiming the cultural indoctrination within Disney amounted to "brainwashing."[17] In order to maintain a strong culture, selection of new staff that embrace an organization's values is critical; therefore, it is unsurprising that Disney encountered these initial problems.[18, 19]

In Tokyo Disneyland, as the purpose is to provide as much of a genuine, authentic American Disneyland experience as possible, such guidelines and protocols were fully expected by the job applicants and cast members. Moreover, Disney's distinguishing feature of high-quality service and delivery is well-matched by the Japanese standards of service quality. Disney has had a far smoother relationship with its employees and the international venture with Tokyo Disneyland. How might the insights gained from Tokyo Disneyland and Euro Disney influence Disney's strategy for its third large-scale international venture, Hong Kong Disneyland?

HONG KONG DISNEYLAND

BACKGROUND

The Hong Kong government contributed a significant amount, HK$22.45 billion (US$2.88 billion), to the park development, which was the deciding factor that lured Disney to Hong Kong, beating out rival cities of Shanghai, China and Kuala Lampur, Malaysia. The park will be held by a joint venture: Hong Kong International Theme Parks, which will be formed with the Walt Disney Company and Hong Kong SAR. In return for their investment, the government will receive $4 billion subordinate shares and 57% ownership, giving a hefty 43% ownership to Disney. Many believe the government conceded too much in their negotiations with the Disney Company in their eagerness to lure the company.

The government maintains that by acquiring Disney, it will attract 3.4 million visitors in the first year, generating an additional $8.3 billion from tourists alone, and increasing to as much as $16.8 billion at the 20-year point and beyond.[20] The travel and tourism industry, which Hong

Kong depends on for much of its revenue, was hit hard after the September 11, 2001 terrorist attacks and the Severe Acute Respiratory Syndrome (SARS) panic in 2003. The Hong Kong government believed that the Disney name would greatly boost tourism visits to Hong Kong and help bolster its faltering economy. The Hong Kong Disneyland theme park will provide 18,400 jobs upon its opening and is projected to boost the economy by more than $148 billion over a 40-year period.[21] The government has also loosened visa restrictions for China's mainland visitors and other countries to encourage travel to Hong Kong and has planned promotional strategies worldwide to highlight the full entertainment options available to park visitors.

The Hong Kong Disneyland Park will be based on the classic Disney approach of its U.S. parks, with separate areas named Tomorrowland and Frontierland and a mixture of rides and shows from all the Disney parks. This approach was an enormous success with Tokyo Disneyland and the company notes the general appeal of Disney characters and products in Asia. The company also does not want to dilute Disney's brand equity by changing too much of the Disney culture and experience. The concessions to its Asian location and Hong Kong's culture will be reflected mainly in the adjustments of the retail, entertainment and dining sector. The park performances will be presented in Cantonese, Mandarin and English.

The second stage of the project will include a 1,400-room Disney-themed resort hotel complex and an entertainment, dining and retail center at Penny's Bay, which the government has planned as a major entertainment area, enticing even more visitors and tourists, especially with the new international airport, Chek Lap Kok, located nearby and linked to several convenient transportation options to the park and the main cities.

THE HONG KONG SPECIAL ADMINISTRATIVE REGION

The population of Hong Kong is close to 6.7 million and is one of the most densely populated locations in the world. Hong Kong is an expensive city to travel to, and it cannot solely focus on the Chinese market and the Hong Kong population.[22] To ensure long-term profitability and sustainability, it must determine strategies that will sufficiently entice and induce people from other countries to travel the long distance to Hong Kong.

Environmental groups have been active in voicing concerns over the theme park. A major concern for Hong Kong Disneyland and the government is the perpetual air pollution in Hong Kong. Dust particles from factories in the Southern China area are often blown into Hong Kong, but the lack of open space and numerous skyscrapers make air ventilation in Hong Kong almost non-existent in some cases. If both Hong Kong Disneyland and the government fail to address this problem, nightly fireworks in Disney can become potentially hazardous to both Hong Kong and the park. Smoke from fireworks will simply remain trapped in the city.[23] The theme park has also received criticism from fishermen who claim that the park would pollute the sea.

Despite the fact that Hong Kong is a unique place with a mixture of the East and West, there are still skeptics of how the city's population at large will feel about Hong Kong Disneyland. Many have grown disgruntled at the way the government has funded most of the park's project.[24] Others are more concerned that the presence of the American theme park would further dilute the Chinese culture in Hong Kong. There were legislators who believed that alternatives to Disney should be considered. The more worrying factor is that Japanese cartoon characters have a much stronger presence in Hong Kong than Disney characters. Thus, Hong Kong Disneyland may face challenges in promoting its icon to the general public.[25]

HONG KONG'S INTERESTS

Hong Kong, known as the Pearl of the Orient, is a major financial city in Asia whose uniqueness lies in its history as a British colony and its position as a financial gateway to China. The island has a GDP per capita of $28,800, greater than the GDP per capita of UK, which is $27,700.

After the Asian Financial Crisis of 1997, Hong Kong had trouble recovering from its recession. As China continues to open its cities to international investments, Hong Kong leaders proposed building a brand image theme park to turn the city into a world class tourist location. After discussions with both Disney and Universal Studios, Disney was chosen as the ideal theme park for Hong Kong to boost its tourist industry. Government officials said that few attractions could rival the international appeal of Disney and recapture the energy in Hong Kong.

DISNEY'S INTERESTS

Disney has its own set of incentives to build a theme park in Hong Kong. The vastness of the Chinese market potential is simply too great to ignore. The mix of culture in Hong Kong makes it an ideal place to test the possibility of other theme parks in the region. Having learned from mistakes in building Tokyo Disney and Paris Disney, the fact that Hong Kong government was offering such lucrative incentives and risk sharing makes it seem that Hong Kong Disneyland will be a good bet. After a deal with

Hong Kong was finalized, talks began with Shanghai in 2002 to explore opportunities there for an additional theme park.

Whereas Europeans largely oppose Disney's American icon image, Hong Kong should have no trouble embracing Mickey Mouse and associates. The people of Hong Kong are well known for their propensity for cultural assimilation. In particular, people are crazy about cartoon characters. During a McDonald's promotion program in 1999, adults queued for hours for snoopy dolls that came along as gifts with value meals. Hong Kong is also probably one of the few places in the world where one will find cartoon characters on credit cards. Therefore, Disney cartoon characters in Hong Kong can potentially be even a greater success than Tokyo Disney.

LOCATION, FOOD, ENTERTAINMENT

Hong Kong is just 1,092 km square, with little flat land for a good site to build a massive theme park. This also makes Hong Kong Disneyland, a day-visit theme park, similar to Tokyo Disneyland, as opposed to vacation destinations like Orlando Disneyworld. The Hong Kong Government and the Hong Kong Disneyland Group decided that the theme park should be situated at Penny's Bay on Lantau Island, a place that has been earmarked for tourism and recreational development.

While Hong Kong Disneyland will retain the strong tradition of Disney storytelling, it also will incorporate elements of Chinese culture into the theme park in order to make itself unique from others. The landscaping is based on story settings, which will include a jungle, a castle, fantasy themes and a journey through space. This pictorial scenery will be made possible with a magical setting of green mountains as its background and the blue South China Sea as its front steps. The idea is to make guests feel as if they belong to the story and to create an unforgettable fairy-tale kingdom encounter for them.

Paul Comstock, director of Landscape Design of Walt Disney Imagineering, commented that Hong Kong Disneyland has borrowed ancient Chinese view principles with thousands of years of history. The principles include view farming, view hiding and water reflection. Such design will be based on hundreds of the Chinese Banyan and other native plants to accentuate the artistic milieu. Tom Morris, creative development vice president for Walt Disney, explained that a successful park in Asia must contain areas with plenty of shade and large pools of water. Specific plant materials are cast to "play roles" as characters in the story creating realistic and magical settings.[26]

When it comes to food, Hong Kong prides itself on the title "Food Heaven," where cuisine from around the world gathers. The people of Hong Kong love to eat, and will readily pay a premium for a fine dining experience. Therefore, only children and teenagers would be satisfied by fast food menus such as that offered by McDonald's. In response, Hong Kong Disneyland put a lot of effort in designing the menu for visitors.

"Hong Kong Disneyland's food will do more than bring people together; it will bring whole cultures together," said Klaus Mager, Hong Kong Disneyland Director Food & Beverage. "The Park's menu will feature a unique combination of Western, Chinese, and Asian cuisines that will be an integral part of the magical experiences enjoyed by Park guests."[27] While the menu features a range of dishes across different cultures and continents, most dishes are primarily focused on Chinese and Japanese tastes, including Dan Dan noodles, cooked in Southern China's Sichuan Province; assorted sushi, prepared in Japanese style; Kashmiri Curry Chicken, cooked in Kashmiri Style.

Hong Kong Disneyland's diverse food menus will be offered at eight Park restaurants, three of which will be table service restaurants and five of which will be self-service eateries, totaling 2,900 seats. In accordance to HK Disneyland's mission to integrate food with amusement, each restaurant will be themed to match the unique, immersive atmosphere of its surroundings.[28]

HOTELS AND RESORTS

Hong Kong Disneyland Hotel and Disney's Hollywood Hotel will be built inside Hong Kong Disneyland to provide customers with the magical paradise experience to stay in a Disney resort. There is only one real resort in Hong Kong, and most other hotels are high-rises; thus, Disney strives to distinguish itself from other city-hotels. Hong Kong Disneyland plans to keep its hotels within eight stories in an effort to avoid the busy city image. The Disney's Hollywood Hotel will capture the locals' fascination with motion pictures, while Hong Kong Disneyland Hotel will keep itself align with Disney's imaginations and fantasies.

"Disney's Hollywood Hotel will capture the fun of movie making with the allure of Hollywood's Golden Era in its Art Deco architecture and style," said Wing Chao, Hong Kong Disney's Executive, "With Hong Kong's love of motion pictures and its international reputation for filmmaking, creating a hotel that celebrates the history and glamour of motion pictures seemed like the perfect fit."[29]

Hong Kong Disneyland has been trying to reveal only bits and pieces of what is going on in the park's development. Apart from regular media briefings, much has still been kept secret to retain the sense of mystery and preserve the Disney fantasies. There are, however, numerous channels to prepare for the grand opening of Hong Kong Disneyland.

In preparation for its grand opening in late 2005, Hong Kong Disneyland began a range of promotion campaigns. It started cooperating with the Hong Kong Television Broadcasts Limited (TVB), the largest broadcasting network in Hong Kong, to start a series of Disney productions. Under the promotion campaign, TVB aired three new Disney TV programs starting in July 2004. This marked the kickoff of Hong Kong Disneyland's pre-launch marketing and publicity efforts, which would increase gradually as the opening of the park drew nearer.[30]

The company has also signed Jackie Cheung, a local singer, to become a spokesman for Hong Kong Disneyland. Cheung has received awards for Hong Kong outstanding individuals, and portrays an image well suited to Disney's culture of honoring the family. He will offer a more wholesome and reputable image in promoting Hong Kong Disneyland. Another figure that Walt Disney is hoping to bring into its promotion campaign is Yao Ming, the most recognizable sports icon in China who has been playing in the NBA for the last three years.[31]

Hong Kong Disneyland expects to serve customers from a vast array of different backgrounds. The dominant dialect in Hong Kong is Cantonese while mainland Chinese widely speak Mandarin. Visitors from other parts of the world are expected to use English. Therefore, employees in Hong Kong Disneyland are expected to be fluent in all three languages.[32] Hong Kong SAR and Disney are faced with a mixture of the factors behind the successes and failures of both Tokyo Disneyland and Euro Disneyland. Irene Chan must ensure appropriate communication of the Hong Kong SAR and Disney's shared vision of the joint venture. She must communicate the uniqueness of Hong Kong Disneyland to not only the Chinese public, but convince travelers worldwide of Hong Kong Disneyland as a complete vacation and entertainment resort.

DISCUSSION QUESTIONS

1. What were the critical issues for Disney to launch the third offshore Disney theme park in Hong Kong?
2. Who are the principal stakeholders to launch this theme park?
3. What can Disney learn from the corporate communication lessons in Tokyo and Paris?

4. Who should mainly manage the project in Hong Kong, the Disney Company itself or the Hong Kong government as the local partner?
5. Which issue should Disney try to address first?
6. How can Disney balance its own identity or corporate culture with the local culture?
7. What actions should Irene Chan and Disney's Global Corporate Communications take to address these critical issues?
8. Based upon the information provided in this case, identify cross-cultural issues using the eight dimensions of culture as discussed in the text: context, identity, learning, environment, change, time authority, achievement.
9. Use the eight dimensions of culture (context, identity, learning, environment, change, time authority, achievement) and identify where Disney:
   • succeeded in their attempts to address cross-cultural issues;
   • failed in their attempts to address cross-cultural issues;
   • should strategize for future cross-cultural issues that may arise.
10. Doing some additional research to find out what has happened since the Hong Kong Disney's opening in September 2005 will help add perspective to these issues.
11. Based upon the information provided in this case (as well as additional research) compare and contrast the complexities and unexpected challenges that each of the Disney theme parks encountered in France, Japan, and Hong Kong. What was similar? Different? What conclusions can you draw from this information? If you were a cross-cultural business consultant hired to advise Disney on issues of doing business internationally, what would you suggest?

SOURCES

1. Susan Thorne, "Magic Kingdom to Get Outpost in Hong Kong," *Shopping Centers Today*. Retrieved 3 December 2004 from http://www.icsc.org/srch/sct/current/sct0500/02e.html
2. "Mickey Learns Chinese in Preparation for Disney's Hong Kong Launch," *Evening Standard* (United Kingdom), 15 January 2003. Database: Ebsco Host Available From: http:web6.epnet.com.libproxy.nd.edu.
3. http://www.hongkongdisney-land.com/eng/discover/20040527.html

4. "The Walt Disney Annual Report —1991," Walt Disney web site, from http://www.disney.com
5. "The Walt Disney Company Fact Book," 31August 1991.
6. Tetsuo Arima, *Disneyland Monogatari* (Tokyo: Nikkei Business Bunko, 2001), 142.
7. *Ibid.*, 146.
8. http://www.climatechangebusinessforum.com/en-us/hong_kong_context_affected
9. "Oriental Land Co., Ltd.," from http://www.olc.co.jp/en/ir/ir.html
10. Tetsuo Arima, *supra* n. 173.
11. *Ibid.*, 174.
12. R. Anthony. "Euro Disney: The First 100 Days," *Harvard Business Case 9-693-013* (1992).
13. M. Du Bois. "Legal beat: Euro Disney's dress code faces challenge by French prosecutor," *Wall Street Journal*, Eastern edition, 28 December 1994: B5.
14. "Only the French Elite Scorn Mickey's Debut", *New York Times*, 13, April 1992:
15. J. Gooding, "Of Mice and Men," *Across the Board*, *29(3)* (1992): 40-44.
16. "Euro Disney's Fitzpatrick Denies report that 3,000 Workers quit over low pay," *Wall Street Journal*, 27 May, 1992.17. "Queuing for Flawed Fantasy," *Financial Times*, 13 June 1992.
18. S.P. Robbins, *Essentials of Organizational Behavior*, 7th Ed., (Upper Saddle River, New Jersey: Prentice Hall. 2003). Chapter 16.
19. Roland Buresund, *Understanding Structures and Cultures*, Book 7. (The Open University Business School, Prof. Cert. Management Text, 1996), Block 4,
20. "Hong Kong Disneyland – An Asset for the Future," Hong Kong Government web site (22 October 2003). Retrieved 15 October 2004 from http://www.info.gov.hk/disneyland/eng.htm
21. *Ibid.*
22. Indira Lakshmanan. "Disney Anticipates Theme-Park Deal with Hong Kong Government," *The Boston Globe*, 1 November 1999. Database: Ebsco Host, from http://web6.epnet.com.lib-proxy.nd.edu/
23. Patsy Moy, "Disney Worry Over Pollution," *Hong Kong Standard*, 12 April 2000. Database: Ebsco Host. Retrieved 22 October 2004 from http://web6.epnet.com.lib-proxy.nd.edu/

24. Indira Lakshmanan,"Disney Plans Theme Park in Hong Kong,", *The Boston Globe*, 20 November 1999. Database: Ebsco Host. Retrieved from http://web6.epnet.com.lib-proxy.nd.edu/

25. Indira Lakshmanan,,"Disney Anticipates Theme-Park Deal with Hong Kong Government" *The Boston Globe*, 1 November 1999: PAGE. Database: Ebsco Host. Retrieved from http://web6.epnet.com.lib-proxy.nd.edu/

26. "Hong Kong Disneyland Unveils Magic Behind Landscape Design," Hong Kong Disneyland web site. Updated 18 Sept., 2003. Retrieved 20 October 2004 from: "http://www.hongkongdisneyland.com/eng/discover/20040330.html"

27. "Hong Kong Disneyland showcases the magic behind its food," Hong Kong Disneyland web site , Updated 10 August 2004. Retrieved Oct. 20, 2004 from http://www.hongkongdisney land.com/eng/discover/20040810.html

28. *Ibid.*

29. "Two Theme Park Hotels Will Offer Guests the Chance to Live the Magic at Hong Kong Disneyland," Hong Kong Disneyland web site. Updated 21 November 2002. Retrieved October 22, 2004 from http://www.hongkongdisneyland.com/eng/discover/2002index.html

30. "Hong Kong Disneyland Launches Hong Kong Marketing Drive," Hong Kong Disneyland web site,14 July 2004, . Retrieved 20 October 2004 from http://www.hongkongdisney land.com/eng/discover/20040714.html

31. Tom Lowry, "Wow! Yao!", *Business Week Online*, 25 October 2004.. Retrieved November 12, 2004 from http://www.business week.com/magazine/content/04_43/b3905010.htm

32. "Disney to build HK Park", *CNN*, 11 November 1999, Retrieved 24 October 2004 from http://money.cnn.com/1999/11/01/worldbiz/hongkong_disney/

This case was prepared by Research Assistants Julianne Lee Baldwin, Alex Liu, and Hidehito Suzuki under the direction of James S. O'Rourke, Concurrent Professor of Management, as the basis for class discussion rather than to illustrate either effective or ineffective handling of an administrative situation. Information was gathered from corporate as well as public sources. This case is used by permission from: Jim O'Rourke Copyright ©2005. Eugene D. Fanning Center for Business Communication. Mendoza College of Business, University of Notre

APPENDIX
Suggested Additional Reading

- Axtell, Roger E., *Do's and Taboos of Hosting International Visitors.* (New York, NY: John Wiley & Sons, 1990).
- Axtell, Roger E., ed., *Do's and Taboos Around the World.* (New York, NY: Benjamin Books, John Wiley & Sons, 1993).
- Brannen, Christalyn and Tracey, *Doing Business with Japanese Men: A Woman's Handbook.* (Berkeley, CA: Stone Bridge Press, 1993).
- Brislin, Richard W. and Tomoko Yoshida, eds., *Improving Intercultural Interactions: Modules for Cross-Cultural Training Programs.* (Thousand Oaks, CA: Sage Publications, 1994).
- Chen, Winnie. *Intercultural Conversation.* (Amsterdam: John Benjamins Publishing Company, 2003).
- Crane, Robert, *European Business Cultures.* (Harlow, England: Pearson Education, 2000).
- Cyr, Donald, *The Art of Global Thinking: Integrating Organizational Philosophies of East and West.* (West Lafayette, IN: Ichor Business Books, 2002).
- Dalton, Maxine et al., *Success for the New Global Manager.* (San Francisco, CA: Jossey-Bass, 2002).
- Earley, P. Christopher and Miriam Erez, *The Transplanted Executive: Why You Need to Understand How Workers in Other Countries See the World Differently.* (New York, NY: Oxford University Press, 1997).
- Earley, P. Christopher, *Face, Harmony, & Social Structure: An Analysis of Organizational Behavior Across Cultures.* (Oxford, England: Oxford University Press, 1997).
- Engholm, Christopher, *When Business East Meets Business West: The Guide to Practice and Protocol in the Pacific Rim.* (New York, NY: John Wiley & Sons, Inc., 1991).
- Engholm, Christopher and Diana Rowland, *International Excellence: Seven Breakthrough Strategies for Personal and Professional Success.* (New York, NY: Kodansha International, 1996).
- Erez, Miriam and P. Christopher Earley. *Culture, Self-Identity, and Work.* (Oxford, England: Oxford University Press, 1993).
- Eun Y. Kim, *The Yin and Yang of American Culture: A Paradox.* (Yarmouth, ME: Intercultural Press, Inc., 1991).

- Fernandez, Juan Antonio and Laurie Underwood, *China CEO: Voices of Experience from 20 International Business Leaders.* (Singapore: John Wiley & Sons, Asia, 2006).
- Gannon, Martin J., *Understanding Global Cultures.* (Thousand Oaks, CA: Sage Publications, 2001).
- Goodman, Michael B., *Working in a Global Environment: Understanding, Communicating, and Managing Transnationally.* (New York, NY: The Institute of Electrical and Electronics Engineers, Inc., 1995).
- Gudykunst, William B. and Young Yun Kim, *Communicating with Strangers: An Approach to Intercultural Communication.* (New York, NY: McGraw Hill, 2003).
- Gudykunst, William B. *Theorizing about Intercultural Communication.* (Thousand Oaks, CA: Sage Publications, 2005).
- Harris, Philip R. and Robert T. Moran, *Managing Cultural Differences,* 4th ed. (Houston, TX: Gulf Publishing, 1996).
- Hofstede, Geert, *Culture and Organizations.* (New York, NY: McGraw-Hill, 1999).
- Hofstede, Gert Jan, Paul B. Pedersen, and Geert Hofstede. *Exploring Culture: Exercises, Stories and Synthetic Cultures.* (Boston, MA: Intercultural Press, 2002).
- McKinniss, Candace Bancroft and Arthur A. Natella, Jr., *Business in Mexico: Managerial Behavior, Protocol, and Etiquette.* (New York, NY: The Haworth Press, 1994).
- Morrison, Terry et al., *Kiss, Bow, or Shake Hands.* (Avon, MA: Adams Media Corporation, 1995).
- O'Hara-Devereaux, Mary and Robert Johansen, *Global Work.* (San Francisco, CA: Jossey-Bass, 1994).
- Ohmae, Kenichi, *The Borderless World: Management Lessons in the New Logic of the Global Marketplace.* (New York, NY: Harper Business, 1999).
- Rhinesmith, Steven H., *A Manager's Guide to Globalization: Six Keys to Success in a Changing World.* (Homewood, IL: Business One Irwin, 1996).
- Rosen, Robert. *Global Literacies: Lessons on Business Leadership and National Cultures.* (New York, NY: Simon & Schuster, 2000).
- Slethaug, Gordon, E. *Teaching Abroad: International Education and the Cross-Cultural Classroom.* (Hong Kong: Hong Kong University Press, 2007).
- Tang, Jie and Anthony Ward, *The Changing Face of Chinese Management.* (New York, NY: Routledge 2002).

- Ting-Toomey, Stella and John G. Oetzel, *Managing Intercultural Conflict Effectively.* (Thousand Oaks, CA: Sage Publications, 2001).
- Ting-Toomey, Stella, *Communicating Across Cultures.* (New York, NY: The Guilford Press, 1999).
- Trompenaars, Fons and Charles Hampden-Turner, *Riding the Waves of Culture.* (New York, NY: McGraw-Hill, 1998).
- Wilson, Meena S., Michael H. Hoppe, and Leonard R. Sayles, *Managing Across Cultures: A Learning Framework.* (Greensboro, NC: Center for Creative Leadership, 2002).
- Zweifel, Thomas D., *Communicate or Die: Getting Results Through Speaking and Listening.* (New York, NY: Swiss Consulting Group, Inc., 2003).
- Zweifel, Thomas D., *Culture Class: Managing the Global High-Performance Team.* (New York, NY: Swiss Consulting Group, Inc., 2003).

More Titles of Interest

- *Cross-cultural Management: Essential Concepts*, by David C. Thomas
- *Seize the Sky – 9 Secrets of Negotiation Power* (Intercultural Negotiation) by Karen Walch
- *Inside Chinese Business: A Guide for Managers Worldwide*, Ming-Jer Chen, Harvard Business School Press
- *The Mindful International Manager: How to Work Effectively Across Culture*, by Jeremy Comfort and Peter Franklin
- *Cultural Differences in a Globalizing World*, by Michael Minkov (follows the work of Hofstede)
- *Global Leadership: Research, Practice and Development*, by Mark Mendenhall, Joyce Soland, et al.
- *Funny in Farsi: A Memoir of Growing Up Iranian in America*, by Firoozeh Dumas
- *Understanding Arabs: A Guide for Modern Times*, by Margaret K. Nydell
- *Encountering the Chinese: A Modern country, an Ancient Culture*, by Hu Wenzhong et al.
- *Speaking of India: Bridging the Communication Gap When Working with Indians*, by Craig Storti
- *Different Games, Different Rules: Why Americans and Japanese Misunderstand Each Other*, by Haru Yamada
- *Latino Culture: A Dynamic Force in the Changing American Workplace*, byNilda Chong and Francia Baez
- *The Art of Crossing Cultures*, by Craig Storti

INTERCULTURAL WEBSITES

- Geert Hofstede, http://geert-hofstede.com/
- Fons Trompenaars, http://www2.thtconsulting.com/about/people/fons-trompenaars/
- Elizabeth A. Tuleja, (Global Business Leader.com) http://globalbizleader.com
- Delta Intercultural Academy: http://www.dialogin.com/
- CIA World Factbook: https://www.cia.gov/library/publications/the-world-factbook/
- Kwintessential (Global Communications Agency): www.kwintessential.co.uk/
- SIETAR – Society for International Education Training and Research, http://www.sietarusa.org/page-87312

OTHER USEFUL WEBSITES

U.S. State Department

- Main Page: http://www.state.gov/index.htm
- Travel and Living Abroad: http://www.state.gov/travel/
- Countries and Regions: http://www.state.gov/countries/
- History, Education, and Culture: http://www.state.gov/history/
- Business Center, Country Background Notes: http://www.state.gov/r/pa/ei/bgn/

Search Engines
- http://www.google.com
- http://www.yahoo.com
- http://www.askjeeves.com
- http://www.dogpile.com
- http://www.thebighub.com
- http://www.search.com

End Notes

CHAPTER 1

1. "Ralph Waldo Emerson cited in: Lawrence A. Samovar and Richard E. Porter, *Intercultural Communication: A Reader*, 4th ed. (Belmont, CA: Wadsworth Publishing Company, 1994), 71.
2. *Ibid.*, 4.
3. *Ibid.*, 27.
4. "U.S. Census Bureau. Population Profile of the United States: 2000 (Internet Release)." Retrieved August 10, 2004, from http://www. census.gov/population/www/index.html.
5. *Ibid.*
6. *Kiplinger Letter*, vol. 79, no. 52 (December 27, 2002).
7. Northeastern University study, retrieved March 10, 2003, from http://www.cnn.com.
8. Uniworld Business Publications, Inc., "Directory of Foreign Firms Operating in the U.S., 11th ed., 2002." Retrieved August 10, 2004, from http://www.uniworldbp.com.
9. "Open Doors 2002, Institute of International Education, November 18, 2002." Retrieved August 10, 2004, from http://open-doors.iienetwork.org.
10. *Kiplinger Letter*, *supra* n.6.
11. Uniworld Business Publications, Inc., "Directory of Foreign Firms Operating in the U.S., 11th ed., 2002." Retrieved August 10, 2004, from http://www.uniworldbp.com.
12. Stefan Lovgren for *National Geographic News*, retrieved February 26, 2004, http://news.nationalgeographic.com/news/2004/02/0226_040226_language.html
13. Marshall R. Singer, *Intercultural Communication: A Perceptual Approach* (Englewood Cliffs, NJ: Prentice-Hall, Inc., 1987), 3.
14. A. L. Kroeber and Clyde Kluckhohn, "Culture: A Critical Review of Concepts and Definitions," *Papers of the Peabody Museum of American Archaeology and Ethnology* 47, no. 1 (1952).
15. Fons Trompenaars and Charles Hampden-Turner, *Riding the Waves of Culture: Understanding Cultural Diversity in Global Business* (New York, NY: McGraw-Hill, 1998).
16. Geert Hofstede, *Cultures and Organizations: Software of the Mind* (New York, NY: McGraw-Hill, 1997).
17. Singer, *supra* n.13.

18. *Ibid.*
19. Concept developed by Jean Piaget in Harry W. Gardiner, Jay D. Mutter, and Corinne Kosmitzki, *Lives Across Cultures: Cross-Cultural Human Development* (Needham Heights, MA: Allyn & Bacon, 1998), 81.
20. *Ibid.*
21. Terry Morrison, Wayne A. Conaway, and George A. Borden, *Kiss, Bow or Shake Hands* (Avon, MA: Adams Media Corporation, 1994), 207.
22. Walter Lippmann, *Public Opinion* (New York, NY: The Free Press, 1965), 53–68.
23. Randel S. Carlock and John L. Ward, *Strategic Planning for the Family Business* (New York, NY: Plagrave Macmillan, 2001).
24. Linda Beamer and Iris Varner, *Intercultural Communication in the Global Workplace* (Boston, MA: McGraw-Hill Irwin, 2001), 18–19.
25. Harry W. Gardiner, Jay D. Mutter, and Corinne Kosmitzki, *Lives Across Cultures: Cross-Cultural Human Development.* (Needham Heights, MA: Allyn & Bacon, 1998), 188.
26. Hofstede, *supra* n.16.
27. *Ibid.*, 3.
28. Edward C. Stewart & Milton J. Bennett, *American Cultural Patterns.* (Yarmouth, ME: Intercultural Press, Inc. 1991), x, xii.
29. *Ibid.*, x.
30. Milton J. Bennett, "A Developmental Approach to Training for Intercultural Sensitivity," *International Journal of Intercultural Relations*, 10 (1986), 179–196.

CHAPTER 2

1. "A Disney Dress Code Chafes in the Land of Haute Couture," *The New York Times*, December 25, 1991, Late Edition, Section 1:1.
2. Philip R. Harris and Robert T. Moran, *Managing Cultural Differences: Leadership Strategies for a New World of Business*, 5th ed. (Burlington, MA: Gulf Professional Publishing, 2000), 29.
3. G. L. Grice and J. F. Skinner, *Mastering Public Speaking* (Needham Heights, MA: Allyn & Bacon, 2001).
4. D. Fabun, *Communication: The Human Experience* (New York, NY: Wm. Morrow, 1968).
5. J. S. O'Rourke, *Management Communication: A Case-Analysis Approach*, 2nd ed. (Upper Saddle River, NJ: Prentice Hall, 2004), 23.

6. Ronald B. Adler and George Rodman, *Understanding Human Communication*, 8th ed. (New York, NY: Oxford University Press, 2003), 15.

7. L. A. Samovar and Jack Mills, *Oral Communication: Speaking Across Cultures* (Boston, MA: McGraw Hill, 1998), 5.

8. Design by: Anne M. Greenhalgh, Undergraduate Leadership Program, The Wharton School.

9. Gay Lumsden and Donald Lumsden, *Communicating with Credibility and Confidence* (Belmont, CA: Wadsworth Publishing Company, 1996), 13.

10. O'Rourke, *supra* n.5, 215.

11. J. Fast, *Body Language* (New York, NY: M. Evans, 1970).

12. Ted Singelis, "Nonverbal Communication in Intercultural Interactions," in Improving Intercultural Interactions: Modules for Cross-Cultural Training Programs, Richard W. Brislin and Tomoko Yoshida, eds. (Thousand Oaks, CA: Sage Publications, 1994), 268.

13. M. Knapp and J. Hall, *Nonverbal Communication in Human Interaction*, 3rd ed. (Fort Worth, TX: Holt Rinehart and Winston, Inc., 1992), 5–6.

14. Knapp & Hall, *supra* n.13, 27.

15. Ricky W. Griffin and Michael W. Pustay, *International Business: A Managerial Perspective* (Reading, MA: Addison-Wesley, 1999), 339.

16. O'Rourke, *supra* n.5, 227.

17. *Ibid.*, 227–28.

18. *Ibid.*, 228.

19. C. K. Ogden and I. A. Richards, *The Meaning of Meaning: A Study of the Influence of Language upon Thought and the Science of Symbolism* (New York: Harcourt Brace, 1927), 11. *See also* Grice & Skinner, *supra* n.3, 7–9.

20. Harris & Moran, *supra* n.2.

21. Peter Drucker, *Management: Tasks, Responsibilities, and Practices* (New York: Harper and Row, 1974).

22. "Avianca, Flight 052." Retrieved August 10, 2004, from http://planecrashinfo.com .

23. For a thorough discussion of how words acquire their meaning, *see* R. L. Benjamin, *Semantics and Language Analysis* (New York, NY: Bobbs-Merrill, 1970). For a thorough and interesting discussion of how language works, both in theory and in practice, *see* R. Hudson, *Invitation to Linguistics* (Oxford, England UK: Blackwell Publishers, Ltd., 2000).

24. Knapp & Hall, *supra* n.13, 5–6.

25. Faris Elashmawi and Philip R. Harris, *Multicultural Management 2000: Essential Cultural Insights for Global Business Success* (Houston, TX: Gulf Publishing Company, 1998), 139.

26. Webb Garrison, *Why You Say It: The Fascinating Stories Behind over 600 Everyday Words and Phrases* (Nashville, TN: Rutledge Hill Press, 1992), 122.

27. Grice & Skinner, *supra* n.3.

28. Carolyn Calloway-Thomas, Pamela J. Cooper, and Cecil Blake, *Intercultural Communication: Roots and Routes* (Boston, MA: Allyn & Bacon, 1999), 141.

29. J. Wallach and G. Metcalf, *Working with Americans: A Practical Guide for Asians on How to Succeed with U.S. Managers* (New York: McGraw-Hill, 1995), 179–80, cited in Carolyn Calloway-Thomas, Pamela J. Cooper, and Cecil Blake, *Intercultural Communication: Roots and Routes* (Boston, MA: Allyn & Bacon, 1999), 141–42.

30. Albert Mehrabian, *Silent Messages: Implicit Communication of Emotions and Attitudes* (Belmont, CA: Wadsworth, 1981).

31. Judee K. Burgoon, David B. Buller, and W. Gill Woodall, *Nonverbal Communication: The Unspoken Dialogue* (New York, NY: McGraw-Hill, 1996), 137, citing R. Birdwhistell (1955) and Philpott (1983) *Background to Kinesics* 13, 10-18; J.S. Philpott, *The Relative Contribution to Meaning of Verbal and Nonverbal Channels of Communication: A Meta-Analysis* (unpublished master's thesis, University of Nebraska).

32. Harry Hoijer in Lawrence A. Samovar and Richard E. Porter, *Intercultural Communication: A Reader*, 4th ed. (Belmont, CA: Wadsworth Publishing Company, 1994), 195 (basic summary of the Sapir-Whorf hypothesis).

33. Calloway-Thomas, Cooper, & Blake, *supra* n.28, 140.

34. Lawrence A. Samovar and Richard E. Porter, *Intercultural Communication: A Reader*, 7th ed. (Belmont, CA: Wadsworth Publishing Company, 1994), 71.

35. Terry Morrison, Wayne A. Conaway, and George A. Borden, *Kiss, Bow or Shake Hands* (Avon, MA: Adams Media Corporation, 1994), 55.

36. *Ibid.*, 94.

37. Bill Bryson, *The Mother Tongue: English and How it Got that Way*, William Morrow Paperbacks, 2001, p. 6.

38. Samovar & Porter, *supra* n.34, 194–96.

39. N. Wolfsen in Russel H. Kaschula and Christine Anthonissen, *Communicating Across Cultures in South Africa* (Johannesburg: Witwaterstrand University Press, 1995), 86.

40. D. H. Hymes, "Introduction: Toward Ethnographies of Communication" in J. J. Gumperz and D. Hymes, eds., "The Ethnography of Communication," *American Anthropologist*, 66, 6 (1964), 1–34; D. H. Hymes, "On Communicative Competence" in J. B. Pride and J. Holmes, eds., *Sociolinguistics*, (London: Penguin, 1972), 269–93.

41. Samuel F. Falcona, Vice President, Corporate Communication, ConocoPhillips, in a personal interview, October 1, 2003, at the ConocoPhillips Headquarters, Houston, Texas.

42. Adapted from Meena S. Wilson, Michael H. Hoppe, and Leonard R. Sayles, *Managing Across Cultures: A Learning Framework* (Greensboro, NC: Center for Creative Leadership, 2002).

43. Samovar & Mills, *supra* n.7, 13.

44. Devorah A. Lieberman in Lawrence A. Samovar and Richard E. Porter, *Intercultural Communication: A Reader*, 4th ed. (Belmont, CA: Wadsworth Publishing Company, 1994), 179.

45. Meena S. Wilson, Michael H. Hoppe, and Leonard R. Sayles, *Managing Across Cultures: A Learning Framework* (Greensboro, NC: Center for Creative Leadership, 2002), 51.

46. Edward T. Hall, *Beyond Culture* (Garden City, NY: Anchor Books, 1977).

47. Samovar & Porter, *supra* n.34, 24.

48. "Jin Shan Ci Ba" the Chinese translation to English of the Chinese Character for "Listening." Kingsoft Powerword Electronic Dictionary (version 2003).

49. Courtland L. Bovee, John V. Thill, and Barbara E. Schatzman, *Business Communication Today*, 7th ed. (Upper Saddle River, NJ: Prentice Hall, 2003), 52.

50. Wilson, Hoppe, & Sayles, *supra* n. 45, 36.

51. Norimitsu Onishi, "Japanese Workers Told from on High: Drop the Formality," *The New York Times*, October 30, 2003: A1, A6.

52. John C. Condon and Mitsuko Saito, *Intercultural Encounters with Japan* (Tokyo, Japan: The Simul Press Inc., 1972), 186.

53. Dave Barry, *Dave Barry Does Japan* (New York: Fawcett Columbine, 1992), 37.

54. Quanyu Huang, Richard S. Andrulis, and Chen Tong, *A Guide to Successful Business Relationships with the Chinese* (New York, NY: International Business Press, 1994), 181–84.

55. Richard R. Gesteland, *Cross-Cultural Business Behavior* (Copenhagen, Denmark: Copenhagen Business School Press, 2002), 69–70.

56. *Ibid.*

57. *Ibid.*, 313.

58. *Ibid.*, 76.

59. *Ibid.*, 72.
60. Fons Trompenaars and Charles Hampden-Turner, *Riding the Waves of Culture: Understanding Cultural Diversity in Global Business* (New York, NY: McGraw-Hill, 1998), 70.
61. Samovar & Mills, *supra* n.7, 353.
62. Min-Sun Kim, *Non-Western Perspectives on Human Communication: Implications for Theory and Practice* (Thousand Oaks, CA: Sage Publications, 2002), 135.
63. *Ibid.*, 135.
64. Gregory Y. Titelman, *Random House Dictionary of Popular Proverbs and Sayings* (NY: Random House, 1996); *see also* "The Phrase Finder," Retrieved August 10, 2004, from http://phrases.shu .ac.uk/bulletin_board/10/messages/749.html
65. R. Kaplan in Lawrence A. Samovar and Richard E. Porter, *Intercultural Communication: A Reader*, 4th ed. (Belmont, CA: Wadsworth Publishing Company, 1994), 181.
66. *Ibid.*
67. Samovar & Porter, *supra* n.34, 177.
68. Samovar & Mills, *supra* n.7, 352.
69. For an excellent discussion of logic and reasons, see Edward P.J. Corbett, *The Elements of Reasoning*, 2nd ed. (Boston, MA: Pearson Longman, 2000).
70. We have used the Yugo brand here not because it is notoriously unreliable, but simply because it is no longer manufactured. Any similar example based on samples from personal experience will provide a useful illustration of how inductive reasoning works.
71. Adapted from Farid Elashmawi and Philip R. Harris, *Multicultural Management 2000: Essential Cultural Insights for Global Business Success* (Houston, TX: Gulf Publishing Company, 1998), 134–36.
72. C. Jaffee, *Public Speaking: A Cultural Perspective* (Belmont, CA: Wadsworth Publishing Co., 1995).
73. William B. Gudykunst, *Bridging Differences: Effective Intergroup Communication* (Thousand Oaks, CA: Sage Publications, 1998), 44.
74. Hymes, *supra* n.40, 269–93.

CHAPTER 3

1. E. T. Hall, *Beyond Culture* (Garden City, NY: Doubleday, 1976).
2. Harry W. Gardiner, Jay D. Mutter, and Corinne Kosmitzki, *Lives Across Cultures: Cross-Cultural Human Development* (Needham Heights, MA: Allyn & Bacon, 1998), 112.

3. Geert Hofstede, *Cultures and Organizations: Software of the Mind* (New York, NY: McGraw-Hill, 1997), 3–4

4. *Ibid.*, 14.

5. *Ibid.*

6. *Ibid.*

7. Hofstede, *supra* n.3, 50.

8. Min-Sun Kim, *Non-Western Perspectives on Human Communication: Implications for Theory and Practice* (Thousand Oaks, CA: Sage Publications, 2002).

9. Gardiner, Mutter, & Kosmitzki, *supra* n.2, 116.

10. Lawrence A. Samovar and Richard E. Porter, *Intercultural Communication: A Reader*, 4th ed. (Belmont, CA: Wadsworth Publishing Company, 1994), 77.

11. *Ibid.*, 417.

12. Gardiner, Mutter, & Kosmitzki, *supra* n.2, 113.

13. Samovar & Porter, *supra* n.10.

14. *Ibid.*, 114.

15. William B. Gudykunst, *Bridging Differences: Effective Intergroup Communication* (Thousand Oaks, CA: Sage Publications, 1998), 45.

16. Tracy Novinger, *Intercultural Communication: A Practical Guide* (Austin, TX: University of Texas Press, 2001).

17. *Ibid.*, 143–45.

18. R. L. Wiseman and R. Shuter, *Communicating in Multinational Organizations* (Thousand Oaks, CA: Sage Publications, 1994), 85.

19. *Ibid.*, 49–50.

20. Hofstede, *supra* n.3, 53.

21. Devorah A. Lieberman, "Ethnocognitivism, Problem Solving, and Hemisphericity," in Lawrence A. Samovar and Richard E. Porter, *Intercultural Communication: A Reader*, 4th ed. (Belmont, CA: Wadsworth Publishing Company, 1994), 178–80.

22. Carolyn Calloway-Thomas, Pamela J. Cooper, and Cecil Blake, *Intercultural Communication: Roots and Routes* (Boston, MA: Allyn & Bacon, 1999), 194.

23. *Ibid.*, 195.

24. *Ibid.*, 199.

25. Terry Morrison, Wayne A. Conaway, and George A. Borden, *Kiss, Bow or Shake Hands* (Avon, MA: Adams Media Corporation, 1994), 204.

26. Samovar & Porter, *supra* n.10.

27. Lieberman in Samovar and Porter, *supra* n.21, 178–80.

28. For a discussion about cultural bias reflected in the work of Piaget and Vygotsky, see Gardiner, Mutter, & Kosmitzki, *supra* n.2, 81–82.

29. Edward C. Stewart & Milton J. Bennett, *American Cultural Patterns* (Yarmouth, ME: Intercultural Press, Inc., 1991), 69.
30. Lieberman in Samovar and Porter, *supra* n.21, 181.
31. *Ibid.*, 182.
32. L. Damen, *Culture Learning: The Fifth Dimension in the Language Classroom* (Reading, MA: Addison-Wesley, 1987), 303.
33. *Ibid.*, 303–06.
34. *Ibid.*, 306.
35. *Ibid.*
36. J. Condon and F. Yousef, *An Introduction to Intercultural Communication* (New York, NY: Bobbs-Merrill, 1975), 213.
37. William B. Gudykunst and Min-Sun Kim, *Communicating with Strangers: An Approach to Intercultural Communication* (Reading, MA: Addison-Wesley, 1984), 50.
38. J. W. Anderson "A Comparison of Arab and American Conceptions of 'Effective' Persuasion," *The Howard Journal of Communications* 2, no. 1 (Winter 1989–90): 81–114.
39. H. S. Hamod, "Arab and Moslem Rhetorical Theory," *Central States Speech Journal*, no. 14 (1963): 97–102.
40. *Ibid.*, 98.
41. Fons Trompenaars and Charles Hampden-Turner, *Riding the Waves of Culture: Understanding Cultural Diversity in Global Business* (New York, NY: McGraw-Hill, 1998), 146–47.
42. Kim, *supra*, n.8, 10.
43. Trompenaars & Hampden-Turner, *supra* n.41, 150–51.
44. David Kellett, "Sheldon." Distributed by United Features Syndicate, Inc. Reprinted by permission. Retrieved at ics.com/comics/sheldon/archive/sheldon-20031119.html.
45. Trompenaars & Hampden-Turner, *supra* n.41.
46. Hofstede, *supra* n.3, 110.
47. *Ibid.*, 113.
48. *Ibid.*, 109.
49. Candace Bancroft McKinniss and Arthur A. Natella, *Business in Mexico: Managerial Behavior, Protocol, and Etiquette* (Binghamton, NY: The Haworth Press, Inc., 1994), 61–62.
50. Gardiner, Mutter, & Kosmitzki, *supra* n.2, 188.
51. Hofstede, *supra* n.3, 109.
52. Florence Kluckhohn and Fred L. Strodtbeck, *Variations in Value Orientations* (Westport, CT: Greenwood Press, 1960).
53. *Ibid.*

54. Edward T. Hall and Mildred Reed Hall, *Understanding Cultural Differences: German, French and American* (Yarmouth, ME: Intercultural Press, 1990), 15.
55. Richard R. Gesteland, *Cross-Cultural Business Behavior: Marketing, Negotiating, Sourcing, and Managing Across Cultures* (Copenhagen, Denmark: Copenhagen Business School Press, 2002), 65.
56. Edward T. Hall and Mildred Reed Hall, *The Dance of Life: The Other Dimension of Time* (New York, NY: Anchor Books, 1996).
57. Morrison, Conaway, & Borden, *supra* n.25, 207.
58. Novinger, *supra* n.16, 111.
59. Gesteland, *supra* n.55, 65.
60. Trompenaars & Hampden-Turner, *supra* n.41, 62–63.
61. Joseph A. DeVito, *The Interpersonal Communication Book*, 5th ed. (New York, NY: HarperCollins, 1989), 248.
62. *Ibid.*, 249.
63. *Ibid.*, 249–50.
64. Michael B. Goodman, *Working in a Global Environment* (New York, NY: Institute of Electrical and Electronics Engineers, 1995), 50.
65. *Ibid.*

CHAPTER 4
1. Robert G. Torricelli (Ed.), *Quotations for Public Speakers: A Historical, Literary, and Political Anthology* (New Brunswick, NJ: Rutgers University Press, 2001), 126.
2. Adapted from an original idea of Anne M. Greenhalgh, The Wharton School, University of Pennsylvania.
3. Marshall R. Singer, *Intercultural Communication: A Perceptual Approach* (Englewood Cliffs, NJ: Prentice-Hall, Inc., 1987), 105.
4. Geert Hofstede, *Cultures and Organizations: Software of the Mind: Intercultural Cooperation and Its Importance for Survival* (New York: NY, McGraw-Hill, 1997), 23.
5. Richard R. Gesteland, *Cross-Cultural Business Behavior: Marketing, Negotiating, Sourcing and Managing Across Cultures* (Copenhagen, Denmark: Copenhagen Business School Press, 2002), 248.
6. Hofstede, *supra* n.4, 35.
7. *Ibid.*, 45.
8. Philip R. Harris and Robert T. Moran, *Managing Cultural Differences: Leadership Strategies for a New World of Business* (Burlington, MA: Gulf Professional Publishing, 2000), 366.

9. David A. Victor, *International Business Communication* (New York, NY: HarperCollins Publishers, 1992), 123–25.

10. Mikhail Moshkov, personal interview, South Bend, Indiana, November 11, 2003.

11. Gesteland, *supra* n.5, 229.

12. Linda Beamer and Iris Varner, *Intercultural Communication in the Global Workplace* (Boston, MA: McGraw-Hill, 1995), 194.

13. David L. James, *The Executive Guide to Asia-Pacific Communications* (New York, NY: Kodansha International, 1995), 42.

14. Lawrence A. Samovar and Richard E. Porter, *Intercultural Communication: A Reader*, 4th ed. (Belmont, CA: Wadsworth Publishing Company, 1994), 88.

15. *Ibid.*, 89.

16. Lecia Archer and Kristine L. Fitch, "Communication in Latin American Multinational Organizations," in Richard L. Wiseman and Robert Shuter, eds., *Communication in Multinational Organizations* (Thousand Oaks, CA.: Sage Publications, 1994), 79.

17. Gesteland, *supra* n.5, 228.

18. Howard W. French, "Japan's Neglected Resource: Female Workers," *The New York Times* (July 25, 2003), A3.

19. Gesteland, *supra* n.5, 46–47.

20. Hofstede, *supra* n.4, 37.

21. Beamer and Varner, *supra* n.12, 197.

22. Norimitsu Onishi, "Japanese Workers Told From on High: Drop the Formality," *The New York Times* (October 30, 2003), A1, A6.

23. Hofstede, *supra* n.4, 54.

24. James R. Stengel, Andrea L. Dixon, and Chris T. Allen, "Listening Begins at Home," *Harvard Business Review* 81, no. 11 (November 2003), 106–17.

25. *Ibid.*, 43.

26. W. B. Gudykunst, *Bridging Differences: Effective Intergroup Communication*, 4th ed. (Thousand Oaks, CA: Sage Publications, 1999), 61.

27. Edith A. Folb, "Who's Got Room at the Top? Issues of Dominance and Nondominance in Intercultural Communication" in Lawrence A. Samovar and Richard E. Porter, *Intercultural Communication: A Reader*, 4th ed. (Belmont, CA: Wadsworth Publishing Company, 1994), 133.

28. Carolyn Calloway-Thomas, Pamela J. Cooper, and Cecil Blake, *Intercultural Communication: Roots and Routes* (Boston, MA: Allyn & Bacon, 1999), 197–201.

29. Hofstede, *supra* n.4, 80.
30. Betsy Morris, "Trophy Husbands," *Fortune* (October 14, 2002), 79–96.
31. Hofstede, *supra* n.4, 79–80.
32. Calloway-Thomas, Cooper, & Blake, *supra* n.28, 198.
33. Hofstede, *supra* n.4,103.
34. *Ibid.*, 96.
35. Meena S. Wilson, Michael H. Hoppe, and Leonard R. Sayles, *Managing Across Cultures: A Learning Framework* (Greensboro, NC: Center for Creative Leadership, 2002).
36. Min-Sun Kim, *Non-Western Perspectives on Human Communication: Implications for Theory and Practice* (Thousand Oaks, CA: Sage Publications, 2002), 99.
37. Judee K. Burgoon, David B. Buller, and W. Gill Woodall, *Nonverbal Communication: The Unspoken Dialogue* (New York, NY: McGraw-Hill 1996), 129.
38. Cecil Adams, "The Straight Dope" Retrieved December 31, 2003, from www.straightdope.com/columns/010302.html.
39. *Ibid.*
40. *Ibid.*
41. Samovar & Porter, *supra* n.14, 106–08.
42. Drew Martin, et al., "International Negotiations: An Entirely Different Animal," in Roy J. Lewicki, David M. Saunders, John W. Minton, and Bruce Barry, *Negotiation: Readings, Exercises, and Cases* (Boston, MA: McGraw-Hill 2003), 340.
43. Russell H. Kaschula and Christine Anthonissen, *Communicating Across Cultures in South Africa* (Johannesburg, South Africa: Hodder & Stroughton, 1995), 88.
44. Terry Morrison, Wayne A. Conaway, and George A. Borden, *Kiss, Bow or Shake Hands* (Avon, MA: Adams Media Corporation, 1994), 180–81.
45. Gesteland, *supra* n.5, 170. Morrison, Conaway, & Borden, *supra* n.44, 207.
46. Fons Trompenaars and Charles Hampden-Turner, *Riding the Waves of Culture: Understanding Cultural Diversity in Global Business* (New York, NY: McGraw-Hill, 1998), 77.
47. *Ibid.*, 76–77.
48. Hiroki Kato and Joan S. Kato, *Understanding and Working with the Japanese Business World* (Englewood Cliffs, NJ: Prentice-Hall, Inc., 1992), 61, 112, 113.

49. David L. James, *The Executive Guide to Asia-Pacific Communications* (New York, NY: Kodansha International, 1995), 42.
50. Kato & Kato, *supra* n.48, 105–06.
51. United States Department of Commerce. Visit http://bisnis.doc.gov/bisnis/fcp1.htm for additional information on the Foreign Corrupt Practices Act.
52. Adapted from Gesteland, *supra* n.5, 99.
53. Hofstede, *supra* n.4, 165.
54. *Ibid.*
55. Kato & Kato, *supra* n.48, 60–61.
56. Adapted from Robert S. Cathcart, Larry A. Samovar, and Linda D. Henman, *Small Group Communication: Theory and Practice*, 7th ed. (Madison, WI: Brown and Benchmark, 1996), 427.

CHAPTER 5

1. Richard R. Gesteland, *Cross-Cultural Business Behavior: Marketing, Negotiating, Sourcing, and Managing Across Cultures* (Copenhagen, Denmark: Copenhagen Business School Press, 2002).
2. James Downs, "Psychocultural Influences on the Process," in William Gudykunst and Young Yun Kim, *Communicating with Strangers: An Approach to Intercultural Communication* (Reading, MA: Addison-Wesley Publishing Co., 1984), 83.
3. LaRay M. Barna, "Stumbling Blocks in Intercultural Communication," in Larry A. Samovar and Richard E. Porter, *Intercultural Communication: A Reader*, 4th ed. (Belmont, CA: Wadsworth Publishing Company, 1994), 337-346.
4. Larry A. Samovar and Richard E. Porter, *Intercultural Communication: A Reader*, 9th ed (Belmont, CA: Wadsworth Publishing Company, 2000), 5.
5. "The Most-Quoted Remarks." Retrieved 18August,2004, from http://www1c.btwebworld.com/ quote-unquote/p0000149.htm.
6. Linel Laroche, "Managing Cross-Cultural Differences in International Projects." Retrieved 18 August 2004, from http://www.itapintl.com/mngdifintproj.htm.
7. Terry Morrison, Wayne A. Conaway, and George A. Borden, *Kiss, Bow or Shake Hands* (Avon, MA: Adams Media Corporation, 1994), 180-81.
8. *Ibid.*, 41.
9. *Ibid.*, 47.

10. *Ibid.*
11. Gesteland, *supra* n.1, 114.
12. For a comprehensive illustration of the full range of human gestures, see Desmond Morris, *Bodytalk* (New York, NY: Crown Trade Paperbacks, 1994).
13. John C. Condon and Fathi S. Yousef, *An Introduction to Intercultural Communication* (Indianapolis, IN: The Bobbs-Merrill Company, Inc., 1975).
14. Fons Trompenaars and Charles Hampden-Turner, *Riding the Waves of Culture: Understanding Cultural Diversity in Global Business* (New York, NY: McGraw-Hill, 1998).
15. *Ibid.*, 201.
16. Geert Hofstede, *Cultures and Organizations: Software of the Mind: Intercultural Cooperation and Its Importance for Survival* (New York: NY, McGraw-Hill, 1997), 4.
17. Milton J. Bennett, "A Developmental Approach to Training for Intercultural Sensitivity," *International Journal of Intercultural Relations* 10 (1986), 179–96.
18. Conversation with Jim O'Rourke (September 2003).

Index

A

Acceptance (stage of), 27, 28, 85, 110, 111, 124, 129, 193
Accommodation, 16, 201
Achievement, 19, 20, 28, 57, 71, 97, 113, 124, 141, 144, 155, 159, 161, 163, 165, 166, 167, 168, 169, 178, 180, 181, 186, 187, 204, 215
Action (emphasis on), 47, 60, 71, 77, 98, 126, 127
Adaptation, 27, 28, 193, 195
African cultures, 66, 74, 78
Ambiguity, 69, 84, 86, 104, 109, 111, 129, 130, 195, 204
Arabic, 8, 53, 98, 103, 115
Arabs, 48, 60, 68, 71, 72, 98, 100, 102, 122, 123, 161, 163, 171, 191
rhetorical style of, 102-104
Asian-Americans, 31, 34
Asian cultures, 60, 65, 66, 68, 76, 87, 96, 173, 185, 189, 191
Assertive (vs. cooperative), 128, 162, 163, 165, 169
Assimilation, 16, 212
Assumptions, 1, 2, 9, 24, 26, 169, 188, 193, 197, 198
Attitudes, 1, 2, 9-11, 13-15, 24, 29, 52, 59, 71-72, 80, 87, 93, 111-112, 124-125, 144, 179, 186, 193, 196, 198, 100
Australia, 63, 88, 97, 105, 154, 159, 188, 204
Authority, 10, 12, 20, 57, 64, 111-12, 120, 125, 143-146, 148, 150, 153-156, 159, 161, 165, 178-180, 185-7, 204
achieved vs. ascribed, 179
Aviation/air-traffic control, 9
Awareness, 2, 10, 16, 22, 29-30, 42, 80, 91, 99-100, 165, 179, 186-187, 196, 200
Axiomatic deduction, 100
Axtell, Roger, 191

B

Beamer, Linda, 204
Behavior, 1, 2, 9-11, 13-17, 19-29, 39-44, 53, 59, 63, 67-70, 80-81, 85-87, 92, 99-100, 106, 109-110, 113, 120, 123-125, 143, 146, 154, 163, 170, 176, 179, 181, 186, 191-193, 195-198, 200
Belgium, 110, 132-133, 137-140, 168
Beliefs, 1, 9-15, 22, 24, 29, 52, 59, 80, 87, 124, 179, 186, 190, 193-194, 196, 198, 200
Bennett, Milton, 26-28
Big Dog Software, Inc., 181-183
Body movement, 39-40, 56, 122
Bond, Michael, 175
Borden, George A., 99, 170, 190
Bow/bowing, 15-16, 68, 143, 178, 189, 190-191, 193
Brazil, 6, 88, 115, 176, 193
Bribes, 149, 175
Buddhism, 22, 68, 71, 90
Business cards, 124, 125, 140
Business letters, 48

C

Canada, 6-7, 60, 63, 76, 88, 97, 105, 114, 154, 159, 167, 176, 188, 201-203
case study involving, 201-204
Canwall Paper Case, 201-204
Categorization, 22
Cell phones, 6, 11, 171
Census (Year 2000), 7
Change, 20, 57, 86, 88, 104, 109-110, 112, 123, 129-130, 147, 154, 158, 186-187, 100, 204, 215
Chinese, 201, 202, 203, 210, 211, 212, 213, 214, 215, 220, 221, 227
case study involving, 201
cooperation and, 98
gifts and, 173
harmony and, 108

high context, 61
  language of, 49, 53, 190
  long-term orientation of, 176
  "saving face" by, 64
Circular thinking, 70, 71, 72, 100,
  123, 127, 131
Clothing, 15, 37, 47, 132
Coca-Cola, 132, 133, 134, 135, 136,
  137, 138, 139, 140, 190
Cognitive orientation, 15, 16, 7, 47,
  70, 84, 86, 99, 101, 192
Collectivism, 24, 70, 87, 88, 89, 90,
  94, 96, 97, 98, 103, 104, 157
  uncertainty avoidance,109-112
Communication, 2, 3, 5, 7, 10, 11, 27,
  28, 31
  behaviors, 40, 44
  codes, 46-48
  competence, 55-56
  context, 60-63
  dimensions, 57-58
  expression, 64-67
  frame of reference, 44-45
  hierarchy, 149-150
  long/short-term orientation,
    175-178
  masculinity, femininity, 162
  nonverbal, 49-52
  power distance, high, 144
  power distance, low, 154
  respect, 170
  space, 120-121
  stumbling blocks, 187-195
  time, 112
  transactional, 40
Competition, 98, 144, 165, 180
Conaway, Wayne A., 99, 170
Condon, John C., 102, 192
Conflict resolution, 10, 59, 65, 69, 85,
  112, 115, 129, 145, 165, 196
Confucian Dynamism, 22, 65, 71, 87,
  90, 91, 115, 161, 175, 176, 177, 178
Confucianism, 22, 71, 91
Conoco, 57
Consensus, 112, 149, 165, 196

Context, 3, 37, 39, 40, 41, 80, 81, 83,
  90, 92, 98, 99, 100, 101, 103, 141,
  186, 187, 191, 203, 207, 215
  high and low, 60-72
  language, 61-66
  learning, 52, 53
  Persuasion, 70
  presentation styles, 76-78
Control, 9, 42, 43, 45, 46, 56, 71, 84,
  85, 86, 104, 105, 106, 107, 110,
  112, 122, 123, 128, 134, 137, 139,
  141, 144, 145, 147, 152, 154, 155,
  161, 163, 170, 171, 175, 178, 179
Cooperation, 38, 98, 125, 179, 180,
  203
Creativity, 38, 76, 98, 147
Cross-cultural, 5, 10, 23, 26, 27, 55,
  67, 68, 85, 91, 92, 109, 120, 130,
  143, 146, 154, 185, 187, 188, 191,
  203, 215
Culture, 1, 2, 5, 7, 8, 9, 13, 15, 16, 17,
  19, 20, 21, 22, 23, 24
  definition, 10-12
  dichotomies and, 23, 101
  ethnocentrism, 2, 25-26, 29, 188,
    193
  example of, 80
  frame of reference and, 27, 27, 39,
    44
Culture, *See also* Cross-cultural
  interactions; Intercultural
    communication
  achievement-oriented, 71
  analogy for understanding, 12
  basic elements of, 9
  dimensions of, 1, 20, 58, 80, 87, 99,
    124, 141, 145, 187, 192, 198
  hidden dimensions of, 1, 15, 23, 80,
    124, 145, 187, 193 145, 147
  identity and, 84 (*See also* Identity)
  language and, 46, 54
  masculine/feminine, 162-165
  power and, 141-161 (*See also* Power)
  norms, 1, 9, 10, 15, 16, 17, 21, 28,
    37, 38, 56, 78, 86, 97, 113, 116,

125, 141, 143, 161, 162, 175, 177, 181, 186, 187, 191, 194, 198
Customs, 7, 12, 13, 15, 70, 108, 109, 116, 129, 147, 150, 152, 180, 186, 188, 189, 191, 194, 197, 199

D

Damen, Louise, 101
Danish, 153
Deductive reasoning, 72-74, 76, 127
Defense (stage of), 27, 193
Dell, Michael, 123
Demographics. *See also* Race/ethnicity 5, 82
   of American cities, 8
   globalization and, 79
Denial, 27, 111, 193
Denmark, 80
DeVito, Joseph, 122, 134
Disney Company, 37, 108-109, 204-215
Diversity, 6
Downs, James, 186
Drucker, Peter, 46

E

Eastern cultures, 22, 50, 66, 68-69, 87, 99, 107-108
   cognitive orientation in, 84, 86, 99, 101
Eastern Europe, 66, 113, 147-148
Education, immigration and, 6
Egyptians, 151
Elpida Memory, 156
Emotion, expressing, 42-43, 61, 65-66, 68-69, 72-73, 79, 88, 98-99, 103, 106, 158, 194, 194-195
Empathy, 28, 81, 91, 198
English, 8-9, 24, 33, 46, 48-49, 53, 55, 59, 64, 71, 81-82, 90, 100, 164, 169, 188, 190, 201, 208, 210, 214
Environment, 16, 19, 29, 31, 34, 55, 57, 61, 71, 84-86, 99, 104-108, 110, 123-124, 128, 134, 137, 141, 151, 167, 186-187, 194-195, 203, 205, 210-211

control *vs.* harmony, 104-107, 110, 128
Eskimo language, 55
Ethics, 84
Ethnocentric, 5, 27-28, 169, 186-187, 198, 200
Ethnocentrism, 2, 25-26, 29, 188, 193115, 123, 132, 147, 167, 205, 207-209
Ethos, 72, 103, 207
European cultures, 32, 38, 49, 60, 63, 66, 68, 86, 76, 86, 88, 105, 212
Eye contact, 27, 47, 86, 109, 124, 142

F

Facial expressions/smile, 40-41, 43, 47, 49, 63, 68, 93, 191, 193
Factual-inductive approach, 100
Fast, Julius, 41
Folb, Edith A., 162
Food, 13, 18, 105, 108, 116, 129, 150, 166, 189, (Disney, 104-115)
French, 15, 37, 53, 54, 76, 100, 105, 115, 133, 137, 146, 152, 156, 168, 191, 205, 208
Fung Shui, 108-109
Future (orientation), 8, 110, 113, 115, 118, 123-124, 151, 176, 187, 195, 203

G

Germans, 6, 31, 49, 66, 68, 73, 86, 113, 117, 132-133, 146-147, 159, 161, 163, 167, 177
Gesteland, Richard R., 67-68, 85, 109, 113, 116-117, 120, 143, 146, 153-154, 186
Gestures, 10, 40, 50, 66, 68 73, 7, 81, 143, 191-192
Gifts and, 170, 173-175, 180, 212
Global market, 6, 20, 29, 186-197, 199
Globalization, 7-9, 79, 117
   demographics and, 1–5
   economy, 113, 117, 158
   village, 5-7

Goodman, Michael B., 123
Great Britain, 97,154-155, 159, 163, 167, 176, 189-190
Greetings, 15-16, 48, 92, 170-171, 189
Grice, G. L., 48
Groups, 10-11, 20, 22, 32-33, 88, 96-99, 105, 106, 112, 145, 178, 192-194, 196, 198, 210
   identity, 186
   language 55
   membership, 88-89
Gudykunst, William B., 103

H

Hall, Edward T., 1, 11, 15, 60, 63, 84, 86, 113, 120-121
Hamod, H. S., 103
Hampden-Turner, Charles, 69, 170
Handshakes, 9–10, 47, 125, 142
Harmony, 50, 62, 65, 71, 86, 90, 101, 125, 149, 167, 175-177
   control vs., 91–92
   risk and, 81
Harris, Philip, 25
Hierarchical societies, 105–109, 130
Hinduism, 10, 108
Hispanics, 3, 61
Hofstede, Geert, 6, 14, 64–65, 69, 105, 116–120, 128
Hong, Y. E., 33
Hong Kong, 128
Hymes, Dell, 56

I

Identity, 10, 17, 20, 57, 84, 86-89, 91, 97, 103, 186-187, 210
   ambiguity/uncertainty and, 79–81
   cognitive orientation and, 73
   collectivism vs. individualism in, 86-97, 107, 124-125
   environment and, 103-104, 141
   learning, 98
   space, time, 10
Immigration, workforce and, 6

India, Indian, 18-19, 73, 113, 115, 117-119, 150, 152, 151, 176
Indians, Southwestern, 60
Individualism (individualistic), 11, 24, 28, 37, 103-104, 114, 123-125
   identity, 84-97
   learning, 98-104
   cognitive orientation and, 73, 76
Indonesia, 97, 115, 147, 152, 190
Inductive reasoning, 72-76, 100, 127
Integration, 27, 29, 193
Intercultural communication. *See also* Cross-cultural interactions; Culture
   applications for, 186
   developing competence in, 196
   stages of sensitivity in, 27-28, 193
   stumbling blocks to, 186-193
   tacit workings of, 38, 55
International finance, 9
Internet, 9, 11, 32-33, 166
Intuitive-affective pattern, 100
Irish, 115
Israel, 31, 155, 159
Italians, Italy, 31, 43, 54, 68, 100, 116-117, 133, 156, 160, 167, 171

J

James, David L., 173
Japan, Japanese, 27, 41, 87, 110, 113, 147, 167l 169
   bowing, 15-16, 143
   business cards, 171, 189-190
   business letter, 48
   cognitive orientation of, 99-101
   collectivism of, 92
   formality, 156-157
   gestures and, 191
   gifts and, 173-174
   harmony and, 144, 149
   high context, silence, 61, 69
   language, 50, 53
   negotiation, 42
   power and, 148-9, 151-152
   respect, "saving face" by, 64-65, 175

seating arrangements and, 172-173
space and, 63-65, 126, 144
Jew, Hasidic, 17

K
Kaplan, R., 70-72
Kato, Hiroki & Joan, 173-174,
    177-178
Kim, Min-Sun, 69-103
Kinesics, 240
Kiplinger Letter, 7
Kluckhohn, 11
Knapp, Mark, 41
Korea, Korean, 24, 50, 61, 68, 86-87,
    92, 98, 176

L
Language(s), 7-8, 9-13, 15, 28, 37-39,
    41, 44, 46-64, 71-42, 92, 170, 188-
    191, 193, 208-214
  assumptions about, 53, 102, 180-
    191
  barriers involving, 81
  codes in, 51-52
  communication and, 38-41, 60
  culture and, 5, 46-50, 99
  differences, 189-190
  grammar of, 46, 52-53, 55, 71, 103,
    power (authority)and, 144-146,
    160-161
  reasoning and, 72-73
  religion, 103
  rhetoric and, 51-53, 74–76
  silent, 11
  slang, 48
  structure of, 52-53
  world view, thought, 54-55, 70-72
Latin Americans, 65, 68, 73, 93-94,
    123, 150-151, 168, 171, 191, 42
  collectivism of, 93, 171
  expression, gestures (abrazo, 191),
    42, 65-66, 68
  fatalism of, 110
  negotiation, 42
  power (*palanca*), 151-152

space and, 123
time and, 167-168
tone of voice and, 171
Laws, 110, 150
Learning, 20, 57, 94, 98, 126, 186
  action vs. observation in, 126-127
  cognitive orientation and, 86, 99,
    101
Linear thinking, 27, 59, 70, 75, 77,
    100-101, 113, 124, 127
Linguistic determinism/relativity, 54
Lippmann, Walter, 20
Logic, 47, 59, 72-74, 77-78, 99-103,
    105, 116. *See also* Reasoning
Logos (logic), 72

M
Madagascar, 78
Malaysia, 152, 176, 209
Martin, Drew, 169
McDonald's, 18-19, 25, 166, 191-192,
    212-213
McKinnisse, Candace Bancroft, 110
McLuhan, Marshall, 5, 7
Mediterranean cultures, 60, 66, 68, 86,
    122
Mehrabian, Albert, 226
Mexicans, Mexico, 6, 63, 93, 98, 153
  power and, 141, 147, 152
  time and, 115
  time off and, 167-168
Middle Eastern cultures, 66, 83, 123
  expression, 66
  space and, 123
  time and, 83
Mindfulness, 194
Minimization, 27-28, 193
Models, 58-59
Moran, Robert T., 38
Morrison, Terry, 99, 170
Muslims, 103

N
Natella, Arthur A., 110
Native Americans, 17

Negotiation, 22, 64-65, 165, 169, 201
  interruptions during, 68, 119
Netherlands/Dutch, 97, 132-133, 154,
  160, 166-167
New Zealand, 63, 88, 97, 113, 154,
  159, 176
Nigeria, 170, 176
Nonverbal communication, 28, 41-42,
  49, 61, 63
  See also Body movement; Eye
    contact; Facial expressions/smile;
    Gestures; Handshakes; Symbols
  codes of, 60-61, 62, 186
  context, 62-63
  visuals in, 52, 59, 62, 77, 79, 101
  vocalics in/tone of voice, 40, 49
Nordic cultures, 73
North America, 103, 121
  Directness, 65, 71
  gifts and, 173
  negotiation, 42
  rhetoric in, 50, 59, 63
  space and, 121, 144
  tone of voice and, 171
Northern Europe, 68, 114, 171
Norway, 160, 165
Novinger, Tracy, 115

O
Observation (*vs.* action), 126-127
Ogden, C.K., 44-45
Organizational structure, 144, 147,
  149

P
Pakistan, 97, 176
Pathos, 72
Pepsi-Cola, 135, 190
Perception, 15, 19, 23
  cognitive, 15-17
  language and, 54-55
  presentation style and, 77
Personal space, 10, 120, 191. *See also*
  Space
"Personhood," 91

Persuasion, 70, 72, 75, 78, 102
Peru, 147
Philippines, 98, 136, 147, 152, 176
Phillips Petroleum Company, 57
Piaget, Jean, 16, 99
Point-dot-space orientation, 101
Politics, 167
Population statistics, 7-8
Porter, Richard E., 169
Portuguese, 150
Power, 141-162. *See also* Achievement
  country clusters, 158-159
  high/low power distance, 152,
    154-155, 157, 160-162
  long-/short-term orientation and,
    128–130
  respect and, 103, 104, 105, 124–128
Power distance, 24, 144, 146-150
Present orientation, 113
Presentation styles, 76-81, 104
  persuasion in, 76-77
Problem solving, 11, 59, 70, 86, 99-
  100, 127
Procter & Gamble, 158
Prototypes, 20-23, 59
Proxemics, 86, 120, 123

R
Race/ethnicity, 7, 146
Rank, 11, 63, 76, 78, 97, 119, 122,
  143-153, 157, 159, 173, 177, 179,
Reasoning, 72-76, 86, 99-101, 104-
  105,
Reciprocity, 91, 176
Reliant Automotive, 141-143
Religion, 73, 87, 103, 110, 165. *See
  also specific religions*
Respect, 41, 42, 63-66, 68, 70, 76-77,
  91, 93, 98, 107, 113, 120, 151, 152
  achievement, 159
  greetings 171
  seating arrangements, 172-173
  gifts, 173-175
  long-term, short-term orientation,
    176-177

Rhetoric, 72-74, 101-103
Richards, I. A., 44-45
Risk, 47, 111-112, 129. *See also*
Uncertainty
Russia/Russians, 31, 54, 73, 99, 100,
136, 148-149, 151, 171, 191

S

Samovar, Lawrence A., 54, 169
Saudi Arabia, 95, 133,
"Saving face," 42, 64, 65, 69, 175, 191
Schemata, 15-16, 44, 187, 192
Scotland, 145
Self-actualization, 12, 88, 98,
Shintoism, 190
Signals, 51-52
Signs, 51
Silence, 39, 51, 60, 63, 69-71, 80, 97,
120, 126
Singapore, 47, 67, 80
Singer, Marshall, 10-11
Skinner, J. F., 48
Social interaction, 9, 99
Sony, 107
Space, 10, 11, 19, 94, 96, 105, 120-123
Spanish, 8, 24, 25, 53, 54, 82, 83, 100,
115, 133, 167
Status, 16, 18, 47, 56, 63, 67, 72-73,
112, 122, 143, 144, 146, 147
achievement, and, 165
long-term/short-term, and, 175-
178
Stereotype, 2, 5, 20-23, 26, 27, 163,
188, 192, 193
prototype, 20, 22, 59
Strodtbeck, 11
Sweden, Swedish, 95, 111, 113, 133,
134, 160, 165, 167
Switzerland, 5, 113, 155, 159, 163
Symbols, 15, 39, 44, 46-48, 51-52,
108, 115, 143

T

Taiwanese, 60, 100, 190
Taoism, 22, 91

Technology, 5, 6, 31, 92, 107, 110,
122, 128, 147, 202
Thailand, 66, 165
Time, 92, 94, 96, 98, 104, 105, 107,
110, 112, 113, 114, 115, 117, 120,
123, 124, 126
fixed *vs.* fluid, 130
polychronic *vs.* monochronic, 113,
114, 116-118
sequential *vs.* synchronic, 70-71,
118
Tone of voice, 40, 47, 50, 56, 170, 171
See Vocalics/tone of voice
Traditions, 12, 13, 93, 113, 123, 124,
125, 152, 180, 205
Triangle of Meaning, 44, 45
Trompenaars, Fons, 11, 69, 170, 188
Trust, 14, 21, 29, 51, 63, 65, 66, 81,
85, 94, 114, 121, 122, 125, 143,
175, 177, 178, 184, 189, 198

U

Uncertainty, 22, 24, 88, 109, 110, 11,
112, 129, 130, 188, 194, 195, 200
United States/Americans, 1, 9, 16, 20,
31, 37, 41, 46, 50, 60, 96, 100, 101,
105, 111, 122, 171, 175
assertiveness, 163, 165
bribes, 149, 175
individualism in, 88
learning, 98
masculinity/femininity, 162
power and, 146, 148, 154-156
presentation style in, 76-77
rhetorical style, reasoning, 100-101
space and, 122
time 166,-167, 171
time off 168
U.S. Foreign Corrupt Practices Act,
174
Universalistic pattern, 101

V

Values, 1, 9-19, 63, 65, 71, 88
achievement, 165-166

assumptions, and, 26-29
Identifying, developing, 144, 196
long-term/short term, 176
power and, 143, 149
vocal/visual codes and, 52
Varner, Iris, 204
Vietnamese, 27, 87, 115
Vocalics/tone of voice, 40, 47, 49, 50,
    170-171
Vygotsky, Lev, 99

W
Western cultures, 23, 60, 63, 68, 72,
    87-89, 99, 104-105, 107, 191
    cognitive orientation in, 23, 99
    environment and, 104-105
    individualism of, 87-89 (*See also*
        Individualism)
Wolfsen, N., 55
Women, 66-68, 94, 151-152, 161-162,
    165
World view, 9-10, 13, 23, 27, 54, 90,
    104-105

Y
Yousef, F., 102, 192